angles on environmental psychology

dedication

To Mum and Dad   CR

To Oliver. In the words of Friends of the Earth:
'Here is the Earth. Don't spend it all at once.'   *JR*

angleson

environmental

psychology

Craig Roberts Julia Russell
Series Editors: Matt Jarvis Julia Russell

First published in 2002 by:
Nelson Thornes Ltd
Delta Place
27 Bath Road
CHELTENHAM
GL53 7TH
United Kingdom

02 03 04 05 06 / 10 9 8 7 6 5 4 3 2 1

A catalogue record for this book is available from the British Library

ISBN 0 7487 5978 6

Illustrations by Oxford Designers and Illustrators
Page make-up by Northern Phototypesetting Co. Ltd

Printed in Great Britain by Scotprint

contents

acknowledgements

We would like to thank a number of people who have helped with the production of this book. First, we would like to thank Rick, Carolyn, Emily and Louise at Nelson Thornes for their support. We'd also like to thank Matt Jarvis for asking us to write our contributions to this book . Finally, our thanks go to all the authors who sent us reprints of their work, especially Evelyn Bromet. Many thanks.   CR/JR

I'd like to thank a number of people who always see the good in me: Tanya, Lindsey, Rebekah, Mum, Dad, Ness and Stuart. Extra special thanks go to Geoff Sheppard for making work fun through turbulent times and whilst writing this book! However, the largest thank you has to go to Javi for simply making life enough fun to cope with. Finally, many thanks to Ju and Em and the fine company they offer – especially to Ju for co-working on this excellent book!

Shall we write another one for the fun of it?   CR

I'd like to thank Craig for having the energy and determination to keep this project going despite my prolonged absence from the real world! Cheers, Ju.   JR

The authors and publishers are grateful to the following for permission to reproduce material:

- Academic Press, an imprint of Elsevier Science (USA), for figures on p. 4, from Duke, M.P. & Nowicki, S. (1972) Diagramming the shape of personal space: a new measure and social learning model for interpersonal distance. *Journal of Experimental Research in Personality*, 6, 119–132.
- Allyn and Bacon for figures on pp. 41, 43, from Carlson, N.R. (2001) *The Physiology of Behaviour*, 7th ed., Figures 3.22 and 18.4; figure on p. 107 from Baron, R.A. & Byrne, D. (1991) *Social Psychology: Understanding Human Interaction*, 6th ed., Figure 9.3, p. 355.
- American Psychological Association for figure on p. 7, adapted from Little, K.B. (1968) Cultural variations in social schemata. *Journal of Personality and Social*

Coverage of examination board specifications

Chapter	Edexcel	OCR
1 Personal space and territoriality	Individual and cultural differences Invasion of personal space Importance of territory Functions of territory	Effects and consequences of invasion Definitions, types and measures Defending territory and space
2 Architecture and behaviour	Effect on communication Effect on residential satisfaction Work of Oscar Newman (defensible space and effect on vandalism, crime and residential satisfaction) Good and bad practice in architectural design with respect to defensible space (Pruitt-Igoe, Van Dyke, Fowler et al)	Urban renewal and building design Theories and effects of urban living on health and social behaviour Community environmental design
3 Sources of stress in the environment	Sources of environmental stress (noise, pollution, travel) Research into environmental stress Effects of stressors on behaviour Strategies for coping with environmental stressors	Noise Negative effects on performance, social behaviour and health Positive uses of noise, e.g. music
4 High density living	Effects of crowding on animals Effects of high-density living on humans Theories of crowding (deindividuation, contagion, convergent, emergent norm)	Animal studies Effects on human health, social behaviour and performance Definitions, measurement and different types of crowding Preventing and coping with effects of crowding Crowd behaviour Crowds in emergency situations Crowd control and preventing problems
5 Encouraging environmentally responsible behaviour	Why behaviour is not environmentally friendly (e.g. recycling) Changing attitudes through promotional material (e.g. Yale Model of persuasive communication)	
6 Climate and weather		Definitions, types and climatological determinism Effects on performance and social behaviour Effects on health (e.g. SAD)
7 Environmental disaster and technological catastrophe		Definitions, characteristics and causes Examples of behaviours during them, and effects on individuals Psychological intervention before and after events
8 Environmental cognition		Definitions, measures, errors and individual differences in cognitive maps Designing better maps; Wayfinding Scenic environment

1

Personal Space and Territoriality

what's **ahead**?

In this chapter we will examine the role that personal space and territory play in human behaviour. For example, what happens when somebody invades that space? Why do humans need territory? We will also examine individual differences in the need for personal space (for example, gender differences and cultural differences) and we will look at how we choose to defend the space around us.

What is personal space?

Think about how it feels to have someone stand very close to you, or what it is like to be on a crowded bus or train. It probably makes you feel a little stressed and irritable, and that is because someone is invading your *personal space*. Katz (1937) was the first person to discuss the term 'personal space'. Bell *et al.* (1996, p.275) define it as a '... portable, invisible boundary surrounding us, into which others may not trespass. It regulates how closely we interact with others, moves with us, and expands and contracts according to the situation in which we find ourselves.' Thus our personal space is like a bubble. It changes shape and size depending on the situation in which we find ourselves.

interactive
angles

Describe how you would feel on a crowded bus, when you are with your best friend or when you are meeting someone for the first time. How does your personal space differ in each situation? Does the 'bubble' around you change for each situation?

Hall (1963) distinguished between zones of personal space (called *spatial zones* by Hall) based around interpersonal relationships that we may have.

Distance	Usual activities and relationships	Input to the senses
Intimate (0.0–1.5 feet [0.0–0.45 m])	Contact is intimate (for example, comforting another or having sex). Physical sports such as judo and wrestling allow invasion of the intimate zone.	Touch is the basic mode for communication. We are intensely aware of other sensory information. Such as smell and heat emitted from another person.
Personal (1.5–4.0 feet [0.45–1.2 m])	Friends are allowed to get within this zone, especially those who are close to us. Your usual everyday interactions will trespass into this zone too.	Speech is the key source of sensory input from others (more so than touch). However, research has shown vision to be a key source of sensory input too (see Gale *et al.*, 1975, p.8).
Social (4–12 feet [0.45–3.66 m])	People we do not really know personally, but whom we meet quite regularly, are allowed in this zone. Business-like contacts are also allowed to enter this zone.	Sensory input from other people is now rather minimal. Vision is less crisp, speech is still easily processed but touch is now impossible.
Public (more than 12 feet [3.66 m] away)	This is for formal contact; for instance, for someone giving a public speech.	Very little sensory input, usually only from speech. Non-verbal communication takes over as a main source of information.

Theories of personal space

There are numerous theories as to why we require personal space. Bell *et al.* (1996) stated that there are *four* main theories:

- *Arousal theory*. When people invade our personal space we usually become aroused. As a result, we try to make sense of this arousal and this dictates how much space we feel that we require. For example, when we meet someone for the first time (for example, on a date), we may either feel good or nervous. Both of these situations could arouse us. In the first situation (feeling good), we may require less personal space than in the second situation (feeling nervous), as we have understood why we are aroused and acted upon that reason.

- *Behavioural constraint theory*. According to this theory, we require our personal space; otherwise, we feel that our behavioural freedom is being taken away. We feel this when people get too close.

- *Overload theory*. We maintain an optimum personal space in situations in order to avoid being bombarded with too much information. This overstimulation needs to be avoided; otherwise, it is impossible to cope with the situation, because we are too busy processing all of the information (for example, facial details, smells and touch).

- *Stress theory*. This theory states that we keep personal spaces so that we do not get stressed about close proximity. Basically, it subsumes the above theories into a more general explanation. Chapter 4 looks into the stressful effects of crowding.

How can we measure personal space?

A variety of techniques have been used to measure personal space. These include the following:

- *Laboratory experiments* in which variables can be controlled and measurements can be taken of personal space. These techniques allow researchers to control many potentially confounding variables, but the artificial set-up may not generalise to everyday behaviour.

- *Simulation techniques* in which participants act out scenarios linked to personal space with symbolic figures, such as dolls or teddy bears (see, for example, Little, 1968, p.6). This is particularly good for measuring the personal space of children but, as with laboratory experiments, the artificial set-up may not generalise to everyday behaviour.

- *Field experiments* in which participants are (unknowingly, in some cases) observed in natural settings. The researchers can still manipulate variables and observe how people react to these manipulations (see Fisher and Byrne, 1975, p.9). The advantage of this method is that it has high *ecological validity*; that is, it is a good measure of everyday behaviour, as it is in a natural setting. However, there are ethical implications associated with experimenting on people without their consent.

- *Questionnaires* in which participants have to imagine a scenario and rate whether they feel uncomfortable in the situation. An example is the *Comfortable Interpersonal Distance Scale* (CIDS) (Duke and Nowicki, 1972), on which participants have to rate where they feel uncomfortable in the situation that they are imagining. An example CIDS is given overleaf:

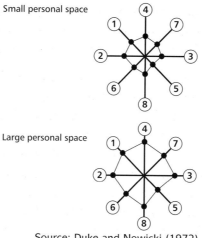

Small personal space

Large personal space

Source: Duke and Nowicki (1972)

The CIDS technique allows a precise measurement of the area of personal space that people require in different situations. However, people could lie when completing the CIDS or not imagine the scenario very well. Also, as with laboratory experiments and simulation methods, the questionnaire technique is an artificial set-up and may not generalise to everyday behaviour.

● *Naturalistic observations* in which participants are observed in natural surroundings, where they would normally be observable. Therefore, people act more 'naturally', and so there is improved ecological validity. Situations do not need to be created to measure personal space, although the measurements may not be as 'controlled' as those in laboratory experiments.

There has been a debate in this area of psychology with regard to whether the above measures actually test the same thing. For example, Knowles (1980) noted that there is some consistency between the various techniques, but in some studies the consistency between various techniques has been low (Wann and Weaver, 1993). It may depend on the type of personal space that you are trying to measure (for example, the distance from strangers or from friends, or informal situations).

Through the use the above techniques, it has been possible for psychologists to measure personal space in different situations, and a variety of individual and cultural differences have been reported.

Individual and cultural differences in personal space

Individual variables seem to affect our levels of tolerance to having our personal space invaded. Sanders (1978) discovered that personal space is affected by the menstrual cycle. Females ranging from 17 to 27 years of age completed a menstrual cycle questionnaire and it was discovered that they tended to maintain a larger personal space during the menstrual period compared to the approximate middle of the cycle.

Prior knowledge about a situation can also affect the amount of personal space that we wish to have. Feroleto and Gounard (1975) examined how close individuals would seat themselves in relation to an interviewer depending on their expectations about the situation. Twenty participants took part in the study, 10 college students and 10 older adults from a residential county home. In both groups of participants, half were told to expect an unpleasant interaction and half were told to expect a pleasant interaction. Those who were told to expect an unpleasant situation sat significantly further away compared to those who were expecting a pleasant situation. The older adults seated themselves further away in both conditions (unpleasant and pleasant). This would appear to indicate that older adults require larger personal spaces, as they may feel more threatened in an interpersonal situation.

An intriguing study conducted by Skorjanc (1991) examined the personal space of participants in relation to the perceived violence level of a criminal. The participants were primed (given information beforehand) into believing that a person they were about to meet in a room was a violent offender, a non-violent offender or someone who had never criminally offended. The measurement of personal space was taken as the number of seats away that the participant chose to sit in relation to the criminal or non-criminal. The results showed that, on average, the participants sat much closer to the person they had been told had never criminally offended compared to the two 'criminals'. There was little difference in the mean number of seats that the participant sat away from either the violent or the non-violent offender. Therefore, attitudes about individuals can affect our personal space preferences in social situations that involve them.

Gender has long been assumed to be one area in which differences are marked with respect to personal space. Early research showed that females have a smaller personal space, especially in same-sex interactions (Andersen and Leibowitz, 1978; Larsen and LeRoux, 1984). Maier and Ernest (1978) asked adults to rate levels of touch in a series of hypothetical situations. Consistent findings emerged: both males and females believed that people, irrespective of gender, would prefer to be touched by a female. Also, both genders reported that females place more emphasis on touch compared to males. However, observational studies have reported there is no difference in the number of times a man and woman touch (Henley, 1973; Willis et al., 1978; Greenbaum and Rosenfeld, 1980; Major, 1981). On the other hand, Bell et al. (1996) noted that females interact at a closer distance compared to males when with people that they like or find attractive.

So, in some studies females are more positive about same-gender touch than males. However, examination of potential cultural differences in same-gender touch has been limited. Willis and Rawdon (1994) examined female and male students from Chile, Spain, Malaysia and the United States. They all completed the Same-Sex Touch Scale (developed by Larsen and LeRoux, 1984), that measures the importance we place on touch in interactions with the same sex: the higher the score, the more importance was placed on touch in same-sex interactions. The average scores for each gender (F = female, M = male) in each nationality are shown in the table below, out of a maximum score of 100:

Nationality	Female	Male
United States	70.6	58.3
Malaysia	54.3	46.1
Chile	64.6	56.8
Spain	69.8	61.9

As can be seen, irrespective of culture, females had more positive scores towards same-sex touch compared to males. With respect to culture, the Malaysian students had the most negative scores. The Spanish males were the most tolerant of all males of same-sex touch. Of all groups, females from the United States had the most positive scores. Of course, the research has its limitations, in that the measure was via a questionnaire rather than *actual* observation of interactions. However, it does note cultural and gender differences in personal space.

Little (1968) examined cultural differences over 19 different social situations in a sample of Americans, Swedes, Greeks, Italians and Scots. The participants had to place dolls at distances that reflected where they would stand in real social situations. The situations that they had to assess included: two good friends talking about a pleasant topic; a shop owner discussing the weather with his assistant; two people talking about the best place to shop; and two strangers talking about an unpleasant topic. Opposite is a graph of the average distances (in twelfths of an inch [1 inch = 2.54 cm]) over the 19 different social situations.

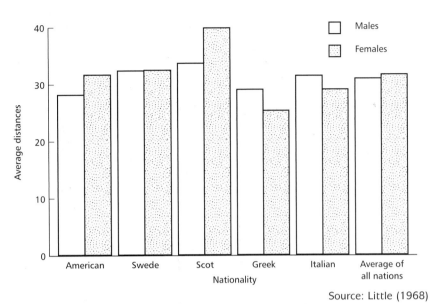

Source: Little (1968)

As can be seen, on average, the Greeks placed the dolls at shorter distances, while the Scots placed them at greater distances, compared to the other nationalities.

There are cultural differences in personal space distances

Effects and consequences of invading personal space

The effects of invasion of personal space have been investigated in a variety of ways. One study involved directly invading the personal space of men in a public lavatory to see if this affected arousal levels.

classic
research

a lav-oratory experiment!

Middlemist, R.D., Knowles, E.S. and Matter, C.F. (1976) Personal space invasion in the lavatory: suggestive evidence for arousal. *Journal of Personality and Social Psychology*, 33(5), 541–6

Aim: To investigate the proposal that invasion of personal space produces arousal.

Method: The setting was a men's public lavatory. According to the researchers, this was an ideal set-up as 'norms for privacy' were already in place (the spaces between the urinals), so the effect that distance had on arousal could be easily measured. The men's public lavatory contained three urinals. Sixty participants were randomly assigned to one of three conditions: (1) the experimenter stood immediately next to the participant; (2) the experimenter stood at the other end of the three urinals to the participant; or (3) the experimenter was absent. Two key measures were taken. The first was a measure of how quickly the participant began to urinate. The second measure was how much time he took to urinate.

Results: The closer the experimenter stood, the longer it took for the participant to begin urination. Also, the closer the experimenter stood, the less time it took the participant to 'complete' urination.

Conclusion: The evidence suggests that invasion of personal space in men produces physiological changes associated with arousal. (The sympathetic autonomic nervous system arousal relaxes the bladder therefore inhibiting micturation. This is caused by the social stimulus of company affecting the autonomic nervous system via the central nervous system.) The more the personal space was invaded, the more aroused the men became. However, the ethics of the research must be questioned!

Another study that examined arousal levels, linked to the invasion of personal space, was conducted by Gale *et al.* (1975). They measured both direct invasion (closeness of a person) and indirect invasion (looking at the participant). For the 18 participants, an electroencephalogram (EEG) reading was taken in varying conditions. The EEG measured electrical activity in the brain and was used as a measure of arousal. The conditions involved a male experimenter either directly looking at the participant or looking away, at distances of 2, 4, 8, 16 or 32 feet (0.6, 1.2, 2.4, 4.8 or 9.7 m) away from the participant. The results showed that the greatest level of EEG arousal was when the experimenter was looking at the participant from a distance of 2 feet (0.6 m) away. The EEG arousal measures diminished the further away the experimenter was from the participant. However, for each distance, the EEG readings showed more arousal when the experimenter was looking at the participant compared to when the experimenter was looking away.

Gender differences in response to invasion have been noted, including a classic study by Fisher and Byrne (1975).

classic
research

girls just wanna have space!

Fisher, J.D. and Byrne, D. (1975) Too close for comfort: sex differences in response to invasions of personal space. *Journal of Personality and Social Psychology*, 32(1), 15–21

Aim: There were two main aims of this study: (1) to examine gender differences in the invasion of personal space; and (2) to examine how gender affects the putting up of barriers to indicate to others where our personal space is.

Method: For the first aim, Fisher and Byrne's confederates (people who knew what the experiment was about) invaded the personal space of 62 males and 63 females in a university library in a number of ways. They either sat next to the participants, sat one seat away from the participants or sat opposite the participants for 5 minutes. After the invasion had taken place, Fisher and Byrne asked each participant to complete a questionnaire about the experience. Questions were asked about how the participants felt during the invasion of their personal space (for example, how happy they felt, how attracted they were to the confederate, their perceived level of crowding and so on).

For the second aim, a different researcher was used, who was not told about the aim of the research (this is called the 'single-blind' technique). The researcher had to observe 33 males and 33 females and record where they placed their personal belongings on a library table.

Results: From the first study, distinct gender differences emerged. Males disliked being invaded by someone approaching from opposite them, but did not mind someone invading the space next to them. For females, different results arose: they did not mind people invading the space opposite to them, but they disliked invasion when someone sat next to them. The following tables of means highlight this trend across all measures taken on the questionnaire:

Happiness rating – the higher the score, the more happy the participant was

	Sitting next to	Sitting opposite
Male	29.15	23.57
Female	23.46	26.79

Attractiveness rating – the higher the score, the more attracted the participant was to an opposite-sex confederate

	Sitting next to	Sitting opposite
Male	10.99	9.14
Female	9.87	10.14

Perceived level of crowding – the higher the score, the more the participant felt crowded

	Sitting next to	Sitting opposite
Male	11.48	17.04
Female	16.60	14.76

The results of the second study backed up those reported in the first study. Males were more likely to place their personal belongings in front of them, while females were more likely to place personal belongings next to them – both males and females were setting up barriers to defend their least favourite direction from which they could be invaded.

The table below shows the number of 'barrier placements' observed on the table at which the participants were seated:

	Barrier next to person	Barrier opposite person
Male	9	15
Female	17	6

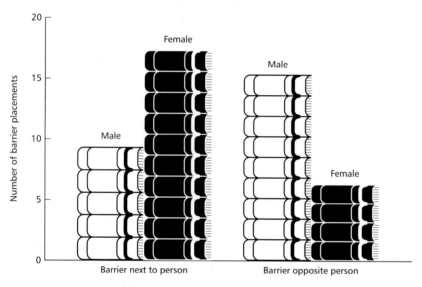

Adapted from Fisher and Byrne (1975)

Conclusion: From this study, it is clear that males do not like to have the space in front of them invaded. Females do not like to have the space next to them invaded. Both genders defend this invasion by setting up barriers to stop people getting too close.

According to Sinha and Sinha (1991), lack of personal space (through continual invasion) may well affect our ability to complete tasks. They examined this idea by getting 60 students to perform tasks under certain conditions. The experimenters manipulated the *social density* by changing the number of people in the same room (the higher the social density, the more chance there is that your personal space will be invaded). They also measured the personal space of all participants using a stop-distance technique: that is, a person approaches and the participant says 'Stop' when he or she begins to feel uncomfortable. The social density and the size of the individual's preferred personal space had effects on difficult tasks, but not on simple tasks. Those participants who preferred a large personal space perceived a high social density as much more crowded compared to those who had a small personal space. This could be because the participants who had large personal spaces were more likely to perceive that their personal space was being invaded. Those with a small personal space, however, would not perceive as much invasion and therefore would report less crowding. In addition, it should be noted that the perceptions only differed during a difficult task. A simple task allowed all participants, irrespective of the size of their personal space, to perceive little crowding.

Recent research has involved the analysis of personal space invasion when using an Automatic Teller Machine (ATM, or cashpoint). Kaya and Erkíp (1999) were interested in the levels of personal space that are comfortable when we withdraw money from an ATM. They observed people waiting to withdraw money under low- and high-density conditions. A total of 100 observations were conducted under both density conditions. They also interviewed a selection of participants. Personal space was predictably invaded more often under high-density conditions, but also if the participant *perceived* the space to be narrow around the ATM (these perceptions were measured using a questionnaire that asked them about the space in the ATM hall). Even so, there was no difference in the amount of personal space that the participants felt was necessary under both density conditions. People wanted privacy when withdrawing money. Gender did not play a main role in the need for personal space in this situation, although participants of opposite genders kept greater distances between themselves and other ATM users. One gender difference reported was that females' approach to males was more distant compared to males' approach to females (for example, in the low-density condition, 76 per cent of females kept more than 46 cm away from males, while for males approaching females this figure was only 46 per cent).

An intriguing study was conducted by Brodsky *et al.* (1999), who examined invasions of personal space in direct and cross-examinations in real-life courtroom trials.

research now

lawyers in yer face!

Brodsky, S.L., Hooper, N.E., Tipper, D.G. and Yates, S.B. (1999) Attorney invasion of witness space. *Law and Psychology Review*, 23, 49–68

Aim: To examine the invasions of personal space by attorneys during direct and cross-examination of witnesses in real-life trials.

Method: Brodsky *et al.* conducted naturalistic observations on 995 courtroom examination questions, of which 372 were direct examinations (questioning a person who you are defending) and 623 were cross-examinations (questioning a person who you are not defending). A total of 12 attorneys were observed over six cases.

Results: It was seen that attorneys invaded the personal space of witnesses most often during cross-examination compared to direct examination. However, Brodsky *et al.* noted that this technique was ineffective in the trials that they observed.

Conclusion: It is presumed that attorneys are invading personal space to increase the stress and arousal of witnesses, so that they 'crack under pressure' and reveal crucial evidence.

Finally, Glover *et al.* (2000) noted the role of personal space in bullying. In order to reduce bullying, one of the crucial aspects was to teach the bully to respect the need of others for personal space. Once this was instilled, the bullies lessened their aggressive behaviour.

What is territory?

Bell *et al.* (1996, p. 304) define territoriality as follows: '... (it) can be viewed as a set of behaviours and cognitions a person or group exhibits, based on perceived ownership of physical space'. This may be permanent, as in owning a house, or temporary, as in controlling your office space but not directly 'owning' it.

Altman (1975) noted that we have three different types of *territory*:

Type of territory	Occupation of territory/ perception of ownership	The extent to which we 'personalise' the territory
Primary territory (for example, own home, office space, bedroom)	*High* degree of occupation and perception of ownership. We believe that we permanently own the territory, and others believe this too!	The territory is personalised in great detail, so that the owner has complete control, and others recognise this almost immediately after entering the territory. Uninvited intrusion can have serious consequences!
Secondary territory (for example, a classroom)	*Medium* degree of occupation and perception of ownership. We believe that we are one of only a limited number of users of the territory.	Personalisation occurs to some extent, but only when the occupancy of the territory is legitimate. For example, within about one month of a new class starting, each person will have his or her own seat, in which he or she will usually stay for the rest of the year. That person legitimately 'owns' that seat during every lesson.

Public territory (for example, an area on a beach, or a seat on a bus)	*Low* degree of occupation and perception of ownership. We believe that we are one of countless people who use this piece of territory.	Personalisation tends to be temporary, as we may not revisit the territory for some time. We tend not to defend this territory in the way we would if it were primary or secondary territory.

The importance and functions of territory

So, on the basis of what we have seen about the importance of territory, what could be the functions of territory for humans? Taylor (1978) believes that one of its functions is to allow us to organise ourselves sensibly:

Type of territory	The function of the territory in terms of organisation
A public place (for example, on a beach or in a library)	It organises a person's space. It allows you to try to dictate the amount of personal space that you would like within that territory.
Primary territory (for example, your bedroom or your desk at work)	It again organises a person's space. It allows you to tell others that you need some solitude. It allows for intimate behaviour to occur. It also allows an outlet for self-expression and personal identity.
Small groups, usually face-to-face (for example, with close friends)	It organises the function of the group. It can aid communication between the group members, with both verbal and non-verbal cues being picked up more easily. Also, 'home court' advantage can play a role (see Schwartz and Barsky, 1977). That is, you feel more confident with things when they are part of your group's territory and not another person's. For example, in sport, most teams will perform better when playing 'at home'.
Communities and the neighbourhood	It organises larger areas of territory as an 'in-group' area or the 'in place to be'. It gives a sense of belonging to a larger group of people. You sense that you can trust the people who commonly use the territory.

Is there a similar sense of territory in the workplace? We spend a great deal of our time there, so is territory important for job satisfaction? Meijanders *et al.* (2000) examined whether having your own 'personal' desk or having to share a desk space had an effect on job satisfaction.

Hotdesking

Meijanders *et al.* (2000) showed that primary territory does have an effect on personal identity, as proposed by Taylor (1978). They examined the regulation of privacy in an office that was non-territorial (that is, where workers use any available desk that happens to be free at a particular time – this is called **hotdesking**) compared to a traditional 'one person per desk' office. The main results showed that employees in both types of office were satisfied with the set-ups. However, the way in which this satisfaction was maintained differed between the two groups of employees. Compared to the employees in the traditional office, those in the non-territorial office placed less emphasis on their personal identities at work. There was no difference between the group identity levels for both sets of employees. This can be explained by Taylor's (1978) model, noted above, as the employees in the non-territorial office were 'deprived' of a definite territory and therefore the opportunity to assert their personal identities. This had a detrimental effect on satisfaction. The consequences that this might have with regard to future job satisfaction, or whether it predicted the length of time that someone might spend in their job, were not reported.

Another avenue of research has looked into whether personalising your office space (for example, with photographs and personal items) has an effect on job satisfaction. Wells (2000) examined the role of *personalisation* on satisfaction in 20 companies in California.

research now

a messy office is a happy office!

Wells, M.M. (2000) Office clutter or meaningful personal displays: the role of office personalisation in employee and organizational well-being. *Journal of Environmental Psychology*, 20, 239–55

Aim: To examine the role of territory in the workplace, especially whether personalisation of office space has an effect on employee well-being and organisational well-being (for example, how much a person likes to work in a particular environment, the morale of workers, and so on).

Method: Wells surveyed 338 office workers from 20 companies in Orange County, California, on the amount of personalisation allowed at work and how they personalised their own office spaces.

Results: For employee well-being, three aspects played a role:

- As the number of personal items displayed on or around a desk increased, so did satisfaction with the work environment.

- There was an association between how much the employee would like to personalise and how much was allowed. The more employees were allowed to personalise, the more they were satisfied with the work environment.

- The more control that a person had over determining the arrangement of his or her workspace, the more satisfied he or she was with the work environment.

Also, satisfaction with the work environment was strongly related to job satisfaction. Those who were happy with their physical work environment were more likely to be satisfied with their job. For organisational well-being, the companies that allowed more personalisation of work space reported a more positive work environment, a more positive social climate among employees, greater levels of worker morale and reduced staff turnover. Finally, females tended to personalise more with items related to personal relationships (especially family, friends and pets), and had more trinkets and more plants compared to males. The only aspect of personalisation where males exhibited higher levels than females was with regard to sport.

Conclusion: This research shows the importance of primary territory – as defined by Altman (1975) and then Taylor (1978) – in the formation of a personal identity, and the subsequent satisfaction of being able to show it to other people.

Having a personalised desk can improve job satisfaction

A sense of territorial ownership appears to be important for many individuals and families. Peluso (2000) examined low-income groups in Brazil, with the idea that a sense of territory to protect the 'self' from the adversities of outside life would be evident, as there appear to be 'grand' ideas about the potential benefit, intimacy and privacy of owning a home. Indeed, this is what Peluso discovered when she interviewed low-income families. Some of the poorest inhabitants of Brasilia considered their houses to be comfortable and adequate for a private life, an important function of territory. However, many of the interviewees did indicate a desire for improvement by stating that they would like, among other things, a bigger and better home. This shows that people want territory to allow them to feel protected.

Intriguingly, the homeless population of Rio de Janeiro also shows levels of territorial behaviour that are linked to home ownership (dos Santos and Duarte, 2000). Observations of homeless people revealed many symbolic forms of behaviour that were indicative of territorial occupation. For example, the use of barriers or urban equipment allowed the homeless to 'map out' bedrooms, bathrooms and kitchens. Therefore, a sense of territory appears to be important in a variety of circumstances.

How do we defend our personal space and territory?

In Chapter 2 we will introduce you to the idea of *defensible space*, an area that we clearly mark out as being owned by ourselves. Any person intruding into this area would soon realise that it is owned by someone else! The idea of defensible space is supposedly linked to criminal behaviour and vandalism, so it seems to be useful to want to defend the space over which we feel we have ownership.

Also, as we have seen on page 9, Fisher and Byrne (1975) noted that when people sat at a desk in a library they defended their territory by setting up barriers (usually books), so that no one could invade without having to move these items.

Smith (1983) noted that there were cultural differences in the extent to which people defended their area on a beach. Germans showed a much more striking sense of territoriality compared to the French. The Germans showed many more actions linked to territorial behaviour. For example, they were much more likely to erect sandcastles to indicate that the particular area of the beach was reserved for them.

Hoppe *et al.* (1972) examined the effectiveness of territorial markers in libraries and public houses. In libraries, when one person on a desk asked a neighbour to defend their space while they went away to do something, leaving a territorial marker such as a notebook was no more effective than leaving no territorial marker at all. However, about half of the neighbours in the 'no territorial marker' group subsequently placed their own territorial markers in the space they had just been asked to save! In the public house study, a half-full glass of beer was found to be very effective at marking territory, compared to a personal marker such as a jumper.

Conclusions

Personal space appears to be needed for a variety of reasons, and it changes depending on the circumstances in which we find ourselves. Personal space can be measured in different ways, so that studies can be conducted to see how personal space changes under different conditions. Research has revealed gender differences and cultural differences in personal space. Psychologists have also examined our reactions to invasion of the personal space around us. Again, gender differences have been reported. Invasion of personal space also appears to cause us stress and to affect our ability to complete tasks. In the courtroom, it is made use of by lawyers – but to no real effect – when cross-examining witnesses, in an attempt to intimidate them.

Territory also plays a key role in our behaviour, allowing us to organise the space around us and feel a sense of personal and social identity. Efforts to reduce territory at work – for example, through 'hotdesking' – may be successful, but they make the employees place less emphasis on personal identities at work. Allowing personalisation of territory has a positive effect on the morale of workers. Defending territory appears to be effective if we place physical barriers around our space in the library or classroom.

where to now?

The following are good sources of information about personal space and territoriality:

▶ **Bell, P.A., Greene, T.C., Fisher, J.D. and Baum, A. (2001)** *Environmental Psychology*, **5th edn. Orlando, FL. Harcourt Brace College Publishers** – a great introduction to personal space and territory in humans.

▶ **Bonnes, M. and Secchiaroli, G. (1995)** *Environmental Psychology: a Psychosocial Introduction.* **London: Sage** – some nice debate about territory and personal space, with some good research highlighted.

1   Using empirical evidence, discuss how personal space differs between individuals and/or cultures.

2   Identify and describe three ways in which we react to our personal space being invaded.

3   Using examples, explain what is meant by **territory**.

4   Using empirical evidence, assess the importance of territory to humans.

2

Architecture and Behaviour: Housing Design and Urban Renewal

what's ahead?

In this chapter, we will examine the role that architecture plays in our behaviour. The effects of architecture on communication and residential satisfaction will be explored. The work of Oscar Newman on defensible space and its effect on crime and vandalism will be examined, alongside good and bad practice in architectural design. This will involve an exploration of urban renewal projects and building design. Urban living will also be discussed, with respect to health and social behaviour. To do this, urban and rural differences will be considered across a number of psychological and health issues. Finally, we will present ideas and research on community environmental design; a process in which the community 'has its say' on building design issues.

The effect of architecture on communication

The architecture, design or layout of a room can have a considerable effect on our communication. For example, there are two main types of chair layout that can affect the amount of interaction we have in a room. The first is the *sociofugal* design. This kind of design is used to keep people apart. It usually features fixed seats that face away from each other. The second type is the *socipetal* design, which promotes interaction between people, usually with movable seats that are placed facing towards each other.

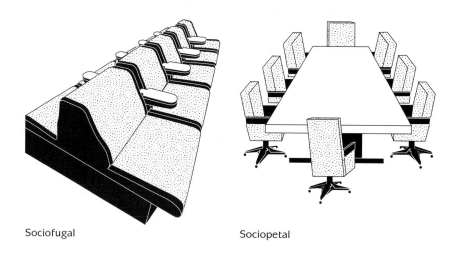

Sociofugal   Sociopetal

Recent research has examined the design of study areas and whether it affects communication, and hence the ability to concentrate and work.

research now

the blues may not make you sad!

Stone, N.J. (2001) Designing effective study environments. *Journal of Environmental Psychology*, 21, 179–90

Aim: To examine how a person's ability to study is affected by setting (open plan or private), colour of room (blue, white or red) and type of task (reading or mathematics).

Method: A total of 144 students took part. Each student was randomly assigned to one of 12 conditions from the combinations of setting, colour and type of material as noted above. The open plan and private settings were as shown oppposite:

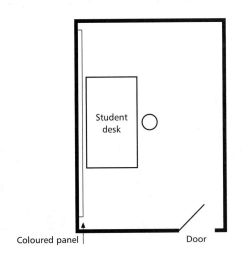

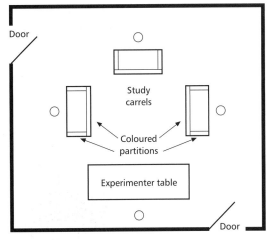

Source: Stone (2001)

In each condition, the participants were either given a mathematics test or a reading comprehension test. After completing the tasks, the participants had to complete questionnaires that measured mood, satisfaction and motivation.

Results: Stone found that there were some differences between the conditions. For example:

- On average, the participants experienced the most positive mood in a blue open-plan room, and experienced the least positive mood in a red open-plan room.

- For the private room, the colour red brought about the most positive mood.

- Participants were the most satisfied with their performance in the white private room and the blue open-plan room.

- There was little difference in the amount of privacy the participants felt they had between the open-plan room and the private room.

- Participants performed significantly worse in the reading task, irrespective of the setting, if the surroundings were red. They performed better in white surroundings.

Conclusion: There were some differences between the two settings (open plan and private) on the measures taken. For example, room colour had effects on satisfaction with performance in the tasks and on mood.

The effect of architecture on residential satisfaction

Lawton *et al.* (1975) examined whether there was any relationship between type of residential building (size, sponsorship of building and height of building) and well-being in older adults. They discovered that residents of non-profit-making privately sponsored housing had higher friendship scores and were more involved in activities compared to other types of dwellings. Those in small communities also had high friendship scores alongside higher residential satisfaction and activity levels.

The main factor that affected residential satisfaction was the size of the community in terms of number of units. The smaller the number of units, the more satisfied the people were. Height of building had a negative effect on residential satisfaction. That is, those who lived in taller buildings were less satisfied with where they lived. However, the cause might have been that friendly people had chosen to live in such places.

In Vietnam, Hanazato (2000) noted the differences in satisfaction between dwellers in two types of housing: pencil-housing (large privately owned dwellings) and apartments (small government-run dwellings). The former type of housing is popular, but poor ventilation and lack of building regulations mean that there is a wide range of conditions and subsequently of levels of satisfaction with the dwelling. In the latter type of housing, satisfaction is increased only with increased space and extensions are often undertaken. Hanazato concluded that there needs to be more control over the housing situation in Hanoi, Vietnam, for there to be overall improvements to dwellings. So, both the condition of the building (for example, ventilation) and the amount of space affects satisfaction with a residence.

The work of Oscar Newman on defensible space

Newman (1972) introduced the concept of *defensible space* to psychology, following after the work of Jane Jacobs. The term refers to an area of physical space that can be perceived as clearly belonging to someone. Any visitors to this space would quickly realise that it is someone else's territory. The idea of defensible space was generated because Newman had noted that many 'new' high-rise residential developments of his time had failed, as evidenced by their rapid decay and high crime rates. Newman proposed that this was the case because people had no control over the secondary territory (see Altman, 1975; see also p.12) within or around the buildings; for example, lobbies, staircases, lifts, parking areas and communal gardens. Residents were not able to feel any ownership of territory in or around the location of their living quarters. Therefore, they had a reduced capacity for surveillance over these areas, and they could not distinguish between people who lived in the same building as them and people who did not. So, residents did not feel any ownership over these areas, which reduced the sense of 'community'.

According to Taylor *et al.* (1984), defensible spaces could reduce crime for a number of reasons:

- Spaces that look 'defended' could well lead potential burglars to believe that the residents will actively respond to them trespassing on this secondary territory.

- Defensible spaces may well increase a 'sense of community', leading to a more cohesive residential group. As a result, people may feel 'safer' and therefore use the defended space more, which will lead to more contact with neighbours. This, in turn, could make people more inclined to intervene if a non-resident enters the defensible space.

- Defensible space may increase people's territorial functioning. As areas become characterised as 'defensible', people will act accordingly and come to the defence of those areas when necessary.

Newman (1972) then argued that if defensible spaces were deliberately designed into new multi-dwelling buildings, residents would feel more ownership over certain areas, and that this would increase informal surveillance and promote some form of cohesion within the community. That is, people would be more likely to 'look out for one another and their properties'. As a result, crime should decrease and a sense of community would be introduced. Newman recommended that certain features in the design of buildings could easily increase the amount of defensible space. These included using boundary markers that would show others where the territory was located. For example, pathways, fences and hedgerows would tell others that the territory was defended. Another approach would be to strategically arrange the windows on a building so that semi-public areas could be watched over by many of the residents. This could help to encourage positive social interaction between members of the community, so that the amount of surveillance increased.

On page 26, we will look at examples that have been shown to be good and bad with respect to Newman's ideas of defensible space.

Newman and Franck (1982) tested the relationship of physical design to crime as outlined in defensible space theory by examining housing developments in America. A total of 2,655 residents were surveyed about defensible space. Newman and Franck discovered some support for the idea that the size of the building affects personal crime and fear of crime. This was the case when participants felt control over the spaces around their apartments and used the spaces outside their apartment as territorial markers. However, the effect of building size on fears of personal crime was not as strong as Newman had originally hypothesised in his defensible space theory.

Ham-Rowbottom *et al.* (1999) examined defensible space theory by assessing police officer's judgements of the vulnerability of residences to burglary. Although Newman's original ideas focused on multi-occupancy dwellings, it is intriguing to see his work applied to other types of dwellings (for example, houses).

research now

will your house get burgled?

Ham-Rowbottom, K.A., Gifford, R. and Shaw, K.T. (1999) Defensible space theory and the police: assessing the vulnerability of residences to burglary. *Journal of Environmental Psychology*, 19, 117–29

Aim: To examine how the theory of defensible space applies to police officer's assessments of the vulnerability of different houses to burglary.

Method: Forty-one police officers were shown a series of 50 photographs of detached houses. Each house had been scored on 55 physical cues that were believed to be good indicators of defensible space. The police officers had to rate each house's vulnerability to burglary on a seven-point scale, from 'highly likely' to 'not likely'.

Results: A total of 10 physical cues were correlated with *less vulnerability to burglary* (in order of importance based on correlation coefficients):

- at least three-quarters of the house is visible from the road
- at least three-quarters of the yard is visible from the road
- a glass panel is not located next to the front door
- a garage is present
- the front door is solid, with no glass
- the backyard is separated from the front yard by an actual barrier
- more windows are visible from the road
- the front door is visible from the road
- the distance from the road is less than 20 feet (6 m)
- a neighbour's house is visible in the photograph.

Conclusion: It would appear that – as judged by police officers – the more physical barriers there are and the greater the road surveillability is (for example, from windows at the front of the house), the less likely a house is to be burgled. This finding is in line with defensible space theory. According to the police, the more physical barriers there are around a house, the less likely it is that it will become a victim of burglaries and other crimes.

Which house do you feel would be more likely to be burgled?

However, MacDonald and Gifford (1989) had discovered that defensible space did not always deter burglars. They surveyed 43 males who had been convicted of breaking and entering, by showing them 50 photographs of single-family dwellings. Each participant had to rate every photograph on a seven-point scale of vulnerability to burglary. The houses that had easy surveillability were rated as the least vulnerable to burglary. However, territorial displays (for example, fences) actually *increased* the attractiveness of the house to burglary. It was argued that having these displays, designed to deter trespassing as Newman stated, actually indicated that the house contents might be of value, as the occupants had chosen to defend their space in such an overt way. Also, barriers can actually help rather than hinder burglars, as they make it easier to climb into the property and can give them somewhere to hide!

Brower *et al.* (1983) noted a down side to defensible space theory: it does not take social factors into account. They surveyed 40 residents split between those who perceived that they lived in a high-problem neighbourhood and those who perceived that they lived in a low-problem neighbourhood. They showed them pictures of a variety of residential backyards. For all participants, the pictures that had real barriers and plants were interpreted as a deterrent towards burglars, because the occupant had strong territorial attitudes. However, for those in a high-problem neighbourhood, the territorial displays were seen as being less effective as deterrents for intrusion. Therefore, the social context overrode the idea that defensible space would deter people from entering. That is, if the neighbourhood is known to have a high crime level, defensible space appears to be less important.

It appears that the work of Newman (1972) still has an impact on the design of urban areas. For example, Yildirim and Kulodlu (2000) recently noted that in Turkey the planning process for urban open areas has to take environmental factors into consideration. If certain factors, such as defensible space, are ignored, then this will ultimately lead to the failure of the plans for the building, causing financial and aesthetic damage to the entire project.

Good and bad practice in architectural design with respect to defensible space: urban renewal and building design

After Newman had proposed the idea of defensible space, researchers examined housing developments and crime rates to see whether his ideas could be translated into the real world.

One such examination of defensible space theory looked into two adjacent housing estates in New York City. The two estates were called Van Dyke and Brownsville. The Van Dyke estate consisted of a series of 14-storey buildings, separated by small areas that had little or no defensible space. The Brownsville estate, on the other hand, consisted of six X-shaped buildings only three stories high. As a result, the entrances were less frequently used and were easy to watch over, as non-residents could be more easily spotted compared to the Van Dyke estate. Within the Brownsville buildings, children played in the hallways and stairwells, and it was common for residents to leave their doors open. Again, it was easier to watch over the immediate space compared to the Van Dyke estate. Due to the greater levels of defensible space in the Brownsville estate, there were stronger bonds between the residents, there was less crime and maintenance costs were reduced.

Central grounds of Van Dyke houses

Entrance to Van Dyke houses – no defensible space, high crime rates and a 'run down' appearance

Brownsville houses from the street – a considerable amount of defensible space and low crime rates

Another example that is used to show bad design is the Pruitt–Igoe project in St Louis, USA (Newman, 1972). The estate was built in 1954, with the ethos of 'no wasted space'. The project was constructed to relocate 12,000 people into 43 buildings, each 11 stories high. The entire complex had 2,762 apartments. The main features of the building included the following:

- the hallways that led to the apartments were narrow
- there were no semi-private areas in which people could meet (so no areas to oversee)
- the project was expensive to build
- the wall tiles were designed so that graffiti could be easily removed
- the light fittings were indestructible
- the radiators and lifts were vandal-resistant.

It appears curious that the project managers appeared to be 'expecting trouble' by introducing many of the above features. But they were correct. After a few years, the entire project was in disarray. Within the buildings there was broken glass and rubbish, the 'indestructible' features had been destroyed, many windows were boarded up or smashed, the lifts had been repeatedly used as toilets and the top floors were no longer lived in. Crime and vandalism were commonplace, with the car park littered with semi-destroyed cars and the children's playground covered in broken glass. By 1970, only 16 of the 43 buildings were still lived in. In 1972, the entire project was demolished. Many people believed that the lack of defensible space had caused the downfall of the Pruitt–Igoe dream.

interactive angles

Can you think of any other reasons why the Pruitt–Igoe project was a failure? Use your knowledge from this chapter so far to see if other reasons besides defensible space could explain the failure.

The Pruitt–Igoe research, which had suggested that defensible space was necessary for the reduction of crime, was backed up by a study conducted by Sommer (1987). He compared the crime rates in high-rise university halls of residence compared to those in cluster halls, which have more defensible space. The latter were seen to have much lower rates of crime and vandalism.

Shon and Kim (2000) have noted that Korean policy has reverted back to a supply of housing that is sustainable (presumably with defensible space so that degradation is lessened and sustainability is increased) compared to a mass production of housing which – as we have seen from the Pruitt–Igoe example – may not be the best type of housing to design.

Brunson (2000) has examined the Department of Housing and Urban Development (HUD) in America, as they have recently invested millions of dollars in the regeneration of urban areas using defensible space theory. Brunson notes that some regenerations have worked, lowering crime levels and bringing about a more cohesive community. However, not all have been so successful. Therefore, Brunson examined whether defensible space is linked to residents' experiences of safety and a sense of community in public housing. A total of 91 residents were surveyed. All were living in an area with a moderate amount of defensible space. Those who defended their near-home space reported that the neighbourhood felt safer and that there was a more cohesive community, compared to residents who did not defend their near-home space. Also, those who spent time outside reported more often that the neighbourhood was a safe place. Those who participated in 'greening' activities believed that the community was more cohesive. All of this tends to back up Newman's (1972) idea that defensible space makes the community more cohesive and safer to live in.

for and against

defensible space theory

+ It appears that when residential areas are constructed with defensible space, crime rates decrease (for example, the Brownsville estate).

+ There are examples in which residential areas have suffered higher levels of crime and vandalism when no defensible space has been present (for example, Pruitt–Igoe and Van Dyke).

− Social factors may have been overlooked in the original theory. If the area has a notorious reputation for crime, then defensible space may not help to reduce it.

− Burglars tend to see more defensible space as an indicator that properties have something to hide.

Theories and effects of urban living on health and social behaviour

There are four main theoretical angles that examine the effects of urban living on health and social behaviour. They attempt to explain why there could be differences in health and social behaviours between people who live in urban areas compared to people who live in rural areas. The four approaches are highlighted below:

- *Adaptation level theory.* This theory states that any stimuli that are intense, complex or novel can lead to either a positive or a negative effect, depending on the past experience of the individual concerned. Due to the differing levels of stimulation in a city or urban area (for example, you may find a quiet park or a busy shopping mall), anyone can find his or her optimal level of stimulation. Those people who initially find urban life too complex or intense usually adapt over time and tolerate such stimulation. Similarly, those who are bored with the country life find pockets of cosmopolitan life in the country.

- *Behaviour constraint theory.* This theory states that people who live in urban areas feel that their behaviour is constrained in some way compared to people living in rural areas. For example, people may feel more fearful of crime in urban areas, or may know that they will experience a potentially crowded shopping centre. This, of course, may lead to the person experiencing negative effects, and as a consequence of this the person may wish to try to reassert his or her freedom from these constraints. In the long term, this may have stronger negative effects, especially if the assertion continually fails. People may then feel that they have no control over their actions and become depressed.

- *Environmental stress theory.* This theory states that specific stimuli in urban areas have negative effects on our lives. For example, crowding and noise (see Chapters 3 and 4) have been shown negatively to affect humans. As we may feel threatened by such stimuli, a stress response may be elicited – emotionally, behaviourally or physiologically (or any combination of the three). Prolonged exposure to these stressful stimuli can have negative long-term effects.

- *Overload theory.* This theory states that people living in urban areas are bombarded with too many stimuli that cannot all be processed. This theory differs from the environmental stress angle above, as it looks at more general and numerous stimuli than just a specific one. The stimuli can come from a variety of sources; for example, other humans living in the urban area, noise, too many people being around, or trying to find the correct amount of money for the car park! All of these overload our senses and lead us to try to cope with the overload caused. However, prolonged overload can have negative effects, such as exhaustion and illness.

The above, remember, are simply theories of the effects of urban living on health and social behaviour. What about actual research that has been conducted? Are there any differences in urban and rural people's health and social behaviour? There has been a great deal of research that has examined urban–rural differences in health and social behaviour as well as urban–suburban differences.

Fisher *et al.* (1994) examined whether there was an urban–suburban difference in eating attitudes.

research now

big in the city

Fisher, M., Pastore, D., Schneider, M., Pegler, C. and Napolitano, B. (1994) Eating attitudes in urban and suburban adolescents. *International Journal of Eating Disorders,* 16(1), 67–74

Aim: To examine any potential differences in attitudes towards eating and weight concern in urban and suburban adolescents. Another aim was to examine whether there are differences in self-esteem between urban and suburban dwellers.

Method: Two groups of participants completed a series of questionnaires that measured attitudes towards eating and self-esteem among others. A total of 268 suburban females (mean age 16.2 years), 389 urban females and 281 urban males (combined mean age of 16.0 years) completed the questionnaires.

Results: One of the main factors examined was the relationship between perceived weight and actual weight. The table below shows the relationship in the sample studied:

Group	Percentage of participants who perceived themselves to be overweight	Percentage of participants who were actually more than 10 per cent over their ideal body weight
Suburban females	63	14
Urban females	35	45
Urban males	19	39

Also, self-esteem was significantly higher in the urban group compared to the suburban group.

Conclusion: Abnormal eating attitudes are present among urban and suburban adolescents. Suburban adolescents are more likely to perceive themselves as being overweight when in fact they are not. Urban adolescents are more likely to perceive themselves as not being overweight when in fact they are.

interactive angles

How could each of the theories described on page 29 explain the findings of Fisher *et al.* (1994) described above?

Another area of research that has interested environmental psychologists with respect to urban living is HIV (Human Immunodeficiency Virus) prevalence rates. Söderberg *et al.* (1994) examined the differences in prevalence rates in rural, semi-urban and urban areas in Tanzania.

research
now

taking risks with HIV

Söderberg, S., Temihango, W., Kadete, C., Ekstedt, B., Masawe, A., Vahlne, A. and Horal, P. (1994) Prevalence of HIV-1 infection in rural, semi-urban and urban villages in southwest Tanzania: estimates from a blood-donor study. *AIDS,* 8(7), 971–6

Aim: To measure the rates of HIV-1 infection in a series of subgroups of blood donors in Tanzania, Africa. This was a test of the idea of risky behaviour in cities.

Method: During the period from March 1988 to April 1991, all blood donors at the Ilembula Luteran Hospital (Tanzania) were asked about their home village, occupation, age and marital status. They were also tested for the prevalence of HIV antibodies in their blood sample. A total of 3,474 males and 1,287 females participated in the study.

Results: The following table shows the prevalence rate of HIV-1 infection split by gender and the type of area in which they lived:

Group	Overall rate (%)	Urban rate (%)	Semi-urban rate (%)	Rural rate (%)
Male	6.6	13.6	7.2	3.7
Female	7.0	15.0	7.9	3.0

Four high-risk groups emerged from the study: males from urban or semi-urban areas, females from urban or semi-urban areas, non-farmers from urban villages (compared to non-farmers in rural areas) and unmarried people.

Conclusion: There is a high rate of HIV-1 infection in this region of Tanzania. However, the highest rates are seen in urban areas. Söderberg *et al.* stated that this is consistent with people exhibiting more risky behaviour in urban communities.

Kovess *et al.* (1987) studied urban–rural differences in depressive disorders in French Canada. They noted that there were lower rates of depression in rural areas compared to urban areas even when age, sex, marital status, education and employment were taken into consideration. Kovess *et al.* also noted that there was no evidence for the urban group feeling less communally supported, which may have explained the differences. When subgroups were analysed, there appeared to be two groups that were causing the urban–rural differences: unemployed males and unpartnered women. Therefore, these two groups were the most depressed in urban areas, despite there probably being more potential for jobs and more opportunities to meet other people.

Yip *et al.* (2000) examined suicide rates of urban dwellers and rural dwellers to see if there were any differences.

research
now

rural lives at risk?

Yip, P.S., Callanan, C. and Yuen, H.P. (2000) Urban/rural and gender differentials in suicide rates: east and west. *Journal of Affective Disorders*, 57(1–3), 99–106

Aim: To examine the differences in suicide rates between rural and urban areas in Beijing (China) and Australia. Previous research had shown that there appear to be more suicides in urban areas. Also, the effect of gender on suicide rates in both urban and rural areas was investigated.

Method: Data on suicides from 1991 to 1996 in both geographical areas were examined.

Results: Contrary to expectations and previous research, the rural suicide rates were higher in Beijing for both males and females compared to urban suicide rates. Also, the elderly had the highest suicide rate. For Australia, rural male suicide was higher than urban male suicide. Urban females had a higher suicide rate compared to rural males.

Conclusion: The idea that there are more suicides in urban areas was not supported. Yip *et al.* stated that cultural factors and socio-economic factors could explain why there were more rural suicides in Beijing and Australia (for example, the stress of making a living in rural areas).

interactive
angles

Read the Yip *et al.* (2000) study again. How could each of the four theories on page 29 predict that suicide should be higher in urban areas? Why do you think that the Yip *et al.* study found the opposite?

Intriguingly, there have been differences in emotion found in schizophrenics from rural and urban dwellings. Chu *et al.* (1982) discovered that rural schizophrenics tended to be more apathetic, angry, aggressive and uncooperative. Urban schizophrenics tended to be more anxious, asocial and disoriented.

Community environmental design

Community environmental design differs from *urban renewal* in that it allows the current residents of a neighbourhood to make their input into the redesign of an area or the new development of an area. It allows insight into what residents really want from an area that they will be living in or near to.

Al-Kodmany (1999) discussed how the Chicago Pilsen neighbourhood had used the Geographical Information System (GIS: a satellite device that can pinpoint any location on Earth), in addition to a graphic artist, to aid community design. The GIS allowed the main community leaders, with the planners, architects and designers, to examine the spatial layout of the existing neighbourhood. The role of the graphic artist was to amalgamate the ideas of the current neighbourhood and sketch them so that all could be merged into a shared vision. Use of the GIS and the graphic artist helped the current residents to visualize the changes that could take place in the neighbourhood. Overall, this allowed for better direction for the planners and designers, in order for the outcome to be a success.

Rohe (1985–6) examined the potential relationship between community design and mental health. Rohe believed that the level of social inter-action and physical stimulation could be used to reduce the stress caused by undesirable interactions that could take place in the community. Rohe stated that citizen participation is important to aid stress reduction, as it gives people a sense of control over the community and the degree of social support that is available as a result. It was noted that high residential density, high traffic levels, poor maintenance of buildings and the presence of commercial activities close by were all related to negative mental health. Therefore, a need for community design was recommended to alleviate any mental health problems that might arise due to urban planning.

interactive angles

Using the findings of Rohe (1985–6) as a basis, choose a local 'problem area' that you know about and redesign it so that the mental health of people who live there can be improved.

media watch

Summary

The municipal leaders must lend their active support to urban regeneration if it is to be a success. In most of the urban regeneration projects, the residents have played a major role in the formulation of a plan for their area; however, things happening on time and sincere co-operation are necessary in order to maintain the resident participation. These are important examples of the experience to date from the seven urban areas that are participating in an extensive urban regeneration experiment. The purpose is partly to improve the individual urban areas as a whole and partly to provide models for urban policy in the future. The article explains the concept of urban regeneration, and then looks at its history and how it is organised. An attempt is also made to evaluate – $2^1/_2$ years down the line – the extent to which the municipalities' integrated approach has been a success and whether the resident participation has succeeded. Lastly, some examples are given of what urban regeneration can offer as a laboratory for urban policy thinking.

What is this Danish urban regeneration experiment?

It is an experiment in citizen participation and integrated and co-ordinated urban regeneration in selected urban areas. Twelve urban areas in Denmark are participating in an extensive urban regeneration experiment. The purpose is partly to improve the individual residential areas as a whole and partly to provide models for urban policy in the future. Seven of the 12 projects started in 1997 and the remaining five in 2001.

The seven residential areas, which have a total population of around 63,000 are: East Aalborg, Tøjhushaven in Randers, Southwest Kolding, Avedøre Stationsby in Hvidovre and the Holmbladsgade area, Kongens Enghave and the Northwest area in Copenhagen.

The urban regeneration project in the Femkanten area of Copenhagen is the precursor to the other six regeneration projects, which are being carried out in the period 1997 to 2001.

The main features of the urban regeneration experiment are as follows:

- The projects concern selected areas, and not individual residents or properties
- The projects are based on co-ordinated and integrated action
- The projects are aimed at increasing local participation
- The projects are part of a controlled process
- Background of the urban regeneration experiment.

The urban regeneration projects have been initiated in order to halt negative trends in seven selected urban areas. Danish cities do not have such massive problems as other European cities. Even so, some urban areas suffer from a concentration of social problems, worn-down buildings, poorly functioning urban spaces and a lack of facilities. And the negative development tends to be a self-increasing process.

The seven areas participating in this urban regeneration project all have serious problems – social problems, an unbalanced composition of the residents, worn-down housing and residential areas, heavy traffic through the area, etc. However, they also have resources on which urban regeneration can be based – in the form, for example, of a good network among the residents or recreational facilities that are at present under-utilised.

Source:http://www.kvarterloeft.dk

Blossom (2000) notes that interior designers are overlooked in community design work. They often help to produce healthier interior environments, which must increase aspects such as residential satisfaction. Blossom states that there has been too much emphasis on building systems (as in the Prutt–Igoe case, for instance), where the focus has been on the actual exterior nature of the building. Interior features may well have an effect on people's perceptions of urban areas.

Kose (2000) reported how Japan (which has one of the most aged societies in the world) has responded to its elderly population. The key concept of housing projects in Japan since 1987 has been to design for all ages, rather than to build specific sheltered housing for older adults. Kose believes that people should be able to age in their dwellings, and that the dwelling should respond to the changing needs of people as they age. In the United Kingdom a very different viewpoint is adopted: once people can no longer live in their own homes, they usually enter sheltered housing. There has been no report on the success of the Japanese project, and it will be intriguing to see if a mixed-age community, with housing specifically designed for this purpose, actually works.

interactive angles

List the advantages and disadvantages of segregating older adults in terms of the type of housing in which they live.

Conclusions

Architecture appears to have a considerable effect on our behaviour and on the way in which we communicate with each other. **Sociofugal** designs keep us apart, while **sociopetal** designs bring us together. The number of buildings around us could have an effect on how satisfied we are with the place in which we live. Oscar Newman introduced the idea of defensible space, a semi-public area that is clearly 'owned' or looked after by someone. He had the idea that these areas should reduce crime rates in residential areas. There is some support for his ideas and modern residential buildings are constructed with areas of defensible space. Previous residential areas that failed to make use of defensible space saw an increase in crime rates, and some were even demolished.

Urban living appears to be more stressful than rural living, at least at a theoretical level. However, research has shown that some rural dwellers are more stressed with their lives than urban dwellers and are more likely to commit suicide.

Community environmental design allows the residents in a particular area to 'have their say' about a new development or new aspects of a current residential area. This allows people to have some control over where they live and it increases satisfaction and a sense of community.

where to now?

The following are good sources of information about defensible space and urban living:

▶ **Cave, S. (1998)** *Applying Psychology to the Environment*. **London: Hodder & Stoughton** – a nice chapter on the role of the built environment in our behaviour.

▶ **Dwyer, D. (2001)** *Angles on Criminal Psychology*. **Cheltenham: Nelson Thornes** – a lovely section in this book is devoted to Oscar Newman's approach.

▶ **http://www4.ncbi.nlm.nih.gov/PubMed/** – search for urban–rural differences to see whether any of the four angles can explain the results. This is a good resource, as abstracts can be printed.

what do you know?

1 Using examples, distinguish between a sociofugal design and a socipetal design.

2 Describe what Oscar Newman meant by **defensible space**.

3 Use empirical evidence to assess how successful defensible space has been in reducing crime and vandalism.

4 In what ways does urban human behaviour differ from that of suburban, and rural human behaviour? Use studies to justify your answer.

3

Stress and the Environment

We begin the chapter by looking at the nature and physiology of stress and alternative explanations of the effects of stress. We also consider a range of sources of environmental stress, including noise, pollution and travel, and discuss research evaluating the importance of these stressors. In addition, we reflect on the way in which some of these same sources of frustration can also have positive effects on our performance. Finally, we consider the effects that stressors can have on our health and behaviour, and discuss the ways in which we can cope with sources of stress.

What is stress?

Stress is a reaction, both physical and psychological, to circumstances that are perceived to be negative and threatening to the individual. The elements of the situation that provoke such a response are called *stressors*. Under particular circumstances, some environmental stimuli may become stressors: How do their effects arise? For example, what effect will a loud, unpredictable noise have on us that a quiet, predictable noise does not? The effects of stressors can be considered in three ways, according to their effects on different aspects of our functioning:

- *physiological effects* on hormones such as adrenalin and cortisol

- *physical effects* on bodily functions such as pulse rate, blood pressure and the immune system

- *psychological effects* such as fear, anger, sensitivity and changes in cognitive functioning.

Some of these responses are, of course, adaptive; they help us to respond to potential dangers. However, they evolved to protect us in an environment that was rather different from that in which we now live. The need to be able to run fast is of far more use when trying to chase a woolly mammoth or to escape from a sabre-toothed tiger than when trying to cope with too much homework or rush-hour traffic! Psychologists have proposed three broad ways of looking at stress, in order to explain how stress arises. These involve looking at stress as existing in the environment, in the individual, or as a complex interaction between environment and individual.

Approaches to the explanation of stress

Stress in the environment

The environmental approach is sometimes called the *stimulus* or *engineering approach*. The focus is on *stressors*, sources of stress in the physical and social environment. In this model, stress is seen as something that happens to you rather than something that happens within you. You suffer stress when levels of stressors, such as pollution, become too high. Holmes and Rahe's life events theory (p.44) is a stimulus approach model of stress, as it suggests that stress arises in response to the stimulus of events in people's lives. Such models are incomplete, as they fail to account for the role of the individual in the stress response.

Stress in the individual

This approach is sometimes called the *response* or *physiological model*. Stress is viewed in terms of what happens to us, physically and psychologically, when we are in a state of stress. In this model, stress is seen as something that happens within you, for example, when you become annoyed by noise. Selye's General Adaptation Syndrome (p.40) is an individual model of stress, as it suggests that stress is an automatic, passive response of the individual to an external stimulus.

Stress as an interaction between the environment and the individual

This approach is sometimes called the *interactional* or *transactional model*. Both the amount of stress in the environment and the individual's response to it are considered. Importantly, this approach emphasises the psychological factors that allow some of us to cope with more stress in our environment than others. Lazarus' appraisal model (p.46) is a transactional model.

Such models provide a more complete account of stress. Stress begins with the appearance of a stressor in the environment. We judge whether this is indeed a problem. If we judge that it is, then there is an emotional and physiological response. A behavioural response follows, as a way of dealing with the emotional and physiological aspects of the experience.

The physiology of stress

Three body systems underlie the physiological effects of stress:

- the autonomic nervous system (ANS)
- the endocrine system (hormones)
- the immune system (our defence against disease).

You need to have a basic understanding of these systems in order to understand how stress affects us.

The autonomic nervous system

When we are faced with an emergency, the sympathetic branch of the autonomic nervous system responds quickly, preparing us for 'fight or flight'. The sympathetic nervous system (SNS) also sends impulses to the endocrine system, which responds by releasing hormones that enhance the preparation for action. This mechanism, which links the SNS to the adrenal medulla (the inner part of the adrenal glands), is called the Sympathetic Adrenal Medullary system (SAM). Although the sympathetic response is very fast, allowing us to respond quickly to an emergency, its effects are short-lived.

The endocrine system

The effects of the endocrine system are slower but longer-lasting. The hormone adrenalin is released from the adrenal medulla in response to environmental stressors, as are related neurotransmitters (catecholamines). These include dopamine and noradrenalin (Arnsten, 1998). This elevated level of catecholamines during stress may be responsible for some of the effects of stress, such as hardening of the arteries (Schneiderman, 1982). The adrenal cortex (the outer region of the adrenal glands) also releases hormones, corticosteroids, under conditions of stress. These processes are discussed further on pages 40–43.

The immune system

This is a collection of structures and mechanisms that our bodies use to fight off disease. It consists of *white blood cells* that engulf bacteria and the *lymphatic system*, a system of branching vessels that drain tissue fluid containing micro-organisms away from the cells of the body back into the blood. On the way, *lymph nodes* filter out the micro-organisms, which are then destroyed by specialised white blood cells called lymphocytes.

Theories of stress

General Adaptation Syndrome

Selye (1956) described the body's response to stress. He induced stress in rats by using a variety of stressors, including heat, cold and fatigue, and concluded that the rats showed the same physiological responses regardless of the nature of the stressor. These effects included enlarged adrenal glands, shrunken lymph glands, and stomach ulcers. Selye proposed that the body responded to any stress by mobilising itself for action. He called this response the General Adaptation Syndrome, or GAS. This is a response that has evolved as an adaptive way to help the individual deal with an emergency situation. You can see how, when our environment was full of physical dangers, this would be an advantage. If you were confronted by a hungry sabre-toothed tiger, you would certainly want your sympathetic nervous system to kick in as soon as possible, so that you could escape. A similar response is not so useful if you are stuck in a traffic jam (you get wound up, but 'fight or flight' is neither possible nor appropriate). However, according to Selye, our bodies have not evolved to take account of our new environment. Selye identified three stages to the body's response to stress through which we pass if a stressor persists over time:

- *alarm* – the body's mechanisms to deal with danger are activated

- *resistance* – we struggle to cope with the stress, and the body attempts to return to its previous physiological state

- *exhaustion* – if the stress persists and the body cannot return to its previous state, physical resources will become depleted, eventually leading to collapse.

The body's response to stress occurs in three stages, as described by Selye. Initially, in the *alarm stage*, we perceive a stressor and the sympathetic branch of our autonomic nervous system prepares the body quickly for action. The sympathetic response also causes the release of hormones adrenalin and noradrenalin (also called epinephrine and norepinephrine, respectively). The combined effect of the SAM ensures that we are physically prepared to respond to the environmental threat; for instance, by fighting or fleeing. The effects of the sympathetic response and the hormones are shown in the accompanying figure.

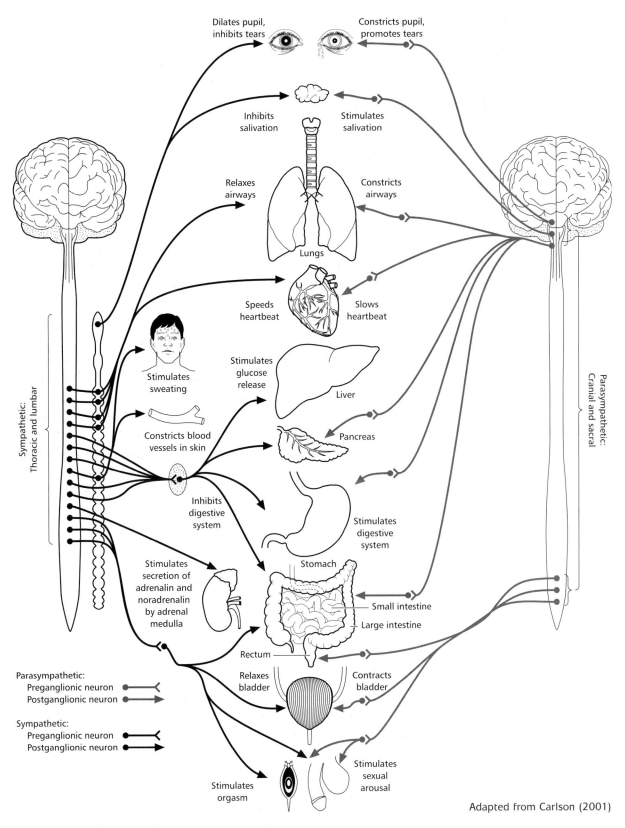

Dilates pupil, inhibits tears

Constricts pupil, promotes tears

Inhibits salivation

Stimulates salivation

Relaxes airways

Constricts airways

Lungs

Speeds heartbeat

Slows heartbeat

Stimulates sweating

Stimulates glucose release

Liver

Constricts blood vessels in skin

Pancreas

Inhibits digestive system

Stimulates digestive system

Stomach

Stimulates secretion of adrenalin and noradrenalin by adrenal medulla

Small intestine

Large intestine

Rectum

Relaxes bladder

Contracts bladder

Stimulates orgasm

Stimulates sexual arousal

Sympathetic: Thoracic and lumbar

Parasympathetic: Cranial and sacral

Parasympathetic:
Preganglionic neuron
Postganglionic neuron

Sympathetic:
Preganglionic neuron
Postganglionic neuron

Adapted from Carlson (2001)

The autonomic nervous system has two branches, the sympathetic and the parasympathetic, which work approximately antagonistically (in opposition to each other). Sympathetic responses, such as to a stressful situation, tend to occur in unison, as the sympathetic chain of ganglia lying alongside the spinal cord activates all the sympathetic functions simultaneously. In contrast, the parasympathetic system, which is active when we are relaxed, can activate target organs individually

inter**active**
angles

Complete the table below, that lists some of the functions of the two parts of the autonomic nervous system.

Sympathetic effects	Parasympathetic effects
Increased heart rate	
Increased blood pressure	
Dry mouth	Maintenance of saliva production
Dilated pupils	
Dilated blood vessels in muscles	
Contracted blood vessels around digestive system	Blood supply to digestive system is increased to remove products of digestion
Increased sweating	
Increased breathing rate	

The sensation of 'butterflies in the stomach' is caused by the contraction of blood vessels around the gut, so that blood supply can be directed to the muscles, supplying them with more oxygen and carbohydrates to be metabolised if physical action becomes necessary. You have probably experienced this response when frightened; for example, before going into a psychology exam! If the stressor is removed, parasympathetic activity in the ANS returns levels of adrenaline and noradrenaline to normal. If the stressor is not removed, the body enters the second stage.

In the second stage of the stress response, the *resistance stage*, levels of adrenalin and noradrenalin fall and levels of three other hormones increase:

- Cortisol breaks down fatty tissue, releasing soluble fats and glucose into the blood. This means that the muscles can obtain more energy from the blood.

- Aldosterone increases blood pressure, maintaining the body ready for action.

- Thyroxine increases the body's metabolic rate. This means that the stressed person can extract energy from food more quickly. Thyroxine also increases the rate at which food travels through the gut, allowing energy to be quickly extracted from the food currently in the gut.

The release of corticosteroids such as cortisol is controlled by another hormone, adrenocorticotrophic hormone (ACTH), which is in turn secreted in response to the release of corticotropin-releasing factor (CRF). CRF is a peptide (a small protein) released by the parvoventricular nucleus, a region of the hypothalamus. Injection of CRF into the brain produces responses similar to those associated with aversive situations, which suggests that some aspects of the stress response are caused by CRF. For example, Swerdlow *et al.* (1986) found that CRF increased the startle response shown by rats to a loud noise. This link between the hypothalamus, the pituitary gland and the adrenal cortex is referred to as the Hypothalamic Pituitary Adreno cortex axis (HPA) and can trigger the release of corticosteroids to minor, but unpredictable, environmental changes. If these are not threatening, the response diminishes. If, however, the stressor is sustained, the action of the HPA is maintained by the forebrain.

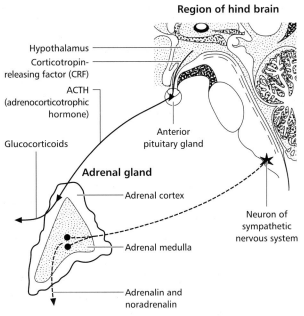

Region of hind brain

Hypothalamus

Corticotropin-releasing factor (CRF)

ACTH (adrenocorticotrophic hormone)

Glucocorticoids

Anterior pituitary gland

Adrenal gland

Adrenal cortex

Neuron of sympathetic nervous system

Adrenal medulla

Brain and endocrine areas responsible for the secretion of hormones involved in the body's response to stress

Adrenalin and noradrenalin

Adapted from Carlson (2001)

If the stressor remains for long enough, and is severe enough, we may enter the third stage, *exhaustion*. Examples of such severe and prolonged stressors include torture, being hunted and/or working in a high-demand profession such as teaching. Exhaustion occurs when the body's supplies of energy and hormones are used up. This may result in collapse and sometimes death.

for and against

the theory of the general adaptation syndrome

+ The idea that the body has certain responses to stressors, and that these responses help us to prepare for danger, is generally accepted.

+ Selye's proposal that the body's response to stress has evolved in order to prepare us to deal with danger is a logical idea.

− It is, however, possible that our responses to stress are learned rather than instinctive.

> — Selye's theory was based on animal research. There are problems in applying this to humans.
>
> + Selye's ideas have helped us to understand the link between stress and illness.
>
> — The main limitation of this approach to stress is that it does not take account either of the effects of different types of stressor in the environment or individual differences in peoples' responses to those stressors.

Life events theory

Whereas Selye's model emphasises the physiological changes associated with stress, the life events model attempts to link stressful events to the incidence of stress. Holmes and Rahe (1967) began by developing a Schedule of Recent Events, a list of potentially stressful life events. People could derive a score on this by counting the number of events that had happened to them in the last year. This list ranged from minor occurrences such as a 'vacation' or a 'change in eating habits' to major traumas including 'death of a spouse' or 'jail term'. While this did demonstrate some links between stress and health status, it was a crude measure because it could not account for the difference in severity of the possible life events that were counted up in the total score. To improve the effectiveness of this system, it was replaced by the Social Readjustment Rating Scale (SRRS). Recent evidence suggests, however, that there is little difference in the power of the two scales to predict ill health (Turner and Wheaton, 1995).

classic research

stress is sickening

Holmes, T.H. and Rahe, R.H. (1967) The social readjustment rating scale. *Journal of Psychosomatic Research,* 11, 213–18

Aim: to develop a weighting system for the critical life events identified on the Schedule of Recent Events.

Method: Records of 5,000 patients were examined for life events that arose in the months preceding the onset of their illness.

Results: Forty-three life events were found to occur often in the prescribed period. Their relative frequency was used to generate the Social Readjustment Rating Scale (SRRS). The SRRS is a list of these life events in order of seriousness; that is, the relative frequency with which they were found to occur in the patients, with weightings according to seriousness. The weightings, called Life Change Units, can be used to calculate a score for subsequent individuals by identifying the number of significant life events that had happened to them in a specified period of time – for example, the preceding 6 months – and adding together the value assigned to each one.

Conclusion: The SRRS can thus be used to predict the likelihood of a stress-related illness arising in other individuals by looking at the total of LCUs. Individuals whose experiences total in excess of 300 LCUs over 1 year are more likely to suffer.

The SRRS includes both positive and negative events, since any deviation from the normal life pattern has the potential to be stressful. However, subsequent evidence suggested that only unpleasant events were linked to increased illness (Ross and Mirowsky, 1979).

The Social Readjustment Rating Scale

Rank	Life event	Mean value	Rank	Life event	Mean value
1	Death of spouse	100	23	Son or daughter leaving home	29
2	Divorce	73	24	Trouble with in-laws	29
3	Marital separation	65	25	Outstanding personal achievement	28
4	Jail term	63	26	Wife begins or stops work	26
5	Death of close family member	63	27	Begin or end school	26
6	Personal injury or illness	53	28	Change in living conditions	25
7	Marriage	50	29	Revision of personal habits	24
8	Fired at work	47	30	Trouble with boss	23
9	Marital reconciliation	45	31	Change in work hours or conditions	20
10	Retirement	45	32	Change in residence	20
11	Change in health of family member	44	33	Change in schools	20
12	Pregnancy	40	34	Change in recreation	19
13	Sex difficulties	39	35	Change in church activities	19
14	Gain of new family member	39	36	Change in social activities	18
15	Business re-adjustment	39	37	Mortgage or loan less than $10,000	17
16	Change in financial state	38	38	Change in sleeping habits	16
17	Death of a close friend	37	39	Change in number of family get-togethers	15
18	Change to a different line of work	36	40	Change in eating habits	15
19	Change in number of arguments with spouse	35	41	Vacation	13
20	Mortgage over $10,000	31	42	Christmas	12
21	Foreclosure of mortgage or loan	30	43	Minor violations of the law	11
22	Change in responsibilities in work	29			

Adding together the weightings for each event that has occurred generates a total of *life change units* that can be used as an indicator of the level of stress experienced

Source: Holmes and Rahe (1967)

Initial evidence supported the predictive power of the SRRS. Rahe (1968) tested 2,500 servicemen in the 6 months prior to tours of duty on Navy cruisers. The life change units (the summed weightings from the SRRS) were then related to medical records at the end of the first 6 months aboard ship. Within the first few months, those individuals with

SRRS scores in the top 30 per cent had nearly 90 per cent more first illnesses than those individuals in the lowest 30 per cent. This trend continued for the entire 6 months. However, subsequent studies have not demonstrated clear relationships between stress (as indicated by the SRRS) and ill health (see, for example, Theorell *et al.*, 1975; Goldberg and Comstock, 1976).

for and against

life events theory

+ Some evidence supports the relationship between life events and ill health.

+ Both the SRE and SRRS seem to be equally effective predictors of illness.

− The degree of stress experienced depends on the individual's perception of the life event (as suggested by the transactional model).

− Ratings of life events tend to be retrospective. They may therefore be unreliable, because of the inaccuracy of memories and the current state of the individual. A person who is ill may perceive his or her life more critically and selectively recall negative events, or may ignore them, blaming his or her condition on some uncontrollable factor such as genetics.

− Life experiences may interact. Coincident negative events may be more damaging than the same events occurring separately, and negative events may be counteracted by positive ones.

− Many studies have obtained rather low correlations.

− Some of the life events are illnesses or illness-related, and so would artificially inflate the correlation.

Lazarus' transactional model of stress

The approach that Lazarus proposes for understanding stress takes account of the ability of people to consider the effect that a stressor is having upon them. Humans can evaluate events, assessing the threat, their own vulnerability and how they might cope. From this perspective, a life event is not necessarily a source of stress; the individual's evaluation of its impact is what determines its stressfulness. A student who misses a deadline but has previously been up to date, and is confident he or she can catch up, may be less stressed by the experience than one who knows that he or she is about to be removed from the course for persistent tardiness. It is the perception of vulnerability and lack of control that creates a stressful situation.

Lazarus and Folkman (1984) suggest that this process of determining whether a situation is threatening, challenging or harmful is one of *appraisal*. Our initial impression, or *primary appraisal*, of the situation generates emotions in relation to the judgement:

- a *threat*, or the anticipation of harm, generates an appraisal of fear, anxiety or worry

- *harm*, or damage already done, generates an appraisal of disgust, disappointment, anger or sadness

- a *challenge*, or confidence in the face of a difficult demand, generates an appraisal of anticipation or excitement.

Following the initial appraisal, a *secondary appraisal* is made. This is the formation of an impression about our ability to cope with the situation. It is a consideration of the possible options, the chances of successfully employing them and whether the action will work. A student with an overdue essay might first consider the options: copying someone else's, missing the lesson when the work is due in, fabricating an excuse and asking for an extension and so on. The student then has to decide whether each action could be implemented – Would a lie be effective? Finally the chances of success need to be evaluated: Would the teacher notice a copied essay or believe the excuse?

Reappraisal may follow in the light of new information. The student may find out that this teacher is a pushover, or that the essay title was the same as one set last year. This knowledge would reduce the judgement of the situation from a stressful to a benign one. Alternatively, additional evidence may suggest that a previously innocent situation is a threat. The student may have believed that to exceed deadlines was permissible, but he or she may subsequently discover that there is a penalty for doing so.

In a recent review of stress in classroom teachers, Jarvis (2001) discusses cognitive factors that affect the experience of stress. He describes the importance of self-defeating beliefs that are associated with higher stress levels and the effect of high expectations. For example, new teachers who find that their initial expectations are not attainable become emotionally exhausted in their efforts to achieve them. Individual differences in coping styles also affect stress. Griffith *et al.* (1999) found that teachers with low social support and a tendency to use disengagement and suppression of competing activities as coping strategies – that is, those who cut themselves off and ignored other aspects of their lives – suffered higher levels of stress. These findings suggest that the nature of cognitive appraisals as described by Lazarus affect our vulnerability to stress.

The importance of control over the environment

A person's control over a potential stressor affects the extent of the stress response that it elicits; for instance, an uncontrollable noise is more stressful than a controllable one (p.54). This relationship can be clearly demonstrated in experimental studies with animals. Seligman and Visintainer (1985) report the effects of controllable and uncontrollable shocks on the health of rats. The experimental animals were injected with live tumour cells, and then exposed to electric shocks. Tumour growth was greater in the 'uncontrollable shock' condition, suggesting that stressors that we are unable to control have a more detrimental effect on health.

Similar results were obtained by Manuck *et al.* (1986) in their study of coronary heart disease (CHD) in monkeys. Prior to the experimental manipulation the monkeys had formed a stable hierarchy with dominant and submissive individuals. New monkeys were then introduced to destabilise the group. Since it would be harder for dominant animals to assert their positions in the new social environment, they would be under greater stress; there would be a mismatch between their expectations of control and the reality of the newly developing hierarchy. The dominant animals did indeed experience a higher incidence of CHD in the unstable condition than did either dominant or submissive individuals in the stable condition.

Although animal studies may rely on assumptions of relevance to people, similar findings have emerged in relation to the human response to stressful environments. Studies in Sweden (Karasek *et al.*, 1981) and in the USA (Karasek *et al.*, 1988) have provided evidence to suggest that job-related stress induced by a combination of high workload, low satisfaction and little control is the best predictor of CHD. Similarly, Haynes *et al.* (1980) found that, in a group of working women, the combination of high job demand, low control and low work support was a reliable predictor of CHD. It appears that, for people as well as animals, control is vital in order to minimise the effects of environmental stress on health.

where to now?

The following are good sources of information about the physiology of stress:

▶ **Kalat, J.W. (1998)** *Biological Psychology*. **London: Brooks/Cole** – this covers both the autonomic nervous system and the physiology of the stress response in detail.

▶ **Pinel, J.P.J. (1997)** *Biopsychology*. **London: Allyn and Bacon** – this discusses the biology of the effects of stress on the functioning of the immune system in an accessible way.

▶ **Cassidy, T. (1999)** *Stress, Cognition and Health*. **London: Routledge** – this offers some alternatives to the biological model of stress.

Sources of environmental stress

Many aspects of our environment act as stressors. Being kept awake at night by street lights, or getting lost in a complicated road layout (as discussed in Chapter 8) or in a crowd (see Chapter 4), can all contribute to making our lives stressful. In this section we consider noise, pollution and travel as sources of stress.

Noise

The intensity of sound (volume) is measured in decibels (dB). Individuals vary in their *threshold of hearing*; that is, the quietest sound that they can detect.

dB	Example		
140	Painfully loud		*Painfully loud*
130	Machine gun fire at close range		
120	Maximum vocal effort		
110	Music at a concert		
100	Chainsaw		
90	Lawn mower		*Hearing damage after 8 hours*
80	Underground train		
70	Fast traffic		
60	Busy office		
50	Conversation		*Quiet*
40	Residential area at night		
30	Clock ticking		*Very quiet*
20	Leaves rustling		
10	Normal breathing		
0			*Hearing threshold*

The decibel scale

In the context of environmental psychology, *noise* refers to sounds that are unpleasant (the word 'noise' derives from the Latin *nausea* – the inclination to vomit). Thus the presence of a sound is necessary, but not sufficient, to produce noise; a noise must in addition be 'unwanted'. While it is rare for noise to have the direct effect of inducing vomiting, noise *can* affect our well-being. The sound of your favourite track played loudly on your own stereo is pleasing, but the same music heard through the wall from your neighbour when you're trying to sleep becomes an annoying noise. Clearly, volume is not the only factor that affects the distinction between wanted and unwanted sounds.

inter**active**
angles

The range of human hearing changes over our lifespan. Young children can hear frequencies between 20 and 20,000 Hz, but with age we lose the capacity to detect higher-frequency sounds. The following is a simple test of your upper register of hearing. Switch on a television and turn the sound off completely. Put your head near the back of the set: Can you hear a soft, high-pitched whine? If so, you can detect a frequency of about 16,000 Hz. As you move away from the set, the sound will become inaudible – you are below your threshold for detecting that frequency. Older people are less likely to be able to hear the sound, and if they can will probably have higher thresholds (that is, will need to be closer).

Why is your own phone a perfectly acceptable sound, but the calls of others an irritating noise?

Glass and Singer (1972) identified three key variables that could affect the extent to which we experience sounds as unpleasant; that is, dimensions along which a sound becomes a noise:

● volume

● predictability

● perceived control.

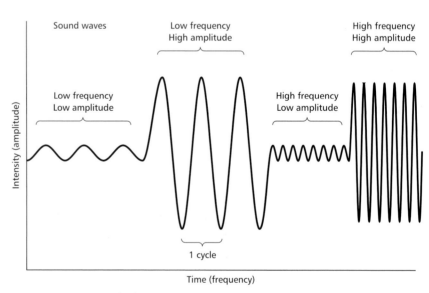

The amplitude of a wave is its 'height'. For sound, amplitude represents volume; sound waves with greater amplitudes are louder. The frequency of a wave is the time between each 'peak' and the next. For sound, frequency represents pitch; sound waves with a lower frequency are 'deeper'. Frequency is measured in Hertz or 'cycles per second'

research
now

noisy student halls

Ng, C.F. (2000) Effects of building construction noise on residents: a quasi experiment. *Journal of Environmental Psychology*, 20, 375–85

Aim: To investigate the psychological and behavioural effects of noise on students living in a hall of residence adjacent to a construction site.

Method: Ninety-four students accommodated in an all-female hall of residence completed a questionnaire about the effects that they experienced relating to the construction of a building nearby. The students were housed in three wings of the hall, providing a comparison between those nearest to, furthest from and in an intermediate position in relation to the noise, the closest being within 5 m of the site. In addition, some students kept an activity log, sound level measurements were taken, observations were made of window opening and closing, and student turnover and achievement were recorded.

Results: Students living in the wing nearest to the construction site were exposed to louder noise and showed significant behavioural differences compared to those in the central or furthest wing. Students living in the noisiest wing were distracted significantly more often, were more likely to be awakened by the noise and had more difficulty with studying and relaxing. The noise interfered with television viewing, conversations and telephone calls. These students coped by speaking more loudly, keeping their windows closed and leaving their rooms. However, there were no differences between residents in different wings with respect to their attitude towards the construction, nor with respect to their academic success.

Conclusion: Noise has significant psychological and behavioural effects on a young, student population, although even the students exposed to the greatest noise did not demonstrate long-term effects of stress. There appear to be few effective strategies to reduce loudness, but students do take action – such as closing windows – which may help to counter the effects by increasing perceived control.

Volume

Higher-intensity sounds are clearly more disruptive. Above 90 dB, sounds become disturbing; for instance, interfering with conversation. In addition, louder noises demand more attention, and increase arousal and stress to a greater extent. However, loudness is not the same as volume. *Volume* is the measurable increase in magnitude of vibration in the air – sounds increase in volume as the amplitude of the waves increases; that is, it is an objective measure of sound intensity. *Loudness* is a subjective measure of the perceived intensity of the sound. This may be affected by several factors:

- *context* – sounds appear louder against a quiet background (when the music in a bar stops, you find that you are shouting)

- *habituation* – we become insensitive to repeated, monotonous sounds (if you live very near to a railway, you may cease to notice loud but continuous noise from trains)

- *pitch* – we attend readily to high-frequency sounds (the screech of an over-excited young child is difficult to ignore).

Stevens (1956) demonstrated that, across most of the audible range, increasing the volume tenfold produces an approximate doubling of loudness. This relationship is illustrated in the accompanying figure. The relationship between intensity and loudness breaks down for very quiet sounds, below 20 dB, where loudness appears to change more rapidly (that is, changes in loudness more closely match changes in volume).

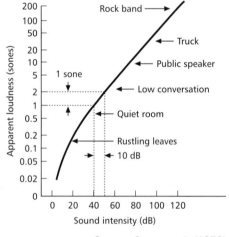

Volume and loudness – across most of the audible range, a doubling of loudness (measured in 'sones') requires a tenfold increase in intensity of a sound (measured in decibels)

Source: Coren et al. (1978)

Belojevic *et al.* (2001) tested participants' ability on a mental arithmetic task under noisy conditions (with recorded traffic noise at 88 dB(A)) and in quiet conditions (42 dB(A)). Extroversion and introversion were also measured using the Eysenck Personality Questionnaire. The introverts (but not the extroverts) suffered impaired concentration and greater fatigue in the noisy compared to the quiet condition, although accuracy was not affected.

Repeated or continuous sounds appear less loud over time: this is *habituation*. As we habituate to the stimulus of the sound, its apparent loudness decreases: this is called *auditory adaptation*. Exposure to intense sounds can induce *auditory fatigue*, which causes a persistent reduction in apparent loudness. Postman and Egan (1949) exposed listeners to an intense (115 dB) noise for 20 minutes. Recordings of their subsequent

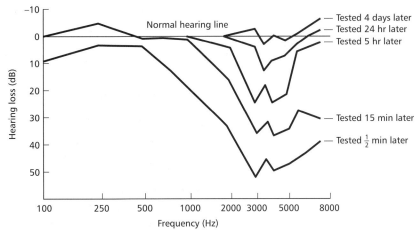

Even brief exposure to loud sounds can have a detrimental effect on hearing. Postman and Egan (1949) found a measurable loss in hearing even 24 hours after exposure to a short burst of loud noise

Source: Coren et al. (1978)

interactive angles

You can observe auditory adaptation using a sound source such as an alarm clock–radio. During the daytime we are continuously exposed to noise – from people, machines, vehicles and so on – and consequently we adapt to the sound intensity. During the night, when noise levels drop, the reverse occurs and we become more sensitive to sounds again. This can be demonstrated by setting the volume of a radio to a comfortable listening level at the end of the day, when the intensity has dropped but you are still adapted to the ongoing noise. In the morning, that same level will seem louder, because you have recovered from the auditory adaptation that you had experienced.

sensitivity showed that there was an immediate, significant hearing loss, which did not reverse for several days (see the accompanying figure).

Predictability

Consider how annoying the occasional cough or sniff is in an exam room. It breaks your concentration far more than the continuous hum of the heater

In addition to acoustic factors (for example, volume and pitch), non-acoustic variables such as predictability alter the effect of noise on mood (Green and Fidell, 1991).

A loud 'clonk' that comes at regular intervals is less disturbing than one that occurs irregularly. For example, the predictable ticking of a clock is less annoying than the erratic scuttling of a pet hamster. This is because we are more likely to be able to ignore an intrusive stimulus that we can anticipate than one we cannot. As a consequence, we can adapt to predictable but not to unpredictable noise. Corah and Boffa (1970) exposed participants to a loud noise either with or without prior warning. Those participants who were told about the noise (that is, those for whom it was predictable) experienced less subjective stress. According to Corah and Boffa, this predictability enabled the participants to feel that they had control over the stimulus. As predictability reduces, a noise is more likely to demand attention and increase arousal and stress.

Perceived control

Being able to control a noise reduces the likelihood of it becoming a problem. A noise that can be stopped, muffled or avoided is less disturbing. If you have control over the noise, such as when you are using a lawnmower, it is less irritating for you – because you can stop the noise whenever you like – than for your neighbour, who has no control over its cessation. Similarly, if the neighbours can block the sound out by closing windows, the noise becomes less annoying to them. Even if they choose not to take any action, they benefit from the sense of having the potential to regain control over the noise. The knowledge that one can avoid a noise, by choosing to go out shopping while the neighbours are mowing, has a similar effect: again one can opt not to and still benefit. However, if you exercise your perceived control and it proves to be ineffectual (you close the windows but can still hear the lawnmower, or you go out in the morning only to find that your neighbours have delayed mowing until the afternoon), the stress of your failure to control the situation will be greater. Ultimately, this can result in *learned helplessness*, the failure to exert control even when it becomes possible. This occurs because prior learning has taught us that attempts to control the situation are not effective. Evans (2000) reports that children and adults exposed to noise, crowding, traffic congestion or pollution develop responses – such as poor decision-making – that resemble learned helplessness.

Individual differences

Unsurprisingly, loud, unpredictable, uncontrollable noises are the most psychologically distressing. In addition to these factors, Borsky (1969) found that necessity, concern, perceived health risk and satisfaction also affected a person's value judgement about whether a noise was annoying. Two further factors – fear and sensitivity to noise – have been shown to be important.

- *Necessity – whether the cause of the noise is seen to be a worthwhile activity.* A lawnmower at least cuts the grass, while loud music may be seen to have no useful function (and is therefore perceived as more annoying).

- *Concern – whether the person responsible is believed to care about those who are disturbed by the noise.* Neighbours who choose to do DIY at night appear to have little concern for the disturbance that they are causing, and the noise is therefore more annoying than, say, their baby crying.

- *Perceived health risk – whether those exposed to the noise fear that they may be damaged by their enforced exposure.* Office workers who believe that noise from a nearby construction site could damage their hearing will find the noise more annoying than those who do not.

- *Satisfaction – whether the individual is content with his or her environment in general.* A neighbour who is in other respects satisfied with the locality will be less disturbed by the noise from a lawnmower than one who is already engaged in a dispute with other residents.

Whether or not an individual associates a noise with a fearful stimulus may affect his or her aversion to that noise. An individual who associates a particular noise with fear will experience greater distress than someone who does not. Thus the buzzing of a wasp against a window will be more problematic for someone who is afraid of insects than for other people.

Some people find noise more aversive than others do; they have higher *noise sensitivity*. This may be due to some personality trait or due to a differing sensitivity to sound, so they may be more intolerant of noise because it is more intrusive for them. It is possible that these two factors are related; people who are more reactive to sound may additionally be more bothered by it as well (Taylor, 1984). This alone does not appear to be sufficient, however, to explain individual differences in annoyance caused by noise (see Staples *et al.*, 1999, p.56).

Sensitivity versus disturbance

Zimmer and Ellermeier (1999) compared measures of noise sensitivity, including behavioural and emotional responses to environmental noises at work, during recreation and while sleeping. They also tested objective disruption during a cognitive task and compared this to the participants' subjective noise sensitivity ratings. Only a weak correlation was found, which suggests that the self-reported effects of noise sensitivity are greater than the actual disruption. The effects of noise sensitivity on annoyance must therefore be mediated by emotional reactions to noise.

research
now

are planes a perk or a pest?

Staples, S.L., Cornelius, R.R. and Gibbs, M.S. (1999) Disturbance from a developing airport: perceived risk or general annoyance? *Environment and Behavior,* 31, 692–710

Aim: To investigate whether people differ in their levels of annoyance according to the long-term benefits they perceive from the disturbance caused by aircraft noise.

Method: Nine hundred and one residents living in close proximity to airports were assessed using the Environmental Noise Risk Scale (ENRS) to measure the costs and benefits that they associated with having an airport close by. They were also tested on a noise sensitivity scale, rating themselves on statements such as 'I find it difficult to study in a noisy setting' and 'I cannot sleep when even a minor noise is present'.

Results: Participants showed a stronger relationship between the ENRS score and the extent to which they were disturbed by the noise than between sensitivity and disturbance. If they were able to perceive economic and community benefits, such as employment opportunities and convenience, rather than focusing on the adverse environmental effects of the airport, they were less likely to be disturbed by the airport noise.

Conclusion: Cost–benefit analysis may be more useful than sensitivity testing in analysing the likely impact of noise on an individual. Where perceived benefits exceed perceived costs, people are likely to be less affected by noise disturbance regardless of their sensitivity level.

Sources of environmental noise

Whilst many sounds can become 'noise' – for instance, if they are loud – some sources of noise, including occupational and transportation noise, present an ongoing problem for many of us.

Occupational noise refers to the unpleasant sounds to which people are exposed in the workplace. There are two reasons why workplace noise is so disruptive. First, in the workplace people may be trying to concentrate, but noise demands attention and increases arousal, thus making the task in hand more difficult. Secondly, workplace noise – particularly in offices – tends to be *wide-band noise*; that is, it is composed of a range of frequencies. This makes it particularly difficult to mask using *white noise* (unpatterned sound, containing a wide range of frequencies, like 'static'). In other settings, the problem may be volume; for example, construction workers may be regularly exposed to volumes of 100 dB, aircraft mechanics to 88–120 dB and coal miners to 95–105 dB (Raloff, 1982). Inside a large barn full of pigs, a farmer may be exposed to 110 dB, or even more at feeding time (Health and Safety Executive, 1995).

inter**active** angles

Try to visit a range of workplaces and identify the sources of noise in each. Some, such as pieces of equipment, will be obvious, while others may be less easy to identify; ambient noise from conversations, intermittent noise from telephones ringing and the hum of air conditioning, for instance. If you have access to a sound-level meter you could ask to use it. Alternatively, you can gauge relative noise in the following way. Write out a long sequence of digits interspersed (say, every 20 digits) with a letter. Record this sequence of digits and letters on to a cassette tape. Using a portable player such as a walkman, set the volume in a silent room so that the speech is clearly audible but quiet when listened to through headphones. In each workplace, play a section of tape (between two letters) and attempt to write out the sequence of digits that you can hear. The accuracy of your record compared to the original list will give you an indication of the interference from occupational noise.

Transportation noise refers to the unpleasant sounds generated by motor vehicles, trains, aeroplanes and other means of transport. One of the reasons why transportation noise is so often reported to be a problem is because it is so loud. Bronzaft *et al.* (1998) found that approximately 70 per cent of residents living along the path of an airport flight corridor reported being troubled by noise from aircraft.

research
now

planes in the parks

Mace, B.L., Bell, P.A. and Loomis, R.J. (1999) Aesthetic, affective and cognitive effects of noise on natural landscape assessment. *Society and Natural Resources*, 12, 225–42

Aim: Many beauty spots, such as the Grand Canyon in the USA and the English Lake District, attract air traffic as well as visitors on the ground. People who may have walked many miles in pursuit of 'restoration' and 'escape' in the natural environment are perturbed to find their isolation violated by helicopters and aeroplanes. The aim of this study was to measure the extent to which enjoyment of the natural environment was affected by noise.

Method: In a laboratory simulation, helicopter noise at 40 dB or 80 dB was played while participants viewed slides of national park scenes. Participants recorded their feelings and rated the slides for scenic beauty.

Results: Participants' feelings of annoyance, solitude, tranquillity, freedom and naturalness were all negatively impacted by the noise, in both the quiet and loud conditions. Furthermore, ratings for scenic beauty (even for some of the most breathtaking views) were reduced by the noise.

Conclusion: Noise both presents a source of annoyance and directly reduces the pleasure experienced from the surrounding environment. Aircraft noise in areas of outstanding natural beauty is an issue that is in need of further attention.

Noise can reverse the stress-reducing effects of the natural landscape

The noise from Concorde (a supersonic jet – one that can fly faster than the speed of sound) on the runway may be as much as 100–120 dB. This is 10–20 dB louder than a subsonic jet. Bell *et al.* (2001) report that a single flight by a loud aircraft is as disturbing as 10 flights by a plane that is 10 dB quieter. In addition to being very loud, transportation noise is intermittent and therefore more disturbing – and may continue into the night, when it is more apparent in contrast to the quiet of nightfall.

The research by Staples *et al.* (1999) accounts for the findings of Fidell and Silvati (1991) that little reduction in the annoyance caused by noise is achieved by adding sound insulation to homes near an airport. Similarly, Nivision and Endresen (1993) studied residents living on a busy street, measuring their health, sleep anxiety levels and attitude towards the noise. Although noise levels were unrelated to either their health or sleep, a strong relationship emerged between the participants' subjective view of the noise to which they were exposed and the number of their health complaints.

Can sounds be beneficial?

North and Hargreaves (2000) used an experimental setting to demonstrate that music was related to arousal. They found that the music selected by participants while riding on, or recovering from, an episode on an exercise bike tended to enhance their mood; they chose fast music while cycling but slow-tempo music when relaxing. Thus noise could be used to enhance mood, providing stimulating environments in gymnasia or relaxing ones in dental waiting rooms.

Music may also serve an emotional role. North *et al.* (2000) conducted a questionnaire study of over 2,000 adolescents, asking them about the role of music in their lives. They found that over 50 per cent played or had played a musical instrument regularly and they listened to music for an average of 2.45 hours per day. They preferred listening to music over other indoor (but not outdoor) activities and perceived different benefits from listening to pop and classical music. North *et al.* concluded that music is important to adolescents because it satisfies their emotional needs and offers a way for them to portray an 'image' to the outside world.

In some situations, a noise can be effectively masked by another source of sound. Burgio *et al.* (1996) studied the effect of such masking for residential patients with Alzheimer's disease, who may become confused by intermittent sounds such as footsteps, vacuum cleaners and voices. By playing tapes of the sounds of a stream running over rocks and of waves crashing against the shore, the distractions were masked and the patients displayed a 23 per cent reduction in verbal agitation.

Belojevic *et al.* (2001; see also p. 52) have shown that, for some people, noisy conditions may enhance performance. While introverted participants found a noisy situation more difficult to work in, the performance of extroverts was enhanced; they worked slightly faster than in quiet conditions.

Pollution

Like noise, *pollution* is an everyday concept. We think of oil tanker spills and billowing smoke from factories. These, and many less visible sources of pollution, result in the contamination of the environment with harmful or poisonous substances. How does this action become a source of stress?

Pollution is not just a recent phenomenon: the seepage of human and animal waste into waterways, for example, has plagued communities for centuries. What has changed, however, is the nature and the scale of the pollution for which we are responsible. For example, radioactive waste is invisible but deadly, and chemical plants and tankers have vast capacities, so that accidents can cause extensive damage and the effects may be long-lasting, such as in the case of nuclear contamination (see also pp.159–65). Furthermore, because of the nature of modern pollutants and the power of their sources (governments and multinational companies), people who are affected may feel that the situation is out of their control. This helplessness enhances their fear.

research
now

muddy waters and heavy metal

Eiser, J.M., Podpadec, T.J., Reicher, S.D. and Stevenage, S.V. (1998) Muddy waters and heavy metal: time and attitudes guide judgements of pollution. *Journal of Environmental Psychology,* 18, 199–208

Aim: To study the changing attitudes of residents living close to the source of river pollution over time following contamination of the River Fal, and to investigate factors affecting differences in perception of risk.

Method: Residents around Falmouth, Cornwall, were sent questionnaires following an environmental incident in which toxic heavy metals such as cadmium and zinc were washed out of a disused mine and into the River Fal. The questionnaires were sent out soon after the event and after 8 months had elapsed. These asked about the perceived seriousness of the spillage (such as the potential effects on employment – for example, fishing or tourism – and at home, as in the contamination of non-mains water) and whether this was believed to be a chance accident or a predictable event for which someone should have been responsible.

Results: The participants' estimates of the seriousness of the contamination (in terms of visible effects, and toxicity of shellfish and drinking water) were higher immediately after the incident than after 8 months, and women were more concerned than men. Those participants asked immediately after the event believed that the toxic effects would be longer lasting than those questioned later. With regard to responsibility, the respondents at 6 weeks were more likely to assign blame than those asked later, and women were more likely to attribute responsibility than were men.

Conclusion: One factor affecting the perceived risk was gender. In general, women were more concerned than men about the potential damage caused by pollution and with assigning responsibility. Both genders became less pessimistic about the effects of the spillage with time. This change may not be related to any real reduction in risk, but to habituation.

Air pollution

We can see or smell some pollutants, but there are others that we cannot detect. Carbon monoxide, for example, is an odourless and colourless gas, but it can be fatal. What makes us concerned about pollution? The level of pollution, perceived or absolute, is not the only factor that affects the stress levels associated with a pollutant. The nature of the pollutant matters too. Smells emerging from oil refineries or breweries are perceived to be more annoying than emissions from a chocolate factory (Winneke and Kastka, 1987).

Atmospheric pollutant	Sources or causes
Particulates	Cigarette smoke Incinerators Vehicle exhausts
Sulphur dioxide (SO_2) Carbon monoxide (CO) Particulates	Smoke from fires burning fossil fuels
Carbon monoxide Nitrogen dioxide (NO_2) Hydrocarbons	Vehicle exhausts
CFCs (chlorofluorocarbons)	Aerosols and old refrigerators
Nitrogen dioxide	Industry

Rankin (1969) found that members of a community who were concerned about air pollution did not complain because they believed that their protests would be ineffective. Such feelings of apathy increase the stress associated with the pollutant. As with noise pollution, even a perception of control over the situation reduces stress. Rotton *et al.* (1979) reported that perceived control over air quality when exposed to a malodorous substance was more important than the level of pollution in determining the level of tolerance of the situation. Feeling less helpless serves to reduce frustration and therefore lowers the stress experienced as a result of the environmental insult.

As with noise, those people who are most anxious are more aware of the threat posed by a pollutant (Navarro *et al.*, 1987). Their fears, unabated by reassurances of safety or reinforced by apathy, can therefore create more stress. Familiarity may also increase the stress associated with a pollutant, although it may also make people less concerned (Medalia, 1964).

Cuthbertson and Nigg (1987) found that episodes of pesticide and asbestos pollution could damage social relationships. This occurred because of differences of opinion about the causes or consequences of the events. These differences, which arose in response to an emotive situation, placed an additional stress on relationships. Similarly, at a group level, following the accident in 1979 at Three Mile Island nuclear power plant, Pennsylvania, USA, differences of opinion arose between local residents, some of whom were worried about the radioactive contamination while others were not, thus dividing the community. Lee *et al.* (1993) found that there were comparable individual differences in perceived danger in relation to Sellafield (a nuclear reprocessing plant) in the UK. Kocher and Levi (2000) found that substantial community conflict followed pollution caused by an oil spill. Technological catastrophes that result in pollution often result in uncertainty about the potential for damage arising from the pollutant (see Chapter 7), and this is a further source of stress.

Travel

Travel, over short or long distances, can be a source of stress. Road rage could happen on a short trip to the shops, an employee who takes the same route to work every day may experience fatigue and a long-haul passenger may suffer the effects of jet lag. Not only can the journey itself be a source of stress, but travelling away from home may present other problems, such as language barriers, differences in cultural expectations and fears about personal safety, or about the safety of food and water.

what's new?

road rage

A study of 526 drivers, conducted by the Automobile Association (AA) Road Safety unit in 1995, found that 90 per cent had experienced 'road rage' incidents during the preceding 12 months. Ward and Waterman (2000) define *road rage* as the expression of aggressive behaviour towards other road users, in response to an angry (emotive) appraisal of the traffic context. Motorists reported being both the recipient and cause of road rage – both of which are stressful. It is interesting that there is a discrepancy between the numbers of each form of behaviour conducted and experienced. This may be explained by subjective perceptions of threat by the recipient. For example, tailgating is frequently experienced but apparently less often performed, perhaps because we perceive the threat of encroachment while failing to recognise our intrusive behaviour towards others. This view is supported by the environmental approach – taken, for instance, by Joint (2000) – which suggests that the car is an extension of our personal space, and is thus defended against invasion by another vehicle cutting in.

Driving behaviour	Percentage of drivers experiencing this behaviour from other motorists	Percentage of drivers admitting to engaging in this behaviour towards other motorists
Aggressive tailgating (driving very close behind)	62	6
Flashing lights	59	45
Aggressive or rude gestures	48	22
Deliberate obstruction	21	5
Verbal abuse	16	12
Physical assault	1	<1
Any other form of road rage	12	40

Road rage experienced and conducted by motorists
http://www.reportroadrage.co.uk/aastat.htm

Rathbone and Huckabee (1999) conducted a review of the literature, legislation and preventive measures in use across the USA. They distinguish between *road rage* and *aggressive driving*. The former is uncontrolled and criminal, while the latter – although potentially dangerous and often constituting a driving offence – is not a criminal offence. They suggest that road rage is most frequent on Friday afternoons at peak travel times, during fair weather, in congested, urban areas. They observe that, although relatively infrequent, the apparent randomness of the victims and perpetrators of road rage frightens the public. This fear is exacerbated by a lack of information about the precursors that lead to road rage incidents and of ways in which to defuse potentially dangerous situations.

Further evidence that aspects of the environment, rather than internal factors such as personality, are responsible for aggressive driving comes from a study conducted by Ellison-Potter et al. (2001), using a driving simulator. The results showed that when students believed that they could not be identified, because they had been told that they were in a convertible with the roof up, they drove more aggressively, had more accidents and killed more virtual pedestrians! The belief that they were visible had the opposite effect, resulting in safer driving (for the effects of anonymity on behaviour, see p.97–100). Aggressive bumper stickers and road signs also made drivers more aggressive but driver anger, a measure of personality, did not appear to be related to aggressive driving. This suggests that making drivers identifiable (for example, printing work telephone numbers on vans) and reminding people to drive courteously (such as signs on Scottish roads, which say 'Frustration causes accidents, please allow passing') could help to reduce driver aggression.

road rage and space-defending space wagons

Commenting on the causes of 'Road-Rage', Matthew Joint, MSc, BSc, MCIT, Head of Behavioural Analysis

Human beings are territorial. As individuals we have personal space, or territory, which evolved essentially as a defensive mechanism – anyone who invades this territory is potentially an aggressor. The car is an extension of this territory. If a vehicle threatens this territory by cutting in, for example, the driver will probably carry out a defensive manoeuvre. This may be backed up by an attempt to re-establish territory, flashing headlights or a blast of the horn are perhaps most commonly used for this purpose. However, this may not always succeed in communicating the full depth of our feelings. As it is usually difficult to talk or even shout to the offending driver, other non-verbal communication (offensive gesticulations) may be employed. Confrontations of this nature are not uncommon and are usually defused as the vehicles move away from each other.

In some circumstances, the defending driver may wish to go one step further and assert his dominance. Many drivers admit to having chased after a driver to 'teach him a lesson', often pressing him by moving to within inches of his rear bumper. This is comparable to the manner in which a defending animal will chase an attacker out of its territory. However, the result of such behaviour in drivers is, of course, potentially fatal.

Some of the worst cases of 'Road-Rage' have occurred where the opportunity for the vehicles to separate and go their own ways does not present itself. Gesticulations and aggressive manoeuvres have been exchanged in a rapidly degenerating discourse. Worked up into a rage, one or both drivers have then got out of their vehicles and physically attacked their adversary and/or his vehicle.

Drivers can adopt simple strategies that help keep frustration, anger and rage in check.

Never assume that an apparently aggressive act was intended as such. We all make mistakes. So don't bite back. If we take an example from studies of animal behaviour in the wild, the dominant animal in a group will rarely get involved in petty fights and disagreements. Although confident in his ability to defeat any opponent, there is always the risk of injury.

Source: http://www.reportroadrage.co.uk

Using the concepts and research discussed in Chapter 1, analyse the evidence for the ideas presented in this article.

Commuting

'Home-working' is increasingly becoming possible as communications networks offer greater flexibility, enabling employees to do their jobs away from the formal workplace. In contrast, as long-distance travel becomes faster, easier and more familiar, so more people are travelling very long distances to their work. People may spend several hours a day commuting, and in addition to the time penalty, they may experience problems on the roads (diversions, hold-ups and, increasingly, gridlock) and on the railways (cancellations, delays and derailments). Such delays inevitably lead to stress, as time is wasted and deadlines are missed. Increasing stress in commuters, both on the road (Gulain et al., 1989) and on public transport (Costa et al., 1988), has been demonstrated. The amount of difficulty experienced on any journey can be measured objectively as *impedance*. This has two elements: *physical impedance* – that is, the actual obstruction to travel encountered (which can be operationalised as the time taken to complete a journey divided by the distance travelled) – and *subjective impedance* – that is, the individual's perception of the problems encountered on the journey. Cassidy (1992) showed that physical impedance rather than distance travelled was the better indicator of perceived stress and health consequences of commuting. An unimpeded long-distance trip is less stressful than a short but interrupted journey. Therefore, a driver can cover many miles if the traffic is free flowing, but a short, queue-ridden trip is more stressful. When covering long distances, a traveller may take the opportunity to work or relax (such as reading on a long flight or train journey) or to learn a new language (using tapes in a car stereo). These options are more readily available to the user of public transport (as their attention is not required for driving), but these commuters report higher levels of perceived stress. This may be the result of the higher perceived control available to drivers in terms of personal space as well as progress (Cassidy, 1997).

For the commuter who spends many hours on the road, there is an additional risk – that of fatigue. Trying to concentrate on a demanding task such as driving when we are in a trough of our circadian cycle is both stressful and dangerous (for a discussion of circadian rhythms, see Jarvis *et al.*, 2000). In particular, drivers on very familiar journeys who are tired or out of phase with their biological clocks are at risk of losing concentration. *Driving without awareness*, a condition in which drivers become mesmerised and fail to attend to road conditions, is a particular risk.

Commuting by air, often for short periods of time to attend meetings at international venues, can lead to poor sleep, tiredness and gastro-intestinal symptoms. This phenomenon, known as *jet lag*, is the fatigue experienced by air travellers as a consequence of crossing time zones, such that their circadian rhythm is desychronised from the local *zeitgebers* (for a full discussion of jet lag, see Jarvis *et al.*, 2000). Since international travel results in sleep loss, commuters experiencing jet lag will suffer both the effects of sleep loss and desynchronisation of the body clock and the local *zeitgeber*.

A further source of stress for air travellers relates to the relative confinement of airline seating. This has several consequences. First, invasion of personal space is inevitable, because neighbouring passengers are well within the intimate zone (see Chapter 1, p.2) and while territory is demarcated by the arm rests and seats themselves, the breaching of these boundaries is inevitable.

A second factor that causes stress on aircraft is the prolonged immobility. This has health implications that are now becoming apparent in direct relation to air travel. Staying still, particularly where legroom and hence movement is restricted, increases the risk of deep vein thrombosis (DVT). Such potential problems serve to exacerbate the stress associated with long-haul travelling. Furthermore, the dry atmosphere on aeroplanes and the tendency to consume (free) alcohol causes thickening of the blood, increasing susceptibility to DVT.

media watch

myth-busting

The Myth: Deep Vein Thrombosis (DVT) is caused by sitting in cheap airline seats. There has been an outcry over the cover-up of so-called economy-class syndrome, after an apparently fit woman of 28 died of DVT after a 15 hour flight.

The Reality: When British Airways said linking DVT (blood clots, to you and me) with economy class seating was a 'red herring', it wasn't exactly right – but it wasn't wrong. BA claimed someone sitting in business class or even driving a tractor could be affected too. This much is true.

DVT is a medical condition that occurs when people develop blood clots in the deep veins of their legs. It can happen when the blood doesn't move through the vessels properly – for example, after a long flight in cramped airline seats, which is more likely in economy class. These blood clots can travel to the lungs or other areas, causing strokes, severe organ damage or death. People have suffered from them after road trips, even after going to the theatre – it's just that long flights seem to pose a greater risk. Ashford Hospital in Middlesex has seen 30 DVT deaths in Heathrow passengers in 3 years.

But a House of Lords report stresses that DVT isn't just a problem for those in cattle-class. It says: 'Economy class syndrome is a misnomer – it seems to be the very act of sitting immobile for 10 or 15 hours at a stretch that causes the problem.'

DVT does not have a single cause but the peculiar environment inside an aircraft generates factors that makes it more likely. Cramped seating is definitely one. Although people have got taller and fatter over the years, aircraft seats have got smaller. Pressure on the knees is a major contributory factor to DVT. Most people would find a seat pitch (the distance between the back of your seat and the back of the one in front) of 30 inches to be the absolute minimum for comfort, but many airlines offer less. Civil Aviation Authority (CAA) guidelines suggest a 26-inch minimum to ensure 'the vast majority of passengers can occupy the seat, stand up and evacuate the aircraft without undue difficulty'. But cramped seating makes it harder for passengers to get up and move around – one of the main preventatives of DVT.

Although they have more stretch-yourself-out capacity, business-class passengers aren't immune. Reclining business-class seats often have footrests, which, if too short, compress the veins at the back of the leg, causing blood pooling. The dry air in the cabin may also contribute to DVT, as blood thickens when the body gets dehydrated. Some experts claim that lower oxygen levels cause the capillaries to shrink, further reducing blood flow, but there's little hard evidence that low pressure in the cabin contributes to DVT. In addition, about 4 per cent of people have a genetic defect called factor V Leiden which makes blood clots more likely. Also, women on the Pill or taking hormone replacement therapy are more at risk from DVT.

So economy class doesn't help the problem, but it isn't the sole cause. However, the CAA has promised to look into the shrinking seat-space issue and airlines have been advised to give information out on DVT with tickets.

Source: *Eve*, April 2000

Summarise the major problems for air travellers and suggest ways to overcome them.

Holiday travel

According to the Holmes and Rahe's (1967) Social Readjustment Rating Scale, taking a holiday is of the 43 most stressful things that can happen to us (see p.44) – which is ironic when you consider that most people take holidays to 'wind down'. To what extent do environmental stressors account for this? Holidays abroad can result in a range of potential stressors relating to the environment, such as questions about the safety of tap water in the new location and cultural differences (these are also considered in Chapter 1, in the discussion of personal space). Further sources of stress when travelling abroad include language barriers, differences in dress code, dealing with approaches from unknown individuals, gender role differences and fears relating to food.

Medway (1999) begins her article 'Fighting the holiday blues' by saying 'Let's face it, the holiday season can be stressful, disappointing, and at times, downright traumatic!' She cites obligations to over-stretch oneself financially, physically and psychologically as primary sources of holiday stress. For some holiday-makers, the stressors can be much more serious; for instance, in cases of food allergy, where home represents a safe haven but eating anywhere else is potentially life-threatening. The website http://www.allergicchild.com/images/holidays.htm is devoted to exactly this problem. When the consequence of eating the wrong foods isn't just a dodgy tummy but anaphylactic shock, holidaying may mean more stress than respite.

where to now?

The following are good sources of information about environmental stress:

▶ **http://www.hse.gov.uk** – the Health and Safety Executive website is a useful source, with many pages devoted to noise at work.

▶ **http://www.le.ac.uk/psychology/acn5** – Adrian North's website describes many of the studies that he has conducted into the effects of noise.

▶ **http://www.reportroadrage.co.uk/experts.htm** and **http://www.reportroadrage.co.uk/aastat.htm** – these websites provide details of reports on road rage.

▶ **http://www.drivers.com** and **http://my.webmd.com** – both have interesting articles about road rage incidents and ways to reduce risk.

Consequences of stress

Effects of stressors on health

The most obvious threat to health from the environmental stressor of noise is damage to hearing. Whilst only very loud sounds (above 150 dB) can actually rupture the eardrum, hearing loss can occur when the sensitive hair cells of the inner ear (which detect sound) are damaged. This may cause temporary or permanent hearing deficits, resulting from exposure to sounds at 90–120 dB, such as are experienced in noisy working environments (for example, construction sites) or at rock concerts. Cohen *et al.* (1973) found that the children in a high-rise block who lived closest to the traffic below had significantly impaired hearing. In addition to the obvious effects of noise, it can also cause raised blood pressure and other effects associated with stress.

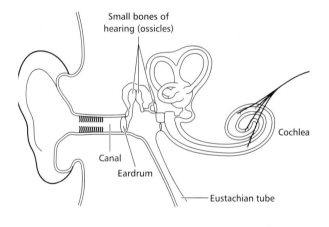

Sound is detected as the pressure of air against our eardrum. Events such as a hammer hitting a nail create vibrations, waves of pressure in the air, which are detected as sound by tiny hair cells in the inner ear

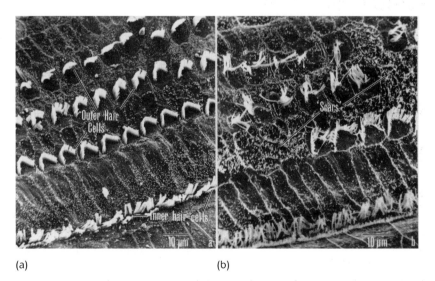

Exposure to loud sounds can damage hearing. (a) A scanning electron micrograph of the hair cells in a normal guinea pig. (b) The disruption to the hair cells caused by exposure of a guinea pig to sound at a level equivalent to that of a rock concert (2,000 Hz at 120 dB for 24 hours)

(a)   (b)

Like noise, pollution has direct biological effects on health; lead can cause brain and liver damage, arsenic is a carcinogen, ozone aggravates respiratory problems, and so on. In addition, pollution can have indirect, psychological effects that influence our well-being. Air pollution may prevent us from going out (see p.75), and may increase the risk of aggression and reduce the likelihood of helping behaviour (Jones and Bogat, 1978; Cunningham, 1979). Furthermore, the stressful effects of major life events seem to be exacerbated by air pollution (Evans *et al.*, 1987; see also p.44).

Many other effects of environmental stress are associated with chronic exposure to stressors, inducing and maintaining the resistance stage of the body's response. The effects of long-term elevated levels of cortisol, aldosterone and thyroxine contribute to a number of serious conditions. We will look at these now.

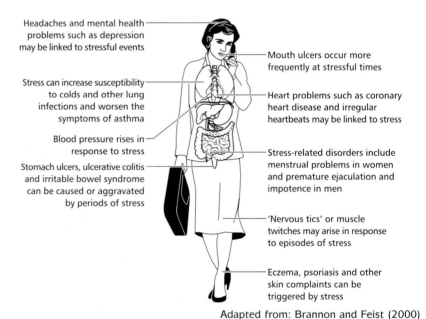

Headaches and mental health problems such as depression may be linked to stressful events

Mouth ulcers occur more frequently at stressful times

Stress can increase susceptibility to colds and other lung infections and worsen the symptoms of asthma

Heart problems such as coronary heart disease and irregular heartbeats may be linked to stress

Blood pressure rises in response to stress

Stress-related disorders include menstrual problems in women and premature ejaculation and impotence in men

Stomach ulcers, ulcerative colitis and irritable bowel syndrome can be caused or aggravated by periods of stress

'Nervous tics' or muscle twitches may arise in response to episodes of stress

How long-term stress can be bad for health

Eczema, psoriasis and other skin complaints can be triggered by stress

Adapted from: Brannon and Feist (2000)

Cardiovascular disorders

The effects of chronic stress include hypertension (high blood pressure) and atherosclerosis (the build-up of fat deposits in blood vessels). Hypertension is a direct result of high levels of aldosterone, and high levels of fat in the blood, caused by elevated cortisol levels, contribute to atherosclerosis. Both atherosclerosis and hypertension can cause serious problems in themselves, but they also increase the probability of having a heart attack or stroke. Talbott *et al.* (1990) compared men working in relatively noisy or quiet industrial settings and reported a positive correlation between hearing loss and raised blood pressure. Comparing men from each setting who had worked there for 15 years, blood pressure was in general higher for those in noisier settings. This shows that workers exposed to the stressor of noise for a prolonged period of time suffer an increased risk of cardiovascular disorders.

In simulated situations, Maschke *et al.* (1995) have demonstrated that noisy work environments increase the level of adrenaline. Evans *et al.* (1995) found similar results with children. Those living close to a noisy airport had higher levels of adrenalin and noradrenalin and higher blood pressure compared to those living further away. The use of protective equipment at work can, however, reduce noise perception, lowering both adrenalin levels and blood pressure (Ising and Melchert, 1980). Job dissatisfaction exacerbates the effects of noise at work. Lercher *et al.* (1993) found that annoyance was related to both noise levels in the workplace and blood pressure, and that this link was stronger in dissatisfied workers.

Cancer

There is considerable evidence for a link between stress and cancer, although there is no evidence that stress *causes* cancer. Animal studies, such as that of Seligman and Visintainer (1985; see p.48), have found that rates of cancer in laboratory animals increase in stressed animals. Eysenck (1988) followed up nearly 400 individuals and found that death rates from cancer were higher for those who reported higher levels of stress at the start of the study. Normally, the immune system finds and kills cancer cells before they can establish themselves as a tumour. Clearly, if our immune systems are functioning less efficiently, then cancer cells are less likely to be eliminated. Once again, strategies such as smoking, which some people use to relax, actually make things worse by introducing carcinogens (chemicals that can cause cancer) into the body.

Gastro-intestinal (GI) disorders

Stress is associated with a number of GI disorders. The sensation of 'butterflies in the stomach' is not dangerous in itself, but if we experience it regularly, it is likely to interfere with our eating patterns. Stress also causes high levels of hydrochloric acid in the stomach. This is believed to contribute to the development of stomach and duodenal ulcers. Whilst this is still a popular belief amongst doctors and the general public (Novelli, 1997), there is now good evidence to show that stress is not the major cause of stomach ulcers: they are caused by bacterial infection (Macarthur *et al.*, 1995). Harris (1999) suggests that the symptoms of irritable bowel syndrome (which include constipation and diarrhoea) are worsened by episodes of stress.

Other effects on health

Cooper *et al.* (1988) stated that the top 20 fatal illnesses in the UK are all caused or made worse by stress. The high levels of cortisol resulting from prolonged stress are associated with allergic responses. This means that allergic conditions such as eczema and asthma are made worse for some people by prolonged stress. Rheumatoid arthritis, an autoimmune disorder causing painful inflammation of the joints, is worsened by stress (Zautra, 1998). The reduced number of lymphocytes in the lymph nodes associated with stress can make us more vulnerable to infection. This is one reason why we may find ourselves constantly catching colds and other diseases when we are feeling stressed. Muscular aches, particularly backache, are made worse by the increased muscle tension associated with stress. This may sound less serious than some of the other illnesses that we have discussed in this chapter. However, backache is one of the most common reasons for sick-leave from work, costing people money and perhaps putting their jobs at risk.

Effects of stressors on performance

Cohen *et al.* (1973) investigated the effects of urban noise on the development of children's reading ability. They compared children living on different floors of a high-rise block over a busy New York City highway. Children lower in the block were exposed to greater noise levels and (despite similarities in social class and exposure to air pollution) were poorer readers than children living on higher floors. Cohen *et al.* suggest that this may be related to the impaired hearing of the children on the lower floors (see p.69). Similar results were obtained by Bronzaft and McCarthy (1975), in their comparison of the reading ability of children at the same school who worked in classrooms adjacent to or away from elevated railway tracks. The reading skills of the children exposed to the noise from the railway were inferior to those of the children on the quiet side. Noise can interfere with the perception of speech sounds; for instance, masking the difference between /p/ and /b/. This could delay the development of verbal skills and reading. Alternatively, the children on the noisy side of the building may have suffered from the 11 per cent loss in teaching time experienced in the classrooms adjacent to the railway.

Evans *et al.* (1995) compared children living adjacent to Munich International Airport with children from less noisy urban areas (see also p.71). Both memory and reading performance were better in children from the quieter neighbourhoods. These differences may be the direct effects of noise or a consequence of other behavioural differences observed; the children from the airport district were more readily frustrated and annoyed and had poorer motivation.

Performance at work is also affected by noise, not just in obviously noisy settings such as construction sites and airports, but in offices and industrial plants too. Banbury and Berry (1998) suggest that the background noise generated by voices is particularly troublesome. Because we tend to 'tune in' to conversations, they are more likely to interfere with our own concentration and communication. Acton (1970) found that we can, however, learn to adapt to working in a noisy environment. Workers from an industrial setting, accustomed to higher noise levels, were more effective at communicating against a background of loud noise than were university employees, whose workplaces are typically quieter.

Although there is little evidence that noise affects workplace productivity directly, it could impact upon effectiveness through employee communication, morale or fatigue. If so, reducing workplace noise could boost productivity indirectly. This might be achieved by the use of sound-absorbing materials on the floors, ceiling and walls, using sound insulation around noisy pieces of equipment and replacing older machinery with newer, quieter models. An alternative technique is to mask noise; for instance, with a constant hum or piped music (see p.59).

Experimentally, air pollution with an unpleasant smell has been shown to affect performance on a complex task (proofreading) but not a simple one (arithmetic). In reality, we may be most likely to suffer the effects of air pollution; for instance, from traffic fumes, when we are engaged in the relatively complex task of driving. How are driving skills affected by the levels of a major pollutant, carbon monoxide? Beard and Wertheim (1967) found that time judgement was impaired by exposure to carbon monoxide, while Breisacher (1971) reports a reduction in manual dexterity and attention with raised carbon monoxide levels. Similarly, Lewis *et al.* (1970) found that participants exposed to air taken at approximately exhaust-pipe height from a busy road did not perform as well as those breathing 'clean' air on information processing tasks. Clearly, the heavier the traffic is and the more dangerous the driving conditions are, the worse our performance may become.

Effects of stressors on social behaviour

As noise can affect attention, arousal and stress, it is likely to have an effect upon social interactions. It seems to have the effect of making people unpleasant; they are more aggressive and less helpful.

classic
research

it's a shocking noise

Geen, R.G. and O'Neal, E.C. (1969) Activation of cue-elicited aggression by general arousal. *Journal of Personality and Social Psychology,* 11, 289–92

Aim: To investigate whether exposure to loud noise increases the incidence of aggressive behaviour and whether this adds to the arousing effect of viewing aggressive media.

Method: Participants were shown a film that was either violent (a prize-fight) or non-violent (a sports film). They were then placed in a situation in which they believed that they were administering electric shocks to another individual (who was, in fact, a confederate of the experimenter and received no shocks). During this phase of the experiment, the participants were exposed to either noisy or quiet conditions.

Results: Exposure to either the violent film or the noisy conditions increased the number of shocks given by the participant. The effect was greatest with the violent film and noise in combination.

Conclusion: Noise increases aggressive behaviour, as measured by the likelihood of administering shocks, and exacerbates the effects of viewing aggression, suggesting that noise may promote aggression by increasing arousal.

Sauser *et al.* (1978) found that participants exposed to a loud noise during a management simulation were likely to assign lower salaries to fictitious job applicants. Loud noise seems to reduce the probability of altruistic behaviour. Page (1977) conducted a field experiment in which a pedestrian (a confederate) dropped a package near a construction site. Under different noise conditions created by the use of a pneumatic drill, the incidence of passers-by stopping to help was recorded. Fewer passers-by helped in noisy conditions, especially when the noise was very loud.

Matthews and Canon (1975) investigated the interaction between the effect of noise on helping behaviour and another factor known to influence the likelihood of altruism, apparent need. The experimenters contrived a situation in which a pedestrian dropped some books on a city street. Two variables were manipulated in the staged incidents; whether the pedestrian's arm was in a cast and noise generated by a nearby lawnmower. Although the noise reduced altruism in both conditions, the effect was most marked in the reduction of offers of help when the pedestrian's arm was in a cast.

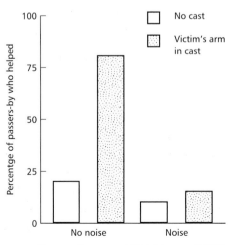

Passers-by are less likely to help when conditions are noisy

Source: Deaux and Wrightsman (1988)

Results such as these may have arisen because people simply do not attend to so many social cues when they are confronted with the sensory overload of a loud noise. For instance, in Matthews and Canon's 'noisy' condition people simply may not have noticed the cast. Alternatively, the noise may affect mood, making people less inclined to help when in a noisy environment.

From the results of a study conducted by Yinon and Bizman (1980), mood seems to be a less important factor than attention. The mood of participants was manipulated by giving them positive or negative feedback on a task that they had performed. During the task, they were exposed to either loud or quiet noise. Finally, the participants were asked for help (by a confederate of the experimenter). If noise affected altruism by having a detrimental effect on mood, it would be expected that the combination of loud noise and a negative report on performance would reduce the likelihood of helping. However, Yinon and Bizman found that in the loud noise condition there was no difference between helping by participants who had received positive or negative feedback. As there was a difference in the low-noise condition, these results suggest that the effect of the loud noise overrides that of feedback, either distracting the participants from the negative feedback or justifying it. It seems that interference from a stressor such as noise is more important than mood in determining social behaviour.

Air pollution can also affect social behaviour. For example, Chapko and Solomon (1976) reported a reduction in visitor numbers to attractions such as New York City zoo and an aquarium when air pollution rose to unhealthy levels. Asmus and Bell (1999) exposed participants to foul smells, mimicking the effects of malodorous pollution. They found that this made the participants feel unpleasant, reduced their willingness to help and increased the likelihood of anger and flight behaviour. These findings support those obtained in the field by Rotton and Frey (1985), who used archive data to demonstrate that high levels of ozone were associated with increased complaints about household disturbances. The effect of such pollution may be either to increase aggressive behaviour (hence *actually* elevating levels of disturbance) or it may increase sensitivity to disturbance (thus elevating the incidence of complaints).

One particularly frequent source of air pollution that causes stress to others is cigarette smoke. In a study of office productivity, Harris *et al.* (1980) found that 35 per cent of office workers smoked, but the smoking of nearby co-workers distressed 26 per cent of the non-smoking majority. In a shopping centre, people on public benches left more quickly if a smoker, rather than a non-smoker, joined them (Bleda and Bleda, 1978). Jones and Bogat (1978) found that volunteers would administer higher levels of aversive noise to another person if they were exposed to cigarette smoke. It is not yet clear whether these responses are a direct physiological response to chemicals in the smoke itself or are simply due to the annoyance that it causes.

Strategies for coping with environmental stressors

Folkman *et al.* (1986) define coping as 'the person's cognitive and behavioural efforts to manage (reduce, minimize, master, or tolerate) the internal and external demands of the person-environment transaction that is appraised as taxing or exceeding the resources of the person'. Coping thus represents the ways in which we attempt to deal with aspects of the world that we find are beyond our normal means to fight.

Like any source of stress, environmental stressors can be tackled from an internal or external perspective; that is, coping strategies can be either *emotion-focused*, aiming to manage the negative effects on the individual, or *problem-focused*, aiming to reduce the causes of stress. In any situation, a combination of these strategies may be employed. Emotion-focused strategies may include keeping busy to take one's mind off the problem, preparing oneself for the worst, praying for strength and guidance, ignoring the situation in the belief that the problem will go away and bottling up one's feelings. Problem-focused strategies may include discussing the situation with a professional, relying on one's own past experiences to tackle the issue and dealing with the situation one step at time. Other strategies are listed in the table below.

Source of stress	Emotion-focused strategy	Problem-focused strategy
Noisy children playing outside	Trying to remember that children need to play and it's good for them to be outside (being objective)	Talking to a friend on the telephone (discussing the situation)
Noise from a nearby lawnmower	Accepting that the grass will look nicer afterwards (seeing the positive side of the situation)	Closing the windows (taking a positive action)
Cigarette smoke from a nearby table in a non-smoking area of a restaurant	Snapping at the waiter (taking anger out on others)	Contemplating asking the waiter to request that the smoker stops, or moving yourself (considering alternative solutions)
Fumes from a local factory	Eating or smoking more (trying to reduce tension)	Trying to find out what the emissions are and why they are released (investigating the issue)

Some examples of strategies that may be employed in response to environmental stressors (note that these are not intended to represent the best ways to cope!)

research now

natural inoculation against stress

Parsons, R., Tassinary, L.G., Ulrich, R.S., Hebl, M.R. and Grossmann-Alexander, M. (1998) The view from the road: implications for stress recovery and immunization. *Journal of Environmental Psychology*, 18, 113–40

Aim: To test whether the natural environment can assist in stress recovery or immunise against the effects of stressful situations.

Method: One hundred and sixty students viewed one of four different videotaped simulated drives through an outdoor environment. Immediately prior to and after the video, the participants were exposed to mildly stressful events. The videos consisted of either predominantly natural or artificial scenes, and the effects were measured as changes in blood pressure and GSR (Galvanic Skin Resistance, a measure of 'sweatiness' indicating activity in the ANS and therefore raised stress) and changes in facial expression (frowning and smiling).

Results: Participants viewing natural scenes recovered from viewing the pre-video stressor more quickly and became less stressed by the post-viewing stressor than those viewing artefacts.

Conclusion: Natural scenes help to reduce the effects of a stressor and can provide immunisation against stress.

How effective are the strategies?

It seems obvious that problem-focused strategies are better, because they deal with the environmental cause. However, it may be beyond the scope of the individual to effect change, so emotion-focused solutions may be essential to enable the individual to feel less stressed about the situation. For example, individuals may be powerless to alter the direction of wind blowing air pollutants from foreign countries or to reverse the effects of an industrial accident.

Of the emotion-focused strategies, evidence suggests that long-term avoidance may be ineffective (Nolen-Hoeksema and Larson, 1999). In fact, avoidance strategies may even be damaging. Epping-Jordan *et al.* (1994) found that in patients using avoidance strategies, the progression of cancer was faster.

Different individuals, circumstances or situations may lead to the availability of differing resources with which to cope. Whilst having wealth may offer the means to avoid many environmental stressors (through avoidance or protection), it may not provide a solution to inescapable sources of stress. Here, intrapersonal resources may be of greater significance. Wealth has been demonstrated to be linked to reduced stress, but this does not apply to everyone (tending only to be important at the lower end of the socio-economic scale: Dohrenwend, 1973). Neither is wealth a buffer against all sources of stress; for example, it is not particularly important following bereavement (Stroebe and Stroebe, 1987).

Type of resource	Examples	Ways in which they may be employed
Material	Wealth	Having more money might enable people to live in rural areas with lower air pollution
Educational	Published research, schools, Internet	Knowing how to protect an employee from hearing damage in a noisy work environment
Physical	Strength, health	Individuals without asthma may be more tolerantof some air pollutants
Social	Family, friends, pets	Being able to talk to a dog about the journey to work may alleviate some of the annoyance about traffic jams
Intrapersonal	Skills, abilities and personality characteristics, such as determination and self-esteem	One individual might be better able to live effectively in crowded conditions than another

Resources for coping with environmental stressors

Gaining control

Earlier in the chapter (pp.54–5) we considered the importance of the sensation of control over a situation to an individual's perception of stress. In many situations, having – or believing that you have – control over a situation helps to alleviate some of the effects of an environmental stressor.

Social support

People gain help, reassurance and other forms of assistance from their interactions with others (including their pets), which helps them to deal with stress; this is called *social support*.

> ### Coping with disasters
>
> Research on the aftermath of disasters such as the nuclear accident at Three Mile Island discusses the coping strategies, such as social support, employed by people from the locality in their attempts to deal with the stress that arises from actual or suspected exposure to pollution. Those residents around the Three Mile Island site who had lower levels of social support showed higher levels of stress (Fleming *et al.*, 1982). In addition, Collins *et al.* (1983) found that residents who focused on managing their feelings in response to the disaster (an emotion-focused strategy) were less stressed than those who attempted to take direct action (a problem-focused strategy). Technological disasters are discussed in detail in Chapter 7.

Coping with stressors at work

The work environment is a common source of stress in the lives that we lead today. Most of the ideas that we have looked at so far have considered how the individual can cope with stressors. This attitude in the workplace puts the responsibility for stress management on the employees, whereas in fact some of the sources of stress could (and for greater efficacy should) be managed by the employer. Increasingly, companies are placing job-stress issues on the agenda. What can be done to reduce stress at work? In Chapter 2 we looked at issues of architectural design including the layout of offices, one factor that can help to relieve stressful aspects of working life.

where to now?

The following are good sources of information about coping with stress:

▷ **Brannon, L. and Feist, J. (2000)** *Health Psychology: an Introduction to Behavior and Health*. **London: Wadsworth, Thomson Learning** – this offers detailed coverage of stress and coping.

▷ **http://www.stressfree.com** – this website focuses on the problems of work-related stress. It considers the measurement of stress as well as strategies for coping.

▷ **http://www.workhealth.org/prevent/prred.html** – this is a more academic site that considers employer-based changes to reduce workplace stress.

Conclusions

Models of stress can focus on the individual and/or the environment. A more complete account of stress is achieved when both of these factors are considered. The body's response to stress is mediated by the interactions of hormones, the nervous system and the immune system, and a biological approach can help us to understand some of the consequences to health of being stressed. Life events theory links the occurrence of stressful events to our experience of stress. This explanation provides further evidence for the link between stress and ill health. Cognitive factors affecting stress are considered by Lazarus. This theory suggests that it is our evaluation of a situation that determines whether or not we will experience it as stressful.

Stressors present in the environment, such as noise, pollution and travelling, are all clearly major sources of stress in modern life. Factors such as predictability and perceived control affect the extent to which we experience these factors as stressful. Such sources of stress can have a negative impact on our health; have detrimental effects on performance, such as impairing learning; and alter social behaviour, making people more aggressive and less helpful. We can attempt to overcome the effects of stressors through problem- and emotion-focused strategies, the former being more effective but not always possible.

what do you know?

1 Describe and evaluate research suggesting that noise affects **either** our social behaviour **or** our performance.

2 Discuss the psychological effects of **two** sources of pollution.

3 How can travelling act as a source of stress? Discuss evidence relating to **two** ways in which travel is detrimental. Suggest ways to combat these problems.

4 Describe the physiological effects of stress. How are these effects linked to stress-related illnesses?

5 Describe **two** techniques for reducing stress. Evaluate **one** of these techniques using evidence.

4

High-density Living

what's
ahead?

We begin this chapter with a consideration of how different types of crowds can be defined. We look at the nature of crowding in both humans and animals, and discuss its effects on health, social behaviour and performance. We then discuss different explanations of the effects of crowding and techniques for preventing crowding and techniques for coping with the problems that arise when crowds form.

What is crowding?

Definitions

There are two ways in which we use the word *crowd*. When we refer to *a crowd*, we mean a large, cohesive gathering of individuals. When we use the term *to crowd*, or *crowding*, we mean the act of coming together to form a tightly spaced group. The *density* of the population is the number of individuals per unit area. In a laboratory this can be artificially manipulated by varying either the number of individuals (*social density*) or the available space (*spatial density*). Laboratory studies are often (but not always) conducted with animals. In some instances, it is possible to observe the effects that different densities have in naturalistic settings. Studies of crowding using people are generally naturalistic, thus avoiding ethical and practical issues. Crowding for humans also refers to the way we feel when exposed to either too many people or insufficient space; in other words, the subjective experience of crowding.

Types of crowds

Crowds may arise for a many different reasons, may be engaged in various activities and may be of differing sizes and compositions. The table below offers one classification of a range of crowd types based on their purpose or activities. Any one crowd may exhibit one or more of these types and may change type over time.

Crowd type	Description	Example
Ambulatory	Walking, usually calm	Shoppers on a pavement during the Christmas period
Disabled, or of limited mobility	Crowd has limited movement	A disability rights rally
Cohesive/spectator	Shared interest of participants – for example, watching a specific activity	Fans at a concert or sporting event
Expressive/revelous	Emotional release	Spectators cheering in unison or rejoicing after an event
Participatory	Involved in an actual event	A community fun-run
Aggressive/hostile	Initially verbal, open to lawlessness	Holiday-makers delayed at an airport
Demonstration	A group that is organised to some extent	Pickets and protest marches
Escape/trampling	Attempts to avoid real or imagined danger	Emergency evacuations following a fire alarm or bomb scare
Dense/suffocating	Reduction of individual physical space such that movement is severely impaired	The crushing of a crowd against barriers or in narrow exits
Rushing/looting	Attempts to obtain or steal something	Ticket-holders rushing to enter a concert that they believe has started without them
Violent	Attacking or terrorising others	Rioters setting light to property

Based on Berlognghi (1993)

Fruin (1981) describes *critical crowd densities* – that is, the number of people per unit area – as a key characteristic in crowd disasters. Critical crowd densities are approached when the floor space per standing person is 1.5 square feet (0.14 m^2) or less. In a moving crowd, space restrictions limit mobility, worsening risks from crowding. At 25 square feet (2.3 m^2) per person, a stream of pedestrians can maintain normal walking speed and avoid one another. As space is restricted to 5 square feet (0.5 m^2) per person, speed is reduced – for example, people exiting a stadium or theatre are reduced to shuffling. By 3 square feet (0.28 m^2) per person involuntary contact is experienced between people, and at 2 square feet (0.18 m^2) per person potentially dangerous crowd forces begin to develop. These situations can arise in situations of panic, when the crowd is trying to get away from a perceived threat (such as escaping from a fire) or in crazes, where people are rushing towards a particular location (for example, a stampede to get autographs or a close look at a celebrity).

Studies of crowding in animals

Animals have been used to study the effects of increasing both social density and spatial density by varying the number of individuals or available space. While on the surface they seem to have the same effect (more individuals per unit area), there are differences. An increase in social density results in an increase in the number of individuals with which any particular individual must interact, and thus there is a potential for social problems. An increase in spatial density generates the key problem of too little space.

classic
research

cramped conditions and non-mating mice

Crowcroft, P. and Rowe, F.P. (1958) The growth of confined colonies of the wild house-mouse (*Mus musculus* L.): the effect of dispersal on female fecundity. *Proceedings of the Zoological Society of London*, 131, 357–65

Aim: To investigate the effect of the restriction of space on colonies of house mice, with particular respect to fecundity (reproductive capability).

Method: Seven colonies were established, each consisting of one adult male and two adult females. Each colony was housed in a pen with high metal walls and eight nest boxes measuring 6 feet (1.8 m) square. Some of these animals had access to much larger pens (more than 100 square feet [9.3 m²]) after 32 or 40 weeks.

Results: In crowded conditions the mice populations increased and then levelled off. The failure to reproduce once a certain population density was reached appeared to be the result of non-fecund (infertile) females. This did not appear to be a direct effect of stress, as aggression was not observed between the females and none sustained injury. In crowded situations the female mice were found to have low fecundity because they could not be penetrated by the males and had inactive ovaries. In addition, they had thread-like uteri and excessive fat deposits. Those animals that remained in crowded conditions did not return to a fecund condition, whereas colonies that dispersed into larger pens showed an increase in birth rate, indicating a return to fecund status.

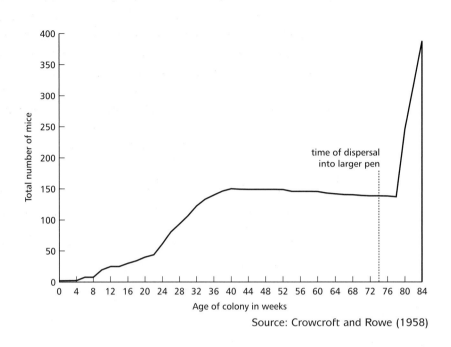

Source: Crowcroft and Rowe (1958)

Conclusion: These results suggest that, for mice at least, populations have a self-regulatory mechanism for limiting reproduction when the population density is high. This appears to act on the reproductive capacity of the females through a reversible change in their physiology and anatomy.

Some of these effects on fecundity described by Crowcroft and Rowe (1958) may have been a consequence of lack of exercise rather than crowding *per se*. Indeed, Schneider (1946) reversed the loss of fecundity in caged house-mice by introducing exercise wheels.

Calhoun (1962) observed the behaviour of a group of rats as it grew to overpopulation and found that dominance relationships also affected response to crowding. The dominant animals defended space and remained in better health than the submissive animals. The latter became confined to a small area of the available space, were more aggressive and were abnormal in their reproductive behaviour and success (96 per cent of offspring died before weaning). While this study clearly demonstrates the negative effects of crowding on social behaviour and reproduction, it can be criticised in several ways. The experiment designed by Calhoun was neither high in ecological validity (rats in the wild would not be confined – they would disperse) nor a simple manipulation of density (as territoriality was also a variable). However, similar patterns of response have been demonstrated in other species, such as frogs (Dyson and Passmore, 1992), pigtail monkeys (Anderson *et al.*, 1977), pigs (Pearce and Patterson, 1993) and hens (Channing *et al.*, 2001; see below). It may be possible that the reduction in reproductive success in crowded conditions occurs independently of the effects of aggression. Within a colony of naked mole rats, sexual suppression mediated by pheromones (airborne chemical signals) released by the queen accounts for the infertility of most of the males and females (Sherman *et al.*, 1992).

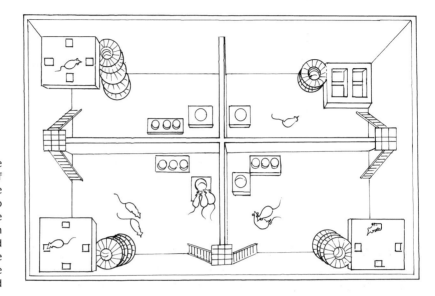

Calhoun (1962) observed the change in behaviour of a colony of rats as the pen became overpopulated. In response to crowding, animals in the *behavioural sink* area (the bottom 2 areas) became aggressive, had higher mortality rates in the females and their reproductive success was reduced

As a consequence of his findings, Calhoun (1971) proposed a mechanism by which crowding could have its effect upon animals. He suggested that each species has an *optimal group size* at which the individuals within it can tolerate the balance between beneficial and non-beneficial contacts with others. Beyond this size, the costs of social contacts (for example, competition and aggression) outweigh the benefits (for example, food sharing and ease of mate location).

research now

happy hen housing

Channing, C.E., Hughes, B.O. and Walker, A.W. (2001) Spatial distribution and behaviour of laying hens housed in an alternative system. *Applied Animal Behaviour Science*, 72, 335–45

Aim: To compare the behaviour of hens in differing social densities.

Method: Perchery-housed laying hens were kept in colonies of eight different sizes from 323 to 912 individuals per pen from age 12 weeks. They were observed from 26 to 61 weeks of age, at 8-week intervals.

Results: In the smallest and largest colony sizes, more standing and fewer feeding behaviours were observed. The distribution of individuals was uneven throughout each pen and this variation was greatest in the larger colony sizes, with individual counts of up to 41 hens per m³.

Conclusion: High social density within a pen leads to uneven distribution of hens and greater crowding in some areas. This may have adverse implications for the welfare of perchery-housed hens. There appears to be an optimum colony size at which birds distribute themselves more evenly and move and feed more freely.

An alternative explanation for the effects of crowding was offered by Christian (1955) in his *social stress theory*. This suggests that high-density existence leads to social consequences that are stressful, such as fighting and competition for food or territory. This would result in a stress-like response mediated by the adrenal glands (see Chapter 3). Increased levels of adrenalin could then be directly responsible for the behavioural and physiological changes that have been identified. Recent experimental evidence from Haller *et al.* (1999) suggests that crowding-induced social instability is more stressful for female rats than for males, resulting in weight gain and hormonal changes associated with stress. Male rats experienced greater stress-related changes in response to increased aggression. This supports the social stress theory, as it demonstrates that crowding may trigger physiological changes associated with stress.

A response to stress may account for the behaviour of wild colonies of Norway lemmings (*Lemmus lemmus*) when the population increases. Contrary to popular belief, this small, hamster-like rodent of the Arctic tundra does not make the ultimate sacrifice in the face of population explosion and head for the nearest cliff to hurl itself off. Rather, colonies reach a size at which they migrate to disperse to new feeding and breeding grounds. These migrations may consist of several thousand individuals, predominantly young males. *En route* to new territories, the lemmings may encounter mountains, rivers and the open sea. Whilst lemmings are good swimmers, and will generally only enter water when there is land in sight, they may swim into open water when many individuals accumulate at the water's edge. As a consequence, many drown (McFarland, 1999).

for and against

studies on crowding in animals

+ Crowding research has provided evidence for the physiological effects of crowding, including stress and reduced fertility.

+ Crowding research has provided evidence for the behavioural consequences, such as increased aggression and changes in dominance and sexual behaviour.

– Studies of crowding cause stress to animals, and so raise ethical issues.

– Studies that manipulate spatial density are confounded by consequent effects on space per individual and absolute space available.

– Studies that manipulate social density are confounded by consequent effects on space per individual and group size.

+ The effects of social and spatial density manipulations may be the indirect result of changes in behaviour, such as territoriality, rather than the direct consequences of crowding.

+ The findings of animal research may help to improve the conditions under which animals are housed; for instance, in zoos and farms.

Studies of crowding in humans

To what extent are the findings from animal studies replicated in the literature on humans? This is difficult to answer, as although laboratory experiments into crowding are conducted, long-term investigations into the effects on humans tend to be naturalistic observations, which means that the results are not directly comparable. The study described below attempted to test Calhoun's 'optimal group size' idea, investigating the pay-off between frustrating and beneficial interactions with others.

Social density

classic research

people, privacy and perceived crowding

Baum, A. and Valins, S. (1977) *Architecture and Social Behavior: Psychological Studies of Social Density*. Hilldale, NJ: Erlbaum

Aim: To investigate the balance between the benefits of increased opportunities to interact as density increases and the costs of such enforced encounters.

Method: The perceptions and behaviour of occupants of two different types of university hall of residence were compared. The accommodation was either corridor-style or suite-style, each offering the same amount of space per individual, the same number of individuals per floor and the same facilities (bathroom and lounge). They differed only in the number of other individuals sharing those facilities (either 4–6 in suites and 34 on corridors) and hence the number of different interpersonal encounters (in other words, the social density varied).

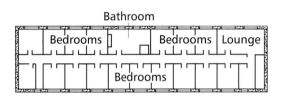

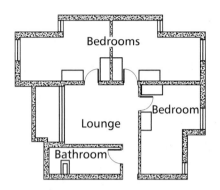

Based on: Baum and Valins (1977)

Results: Residents in corridor-style accommodation perceived their floors to be more crowded. They were more likely to feel that they had to engage in inconvenient and unwanted social inter-actions, and they expressed a greater desire to avoid other people. Their feelings of helplessness were reflected in their social skills. They were less likely to initiate a conversation with a stranger, were less able to reach a consensus after a discussion, were less socially assertive and were more likely to give up in a competitive game.

Conclusion: Exposure to a large number of other people – especially when the group lacks social structure – has negative consequences, resulting in less sociable behaviour. The enforced, uncontrollable personal contacts experienced by the corridor residents led to a feeling of helplessness, so they tended to avoid social interactions and were less assertive in ambiguous situations because they had learned that they had little control over their social environment.

As with animals, studies of social density in humans suggest that crowding results in negative consequences. For example, Saegert (1975) reported increased anxiety during a task performance under crowded compared to uncrowded conditions. As well as worsening difficult situations, crowding also seems to affect the pleasure that we derive from positive situations. Stewart and Cole (2001) reported that backpackers visiting the Grand Canyon National Park had poorer-quality experiences if they encountered more groups of other people. Crowding in the natural environment seemed detrimentally to affect their enjoyment (see also Chapter 8). Similar effects have been demonstrated in the work environment. Rishi *et al.* (2000) assessed the work satisfaction of employees at a bank in Bhopal, India. They found that work satisfaction was negatively correlated with crowding; the more crowded the employees felt, the less satisfied they were. The following study illustrates the way in which social density affects our perceptions of crowding.

classic
research

crowded caravans

Eoyang, C.K. (1974) Effects of group size and privacy in residential crowding.
Journal of Personality and Social Psychology, 30, 389–92

Aim: To distinguish between the effects of group size and social stimulation.

Method: A field survey was conducted using students who were residents of a trailer (caravan) park at Stanford University that consisted of 118 identical housing units. The 58 participants from different trailers rated their living space and satisfaction with aspects of their accommodation and location.

Results: Individuals living in more crowded conditions (either because of larger numbers of occupants per trailer or because they were sharing bedrooms) were less satisfied with their living space. Of these two factors, the absolute number of people appeared to be the more important factor and resulted in generally lower ratings of the living space, its furnishings, their own rooms, tidiness and noise.

Conclusion: Both situational characteristics of occupancy (increased density of residents) and lack of privacy (having to share a bedroom even when it is large) contributed to individuals' perceptions of crowding. Residents in larger group sizes were less satisfied with their living conditions as they were more crowded.

Spatial density

With regard to human responses to increasing spatial density, there seems to be a gender difference; males experience more negative mood states in high compared to low spatial density environments, the reverse being the case for females (Freedman *et al.*, 1972). In Chapter 1 we discussed gender differences in personal space, which could explain this finding. Alternatively, it may be the result of differences in response to socialisation. Women tend to be more friendly, seeking opportunities to associate with others, whereas men tend to be competitive in their social encounters, and thus may view others close-by as a threat (Deaux and LaFrance, 1998). However, some studies report no differences between the genders in their preferences for isolation (see, for example, Demirbas and Demirkan, 2000).

research
now

the benefits of being on top

Kaya, N. and Erkíp, E. (2001) Satisfaction in a dormitory building: the effects of floor height on the perception of room size and crowding. *Environment and Behavior*, 33, 35–53

Aim: To investigate the effects of room location (floor height) on students' perception of the size of their room and how crowded they felt.

Method: Residents occupying two dormitory blocks (one for men and one for women) at Bilkent University, Ankara, were studied. The identical five-storey buildings contained identical rooms and had equal densities. The occupants were surveyed with regard to their perception of their room size, privacy and satisfaction.

Results: Residents on the highest floor perceived their rooms to be larger and felt less crowded than residents on the lowest floor. Participants who perceived their rooms as being larger expressed greater feelings of privacy and were more satisfied with their dormitory rooms.

Conclusion: The perception of density as well as the actual density affect the sensation of crowding and hence satisfaction with accommodation.

Recent evidence suggests that the sensation of crowding is affected not only by our perception of density but also by our expectations – if we correctly anticipate crowds, this helps us to tolerate them.

research
now

crowded shops and crabby shoppers

Machleit, K., Eroglu, S. and Mantel, S.P. (2000) Perceived retail crowding and shopping satisfaction: What modifies the relationship? *Journal of Consumer Psychology*, 9, 29–42

Aim: To examine the relationship between retail store crowding and shopping satisfaction.

Method: A total of 1,006 participants were used in two field and one laboratory experiment to investigate the importance of high density on emotions and satisfaction.

Results: Shopping satisfaction was shown to be reduced by the emotions associated with crowding. However, this effect was moderated by expectations of crowding and personal tolerance for crowding. These relationships were found in both laboratory and field settings.

Conclusion: People who expect shops to be crowded and who are relatively tolerant of crowds are more likely to find shopping satisfying under high-density conditions than those who have less realistic expectations or are less tolerant.

for and against

studies on crowding in humans

+ Laboratory experiments are well controlled and are comparable to animal studies.

− Laboratory experiments of crowding lack ecological validity.

− Laboratory studies of crowding in humans can only study the short-term effects.

+ Research has shown that crowding affects social behaviour, causing people to become less sociable, avoid one another and take less interest in their neighbours.

+ Expectations of crowding as well as actual density affects our experience of crowding.

Effects on health

Animal studies have shown that high-density living may affect health because there is a greater risk of the spreading of disease (Hoogland, 1979) and the same effect may arise in human populations (Paulus, 1988). Studies on death rates in prisons suggest that inmates in higher-density settings are at greater risk, even when factors such as violent deaths have been controlled for (see the accompanying figure).

Evans (1979) reports that varying spatial density – for instance, by putting 10 people in an 8 foot by 12 foot (2.4 m by 3.6 m) room – increased blood pressure and other physiological indicators of stress. Students living in high-density accommodation make more frequent visits to the infirmary (Baron *et al.*, 1976) and Fuller *et al.* (1993) report a higher level of physical illness in crowded conditions. Fleming *et al.* (1987) compared the effect of a challenging task on blood pressure and heart rate of people living in crowded or uncrowded neighbourhoods. Those participants experiencing chronic crowding demonstrated greater cardiovascular reactivity (higher heart rates and blood pressure) than

A higher population size in a prison setting is associated with a higher mortality rate (Paulus *et al.*, 1978)

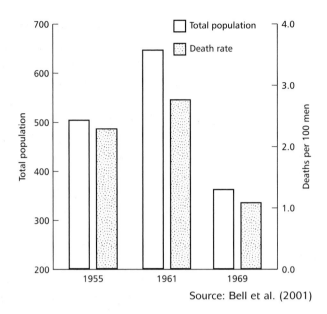

Source: Bell et al. (2001)

those from uncrowded environments. The effect of crowding seems to be an enduring one, affecting performance even away from the stressful environment itself.

Pandey (1999) asked participants living in high- or low-density areas of Gorakhpur City, India, about their health status. A positive relationship between crowding and illness was found; that is, people living in more crowded areas exhibited poorer physical and mental health. These people also reported a strong sensation of crowding (in other words, there was a positive correlation between objective crowding and feelings of crowding) and reduced perceived control. However, Chan (1999) tested 414 urban residents from the hyperdense metropolis of Hong Kong and found that residents in spatially constrained dwellings did not necessarily feel crowded. Where architectural designs met expectations – that is, the participants were satisfied with their physical surroundings – this helped to alleviate feelings of crowdedness.

Not only may high-density living conditions pose greater health risks, but it also seems to impair our ability to care for our own health. Menezes *et al.* (2000) studied a range of factors that could have been related to discharged psychiatric patients failing to comply with outpatient treatment. The only variable associated with poor compliance was residential crowding. Patients living in very crowded homes were twice as likely to miss outpatient appointments as those living in less-crowded homes.

Effects on social behaviour

Baum and Valins (1977) showed that increasing the apparent social density by increasing the number of people encountered affects social behaviour. Under crowded conditions, people became less sociable, less assertive, avoided one another and took less interest in their neighbours (see pp.87–88). At higher social densities – for instance, with three people sharing a room rather than two – room-mates' perceptions of each other become less positive (Baron *et al.*, 1976). Crowding appears to reduce our liking for individuals, as well as for social interaction in general. Furthermore, the effects of crowding on social interaction seem to reduce our ability to seek out others when we need them. Lepore *et al.* (1991) found that individuals who had high levels of social support lost this buffering effect after 8 months in crowded conditions; they no longer sought the assistance of other people as a resource in times of psychological distress. Crowding results in withdrawal: it seems to erode the social support networks that are most important in stressful situations.

Crowding also impacts on prosocial behaviour; that is, the extent to which people will help others. Bickman *et al.* (1973) compared helping behaviour across three conditions: high-, medium- and low-density dormitories. The experimenters 'accidentally' dropped envelopes that had been stamped and addressed into each dormitory and observed the helping behaviour – that is, the number of envelopes that were picked up and put into the postbox. The graph illustrates the rate of prosocial behaviour in each condition. Crowded conditions seemed to reduce the likelihood of helping fellow residents.

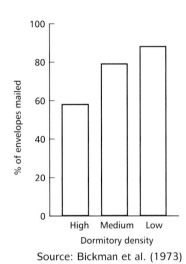

Source: Bickman et al. (1973)

Residents in crowded dormitories are less likely to pick up and post apparently lost items of mail for other residents

If crowding reduces prosocial behaviour, does it also increase antisocial behaviour? The evidence here seems to be contradictory, with effects dependent on age, gender and access to resources (Bell *et al.*, 2001). Since much research on the effects of crowding on aggression is conducted in laboratories, its validity in the real world is questionable. However, research conducted in settings such as prisons (see the accompanying figure) avoids this criticism – although, arguably, the prison population may not be representative in terms of aggressiveness.

Patterns similar to those of Cox *et al.* (1984) have been found with both elderly residents in long-term care and young people in crisis centres. Morgan and Stewart (1998) found that increased social and spatial density were associated with more disruptive behaviour in elderly residents with dementia, while Teare *et al.* (1995) found that the probability of problem behaviour arising in young people at a shelter increased as it became more crowded. In hospital settings with psychiatric patients, Ng *et al.* (2001) and Nijman and Rector (1999) have found that occupancy levels affect the behaviour of patients, with crowded conditions leading to increased verbal and physical aggression.

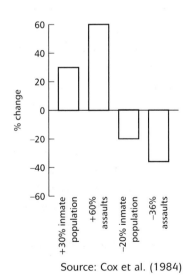

Source: Cox et al. (1984)

Cox *et al.* (1984) found a strong relationship between density in prisons and inmate aggression

Effects on performance

If crowding detrimentally affects our physiology and social behaviour, it seems likely that it will also have negative effects on task performance. If so, this would have implications for the ideal density experienced in

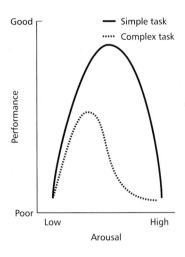

The Yerkes–Dodson law predicts a relationship between arousal level and performance on tasks of differing difficulties. According to this law, when we are highly aroused (such as in crowded situations) we perform best on simple tasks

learning and working environments. Although early studies suggested that there was no decrement in performance with increased density (see, for example, Freedman *et al.*, 1971), subsequent studies, using more complex tasks, have demonstrated some effects (see, for example, Aiello *et al.*, 1975). Since crowded conditions raise arousal level, the Yerkes–Dodson law would predict that we would perform better on simple tasks in relatively crowded conditions, but relatively poorly on more difficult tasks under similar circumstances (see the accompanying figure).

Karlin *et al.* (1979) found that students living in crowded accommodation (with three people in a room designed for two) suffered a decline in their grades. More recently, Bruins and Barber (2000) conducted a field experiment on 80 members of the public recruited outside a supermarket during crowded or uncrowded periods. The participants were required to complete a 'shopping list' of physical and mental tasks. Under crowded conditions the performance of the participants, particularly on the mental tasks, was impaired.

Preventing and coping with the effects of high-density living

High-density living is detrimental to our emotional state, health, performance and social behaviour. Psychologists are attempting to tackle these issues in order to find ways to limit these effects. One solution, perversely, appears to be to inoculate people against the effects of crowding by exposing them to high-density living! Evans *et al.* (2000) have shown that living in crowded conditions can enable people to develop strategies to limit their exposure to others.

research
now

crowded homes, reclusive occupants

Evans, G.W., Rhee, E., Forbes, C., Allen, K.M. and Lepore, S.J. (2000) The meaning and efficacy of social withdrawal as a strategy for coping with chronic residential crowding. *Journal of Environmental Psychology*, 20, 335–42

Aim: To examine whether social withdrawal as a strategy for coping with chronic residential crowding is related to changes in the way in which information about social situations is processed.

Method: Two studies were conducted. The occurrence of social withdrawal was observed through contrived but apparently 'incidental' encounters in a naturalistic, uncrowded condition.

A situation was contrived in which each participant overheard a conversation (between two confederates) about a boyfriend. The conversation contained information about sex, jealousy, friendship, love and anger. The participants were subsequently asked questions about the dialogue such as 'What was Diane doing when BJ barged into her room?' to test their knowledge of the social encounter that they had overheard. In addition, the efficacy of social withdrawal as a means of reducing stress was measured under highly crowded conditions in the laboratory, to compare the responses of individuals in crowded and uncrowded homes.

Results: The field study showed that individuals from crowded residences recalled fewer facts about the overheard conversation than those from uncrowded homes. Similarly, the laboratory setting showed that individuals living in crowded homes appeared to be less aware of personal information about strangers, as shown by the graph.

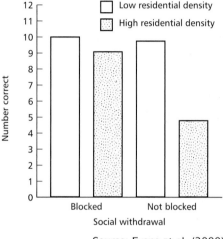

Source: Evans et al. (2000)

When unable to avoid social interactions in this experimental setting ('blocked' condition), participants from crowded accommodation felt more stressed than residents of uncrowded homes.

Conclusion: Living in high-density accommodation appears to predispose individuals to employ social withdrawal as a strategy in crowded conditions, as demonstrated by their low processing of social information about strangers. For individuals who have learned to use this technique while living under chronically crowded conditions, social withdrawal in response to acute crowding appears to be an effective strategy for reducing short-term stress.

Where possible, crowded living spaces should be subdivided, to limit the number of unnecessary social contacts that each individual has to endure. Thus, as in Baum and Valins (1977) study, accommodation could be divided into several smaller units where facilities allow, rather than sharing larger areas and forcing unsolicited interactions.

Crowd behaviour

So far, we have only considered the effects of crowding, particularly those pertaining to high-density living; that is, the consequences of chronic exposure to crowded conditions. Psychologists are also interested in the processes that lead to the formation of short-term crowds, such as are seen at demonstrations or public events. Such crowding falls under the term 'collective behaviour', which can be defined as spontaneous in origin, structureless and dependent upon stimulation from within (Milgram and Toch, 1969). Several theories have been proposed to account for the behaviour of people in crowds, three of which are discussed below.

Contagion

Le Bon (1879) suggested that the behaviour of an individual within a crowd is irrational and uncritical; an individual within a crowd loses the measure of the norms that usually govern his or her behaviour and so becomes 'primitive': hence mob violence results. Contagion theory thus suggests that riotous behaviour spreads through a crowd like a *contagious* disease. Le Bon proposed four situational determinants of crowd behaviour:

- *suggestibility* – individuals become more inclined to respond to the ideas of others, especially when proposed in an authoritative manner and in the absence of a clear leader

- *social contagion* – individuals within a crowd arouse and respond to one another, thereby amplifying the intensity of their interactions

- *impersonality* – individuals lose their appreciation of others as people and so cease to treat them as such

- *anonymity* – within a crowd each individual loses his or her sense of individuality and hence the responsibility for his or her own behaviour.

Of these, social contagion and anonymity have continued to receive the attention of psychologists as key issues in crowd behaviour. When an individual is anonymous, as in a crowd, he or she may lose his or her sense of being an individual. Festinger *et al.* (1952) called this process *deindividuation*. Group members cease to pay attention to individuals *as* individuals, thus losing their self-consciousness and with it the belief that they are accountable for their own actions – moral responsibility shifts from the individual to the group. This loss of the internal constraints that normally inhibit socially unacceptable behaviour could therefore explain the criminal activity of crowds – such as the looting and violence seen during riots. The concept of deindividuation is discussed further on pages 97–107.

Social contagion has been observed in animals: behaviour patterns demonstrated by some animals appear in others that can see or hear them. For example, one barking dog is liable to set off all the others in the neighbourhood. Such social transmission of behaviour can also be seen in people – when one person yawns, those around that person find it irresistible not to follow suit. Although this resembles social learning, it is much simpler. Unlike social learning, contagion does not require that a *new* behaviour is learned; nor does it demand that the models for the behaviour are in any way responsible for tutoring those acquiring the behaviour. Contagion simply occurs when a pre-existing behaviour is triggered in one individual by observing that behaviour in another. Thus, for individuals in a crowd, the nature and intensity of their interactions is likely to escalate; once aroused, individuals seek an outlet for their intense emotions. Horton and Hunt (1976) report an incident in which the victim of a lynch mob was protected by the mayor, resulting in the redirection of the attack on to the mayor. Once incited to attack through social contagion, the group sought an alternative target for their aggression.

Members of a crowd may also share aspects of behaviour, emotions and motivation because of the nature of the crowd; for example, people at a concert all enjoy the same music. Durkheim (1898) suggested that *controlled emotional contagion* (the spread of feeling in a peaceful situation) can be useful in allowing the expression of otherwise pent-up feelings. This tendency of like-minded people to congregate forms the basis of *convergence theory* – the suggestion that crowds are composed of similar individuals because they 'converge' or come together. Benewick and Holton (1987) found that members of a congregation of 80,000 at Wembley Stadium in 1982, attending a mass said by Pope Paul, reported strong feelings of unity with other members of the crowd.

Deindividuation

Diener (1979) suggests that, once within a crowd, an individual loses his or her sense of separateness, because self-awareness is blocked and the person is unable to monitor his or her own behaviour. We frequently perform certain forms of behaviour without self-awareness, but we are accustomed to returning to a higher level of conscious control when the situation or outcome is unexpected, or when we feel that we are being judged.

Think about situations in which you lack conscious awareness of yourself as an individual. Generate a list of circumstances or activities where you 'do it without thinking'. These might include actions that you perform often that have become automatic, such as doing up buttons, and instances of social behaviour where you 'know the protocol', such as replying to 'Hello, how are you?' or requesting a bus to stop.

According to Diener (1979), self-regulation is also lost when we become part of a crowd, and this results in deindividuation. Without the appropriate self-regulatory restraints, we become less concerned about others' opinions of our behaviour, less rational and more impulsive. These are exactly the kinds of behaviour that we see in crowds.

media
watch

To what extent did this crowd demonstrate the impulsivity and lack of rationality predicted by Diener (1979)?

How does being part of a crowd result in this change in behaviour? Prentice-Dunn and Rogers (1982) suggest there are two routes via which socially inappropriate behaviour in crowds could increase. These derive from two kinds of self-awareness, private and public. *Private self-*

awareness refers to the self-regulation described by Diener: it is our conscious attention to our own beliefs, feelings and behaviour. *Public self-awareness* is the extent to which we care about how other people regard our behaviour.

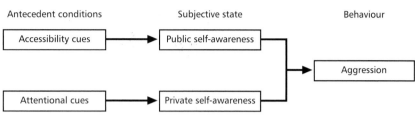

A model of the independent effects of different types of self-awareness impacting on behaviour in a crowd (Prentice-Dunn and Rogers, 1982)

Source: Prentice-Dunn and Rogers (1982)

Being part of a crowd can reduce private self-awareness because our attention shifts from ourselves to others: the noise, arousal and participation in events cause us to focus 'outwardly' on the situation around us. This, in turn, results in a lowering of attention to ourselves, so we are less aware of our internal beliefs and standards, and thus an internal state of deindividuation arises. We experience a loss of individual identity and become more likely to perform kinds of behaviour that we would otherwise regard as unacceptable.

Public self-awareness is also affected by the presence of a crowd, since we become relatively anonymous as the number of other people increases. Other factors such as wearing masks or identical clothing also increase our sense of anonymity. In addition, larger groups result in *diffusion of responsibility*; we feel less accountable when there are other people around – the responsibility is shared (that is, diffused) when the numbers in a crowd rise, so no particular individual feels responsible. Since people feel that they can neither be identified nor held responsible for events, this will compound their disregard for social norms and laws.

The importance of anonymity is supported by evidence such as that of Zimbardo (1970), who demonstrated experimentally that identically dressed participants whose faces were covered (who were therefore unidentifiable members of a group) delivered stronger electric shocks than participants who were dressed normally and wore name tags. This suggested that deindividuation was related to an increase in antisocial behaviour (however, see also Johnson and Downing, 1979, p.100). Mullen (1986) studied lynchings reported in newspapers between 1899 and 1946. He found a strong relationship between mob size and the atrocity of the crime; the larger the group was, the more aggressive and destructive were their actions. This suggests that members of larger groups did indeed lose their self-awareness to the group, felt less identifiable and less responsible, and were therefore more antisocial in their behaviour.

Finally, Prentice-Dunn and Rogers (1982) suggest that when the effects of the loss of private and public self-awareness are combined with behavioural cues, such as weapons and aggressive models, aggression and other socially inappropriate forms of behaviour arise.

classic research

nurses get nicer

Johnson, R.D. and Downing, L.L. (1979) Deindividuation and valence of cues: effects on prosocial and antisocial behaviour. *Journal of Personality and Social Psychology*, 37, 1532–8

Aim: To investigate the effects of deindividuation on the incidence of antisocial behaviour.

Method: Participants were either dressed in robes with hoods (having negative connotations, such as association with the racist Ku Klux Klan group or with executioners) or in nurses' uniforms (having positive associations with helping and caring). In addition, the participants were either identifiable – they had name tags on their costumes – or anonymous. Photographs were taken of each individual and each was told that these were on view to other participants, thus achieving individuation and deindividuation conditions. The participants were required to decide the level of shock to be administered to another person if the participant failed to perform a task correctly.

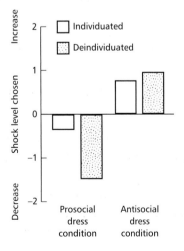

Source: Smith and Mackie (2000)
Mean shock selection

Results: Clothing with aggressive associations increased the likelihood of participants using higher shock levels, and this effect was increased when the participants were deindividuated. Prosocial clothing resulted in lower shock levels, and this effect was also exaggerated when the participants were deindividuated; that is, the nurse-like participants gave even lower shocks when they felt anonymous.

Conclusion: The effects of increasing deindividuation increases people's tendency to follow salient social norms, in this instance to behave in keeping with their 'uniform'. Antisocial behaviour was thus only increased in those participants who wore aggressive-style clothing. This suggests that deindividuation does not result in a freeing from internal standards, but in people altering their behaviour in accordance with the social norms of the group with which they are identified at the time.

for and against

deindividuation

+ It can explain people's actions when 'deindividuated', or when they believe they cannot be identified.

+ It explains the apparently irrational and impulsive nature of behaviour seen by members of crowds.

− It cannot explain why some crowds become violent and others do not: it takes no account of the intent of the crowd.

Emergent norms

From the research that we have looked at so far, it is clear that some groups become antisocial while others become prosocial. We have not yet considered a theory that can explain how these differences in outcome arise. Contagion theory (p.96) can explain how a crowd might become riotous if some angry individuals exacerbate feelings of aggression and desire for revenge in those around them. Also, deindividuation theory (p.97) would predict that the behaviour of individuals will contravene societal norms as they become unconstrained. Emergent norm theory enables us to explain how members of a group might in fact be conforming to a new, emerging set of standards for behaviour. Turner and Killian (1972) suggest that two key factors need to be present for crowd behaviour to change:

● the crowd must develop a new – that is, *emergent* – norm for behaviour (such as aggression)

● individuals in the crowd should be identifiable, thus increasing social pressure on them to conform to the new norms.

This contradicts the predictions of deindividuation theory in that it relies on individuals being identifiable. In a test of the two explanations, Mann *et al.* (1982) produced evidence to suggest that both emergent norm formation and deindividuation may occur. The former was supported, as participants behaved more aggressively when told that the group norm was aggressive. The latter was also supported, as identifiable participants were less aggressive than anonymous participants.

research
now

is litter the norm?

Cialdini, R.B., Reno, R.R. and Kallgren, C.A. (1990) A focus theory of normative conduct: recycling the concept of norms to reduce littering in public places. *Journal of Personality and Social Psychology*, 58, 1015–26

Aim: To find out whether evidence of people behaving contrary to a social norm caused others to adopt this new standard of behaviour.

Method: Five separate studies were conducted, two of which are described here. In study A, participants were observed as they crossed a car park that was either clean (anti-littering norm) or littered (pro-littering norm). Half of the participants saw a confederate dropping a leaflet that said 'THIS IS AUTOMOTIVE SAFETY WEEK. PLEASE DRIVE CAREFULLY' and all, on returning to their car, found an identical leaflet under their windscreen wiper. The participants were observed to see whether this leaflet was dropped into the environment around the vehicle.

In study B, conditions were created by introducing different amounts of litter along a path on different occasions (between none and 16 items of rubbish). Passers-by were given leaflets and observed as they turned a corner and walked along the previously littered path, to see whether and how quickly they dropped their leaflet.

Results: Study A: participants more often dropped litter in a littered environment than in a clean one, and this effect was greater when attention to the norm was reinforced by seeing the confederate littering. However, they were less likely to drop litter in the clean environment when the confederate did so; again, their attention was being drawn to the norm (of anti-littering in this case).

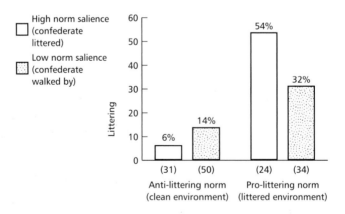

Source: Cialdini et al. (1990)

Study B: the participants were more likely to drop their leaflet if the path was already littered; and the more litter there was, the more likely they were to do so. Virtually all participants who had not littered by the end of the path placed their leaflets in a rubbish bin that was visible only when they reached the end of the path.

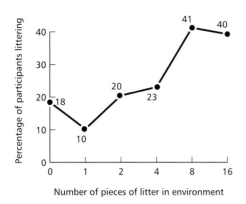

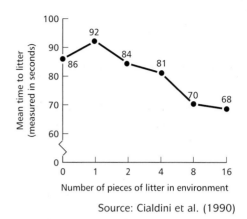

Source: Cialdini et al. (1990)

Conclusion: The litter appeared to draw the participants' attention to the prevailing norm: where that was disregard for the environment, this induced littering behaviour. The participants' perceived an emerging norm (which may have differed from their internal standards) and behaved accordingly.

The findings of Mann *et al.* can be explained by Postmes and Spears' (1998) proposal that the process of deindividuation results in individuals being more likely to respond to emerging group norms which are reliant on the situation or context. This arises because deindividuation has three characteristics:

- a decreased focus on personal identity (but not a loss of self-awareness)

- an increased responsiveness to situational group and context norms

- it is neutral with respect to general social norms.

This can therefore explain why crowds behave differently: deindividuation may or may not occur, and when it does, the behaviour of the crowd will be affected by the locally arising emergent norms. Furthermore, it can explain the selectivity of behaviour exhibited by members of a crowd.

Reicher and Potter (1985) studied scientific and lay accounts of the riot that arose in the deprived area of St Paul's, Bristol, in 1980. They concluded that the police raided a café in the belief that illegal drinking was taking place. When they tried to leave, bricks were thrown and they requested back-up. A 3,000-strong rioting crowd amassed but, contrary to the predictions of contagion theory or deindividuation, the rioters were not an irrational, irresponsible mob. Instead, they were highly selective in their destruction, for example:

- damage to property was restricted to police buildings, banks and other symbols of the establishment, rather than local shops or houses

- damage to other property (such as cars) was restricted to those believed to be unmarked police vehicles

- the effects of the riot were confined to the St Paul's district and did not spread to other parts of the city

- the rioters denied that they had lost their sense of identity – rather, they felt a strong sense of pride in their community.

These findings suggest that the attention of members of the crowd shifted from themselves as individuals to a focus on other members of the group. Since the emerging group norm was one of specific aggression towards the establishment, this provided a cue for the behaviour of others. This theory is based on the ideas of social identity theory (see Jarvis *et al.*, 2000). Reicher's (1984) view sees the rioters as an 'in group' who adopted a shared social identity (based on their location and behaviour) and could justify their behaviour because the initial police presence was judged to have been illegitimate.

Reicher's explanation would support the findings of Marsh *et al.* (1978) after an extensive study of football supporters. They concluded that much of the fans' behaviour followed established social rules which imposed restrictions on their aggressive behaviour, and that uncontrolled violence was more likely to arise when police intervention interfered with the fans' own self-regulation. Similarly, Waddington *et al.* (1987) observed and interviewed demonstrators on two rallies that took place during the 1984 miners' strike. On both occasions, the crowd held the same political views and was in the same town. The rallies were only 2 weeks apart, but one was violent while the other was not. At the second rally, the peaceful demonstration, marshalling of the protesters had been organised from within, barriers had been erected to keep the police at a discreet distance and alternative channels for arousal were provided by speakers and entertainment. Thus, the 'in group' were following their own, predetermined rules, rather than having those of the police (who were viewed at the time as allied to Margaret Thatcher's Conservative government) thrust upon them.

So, in addition to explaining riotous crowds, it is possible to see how, if alternative norms were to emerge from the behaviour of a crowd – such as in the situation described by Waddington *et al.*, at the funeral of Princess Diana or during the Pope's visit (see p.103) – entirely different crowd behaviour could arise. If the 'in group' favoured peaceful behaviour, this would become the behavioural norm.

However, Reicher's research is not without problems. Observers who are present at the time of a riot are unlikely to be without bias. Furthermore, recollections during interviews after the event will be subject to confabulation, the changing of memories after they have been stored, as demonstrated by Loftus (see, for example, Loftus and Palmer, 1974; Loftus *et al.*, 1978: see also Jarvis *et al.*, 2000). In a series of studies, Loftus showed how the recall of eye witnesses was not just inaccurate but could be altered with expectations created by hearing various verbal suggestions. Such evidence indicates that interviewees who had discussed the day's events amongst themselves would be unlikely to have unbiased recall of the riot, and would have tended to mould their memories in line with expected behavioural norms. Since it is not ethical to perform studies of riotous crowding, researchers are faced with either the pitfalls of interviews (see, for example, Reicher and Potter, 1985; Benewick and Holton, 1987) or analyses such as Mullen (1986).

Not all studies of riots generate such a clear pattern as asserted by Reicher and Potter (1985) or Marsh *et al.* (1978). Acts of destruction may spread out from the affected community and may appear in different locations at different times, as observed in the 1965 riot in the Watts district of Los Angeles. In such instances, it seems less likely that social identity and emergent norms are responsible for such forms of behaviour.

for and against

emergent norm theory

+ It can explain why some groups become riotous while others remain calm.

+ It sees crowds as groups of individuals with a shared purpose, who are capable of interpreting events around them, rather than an uncontrollable mass.

— It can be criticised for suggesting that individuals are unable to make appropriate judgements in a crowd situation. There is good evidence of individuals making rational choices about alternative courses of action (see, for example, Berk, 1974).

Crowds in emergency situations

While we have seen that crowds can be peaceful, problems do arise and, should an emergency occur, the risks are compounded by the large numbers of people. Disasters such as the deaths at Hillsborough football stadium and in the Kings Cross Underground fire were worsened at least in part because of the crowded conditions. In addition to sheer numbers, the presence of a crowd seems to reduce the capacity of any individual to act appropriately in an emergency situation.

classic
research

size matters!

Darley, J.M. and Latané, B. (1968) Bystander intervention in emergencies: diffusion of responsibility. *Journal of Personality and Social Psychology*, 8, 377–83

Aim: To investigate the effect of group size on helping behaviour.

Method: The participants, who were naïve to the purpose of the experiment, joined into groups of two, three or six. They could not see the other members of their group, but could communicate with them via an intercom. Each participant believed themselves and those in their group to be bystanders when an emergency arose – a fellow student appeared to be having a seizure. The time taken for the participant to offer help was recorded.

Results: The likelihood of helping at all reduced as the group size increased, and those who did offer assistance did so more slowly when others were present.

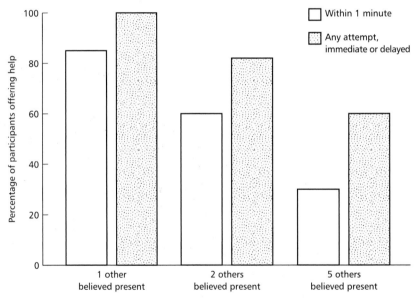

Source: Smith and Mackie (2000)

Conclusion: In an emergency situation, individuals are less likely to act when there are other people around. This is called *diffusion of responsibility*, because individuals do not feel as accountable as they would if they were alone, as the responsibility is shared between members of the group. The inaction of other bystanders appeared to prevent any individual from acting.

Latané and Darley (1970) proposed a model to explain the relative disinclination of people to help in emergency situations when others are present. Their model of bystander intervention (illustrated below) shows that there are several stages in the decision to help. The critical stage in terms of group size is whether they assume responsibility. As we have seen earlier (p.93), individuals are less likely to take responsibility themselves in a crowd, and so may stall at stage 3. In addition, they may judge appropriate behaviour (stage 5) on the basis of the responses of others; so if no one appears to be taking action, that becomes the new norm, even though any individual on his or her own may have acted differently. This use of the responses of others to guide our own behaviour, that then causes us to fail to act (even when we believe we should do), is termed *pluralistic ignorance*.

Since Latané and Darley's original research, many factors other than group size have been shown to affect the probability of prosocial behaviour being exhibited. Such factors include: the ambiguity of the situation (Brickman *et al.*, 1982); the characteristics of those affected (Piliavin *et al.*, 1969); their similarity to the potential helper (Suedfeld *et al.*, 1972); and the characteristics of the bystanders, such as expert knowledge (Huston *et al.*, 1981), gender (Eagly and Crowley, 1986) and personality (Dovidio *et al.*, 1991).

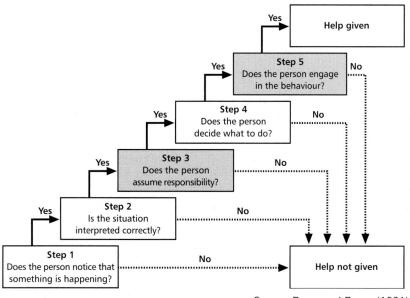

Source: Baron and Byrne (1991)

Levine (1999) has considered possible causes for the absence of bystander intervention in the murder of the 2-year-old James Bulger by two 10-year-old boys. He analysed the testimonies of 38 bystanders and concluded that they had assumed, or had been told, that the three boys were brothers. It would appear that it is not only the presence and nature of the group that affects the likelihood that anyone will intervene, but also *who* they are perceived to be, within the immediate social context.

Crowd control and preventing problems

There are five factors that may increase the risk for individuals within a crowd:

- an increased probability of a dangerous occurrence
- an increased potential number of victims
- a decreased speed and ease of communication
- a decreased speed and ease of changes in action
- diffusion of responsibility.

Since crowds present such risks, there is a need to develop successful strategies for approaching crowd control. As we have seen, some tactics, such as a strong police presence, may be counterproductive, inciting rather than reducing violent incidents. So, what can be done to tackle crowds effectively?

Waddington *et al.* (1987) developed a model to analyse social disorders such as the political demonstrations that they observed (see p.104). This model provided not only an explanation of the events but possible routes for intervention to reduce violence in such situations. These levels of analysis are ways to understand factors involved in the transition of a crowd from peaceful to violent, and are not intended to be hierarchical – one does not cause another:

- *structural* – aspects of the organisation of society, in other words its *structure*, which affect the way some individuals will respond, such as the effect of a factory closure on the workforce
- *political/ideological* – problems may arise because of governmental decisions, such as the reduction of union power, which leaves employees feeling that they are unable to help themselves
- *cultural* – shared norms and beliefs, including standards of behaviour and values such as human rights
- *contextual* – the sequence of events leading up to development of the crowd, including initial triggers and subsequent incidents
- *spatial* – the environment the crowd is in; for example, if a demonstration is held outside a particular location or arises in a specific community district
- *interactional* – the nature of the *interactions* between individuals, such as the manner in which arrests are conducted.

Returning to the account of the miners' strike, described on page 104, we can see that although the political/ideological and cultural factors were unchanged, in the second demonstration many other factors had been carefully considered. Some contextual factors were controlled through consultation with the police (although others, particularly in relation to the reasons for the miners' strike, were not). Spatial factors were more conducive to a peaceful event, as appropriate barriers were erected and the protesters' mood and movements could be manipulated by the judicious use of speakers and entertainment. Finally, interactional factors were improved, as crowd control was conducted by the organisers of the rally rather than by the police.

media watch

'Segregate Oldham'

Firebombed

Petrol bombs were thrown at officers and the *Oldham Evening Chronicle* was firebombed in what has been called Britain's worst race riots for more than a decade. Twelve people, seven white and five Asian, were arrested for public order offences on Sunday night – the second night of violence in the town – and 30 people were injured.

- The violence was sparked on Saturday by a gang of white men who threw a brick through the window of a house where a pregnant Asian woman lived.
- A group of Asian youths later fought their way into the Live and Let Live pub, where far-right activists are believed to have been drinking.
- A barricade of furniture and tyres was set on fire in Ward Street, in the Westwood area.
- Forty Asians threw bricks at and fought outside the Jolly Carter pub, one of five that came under attack.
- Later 200 Asians, mainly young men, congregated in Hardy Street, Glodwick.
- Thirty white people on a pub crawl chanted racist songs but were dispersed by police.
- Around 100 riot police with body armour and shields sealed off the main roads in Glodwick while a police helicopter circled overhead. Cars containing youths were monitored.

But BBC reporter Asad Ahmad said many Asian youths on the streets had considered the huge numbers of riot police, vans and dogs out in force in their community was provocation enough for more disturbances.

At some stages during the night officers faced stand-offs with both white and Asian youths, gathering in groups of up to 200.

A police spokeswoman assured residents that officers would be staging 'high profile policing' for the remainder of the Bank Holiday weekend. BBC correspondent Richard Wells said the tension seemed to have eased during the day on Sunday. 'However, community leaders are still on their guard,' he said. 'They've asked for urgent meetings with both the police and the local authority and have appealed to everyone to be calm.'

Source: http://news.bbc.co.uk
http://skynews.co.uk

Consider the above article in the light of the six factors listed above. Can you identify the factors that were present in the crowd at the time of the riot?

As a consequence of their observations and subsequent analyses, Waddington *et al.* made five recommendations for effective crowd control:

- crowds should be allowed to police themselves where possible

- effective liaison should be encouraged between the police and key members of the crowd

- where the police are involved, they should use minimum force to avoid their actions being interpreted by the crowd as trouble-making

- individuals who are responsible for managing the crowd should be trained in interpersonal communication

- enforcement agencies, including the police, should be seen to be accountable to the community rather than autonomous.

Each of these factors could provide a flashpoint, turning the crowd from peaceful to violent by acting as a source of grievance of the assembled individuals. Once frustration and aggression have erupted and violence ensues, the crowd becomes more difficult to police effectively.

interactive
angles

Identify a recent incident where crowd trouble has arisen. Find some reports about this situation from different sources (such as newspapers, magazines and the Internet) and try to identify the extent to which each of these recommendations was followed.

In addition to studying the cognitive and emotional factors affecting a crowd, recent research has focused on the behavioural element of movement. The traditional 'physical flow' approach to predicting crowd movement assumed that a crowd was a homogeneous mass, with people moving along corridors like water through a pipe. However, unlike people, water does not make decisions or have preferences, and cannot experience pain and fear or stumble and fall (Low, 2000). In distressing situations, people attempt to move more quickly. Consequently, they bump into one another, creating friction and slowing each other down – the 'shock wave' effect. As movement becomes more difficult, people become less stable and may fall, creating an obstruction in the path of others (Helbing, 2000). Proulx (1997) suggests that to improve computer modelling of human movement in emergency situations such as fires, we should consider the way in which people:

- tend to move in familiar directions (rather than following instructions or signs)

- turn back on themselves

- may move back towards the source of danger

- move at different speeds.

Using a computer simulation that takes account of the 'particulate' nature of the motion of people in a crowd, Johnson and Feinberg (1997) suggest that some of the problems arising in emergency situations can be overcome. The issuing of clear instructions from someone in authority to ensure that all available exits are used should reduce crowding along familiar routes. This, they suggest, was one of the key contributory factors in the failure to evacuate safely from the Beverly Hills Supper Club Fire, in which 165 people died (Johnson et al., 1994).

interactive
angles

The Canadian government has produced, as part of its *Spectator and Management of Crowd Control* advice, the following guidelines for defusing potential unrest in crowded situations, each of which has been used successfully:

- playing up-tempo music (of a type consistent with the age group of the crowd) over the public address system

- a humorous, animal-costumed individual (such as a mascot) walking up and down the line giving handshakes, pats and waves

- a large inflated beach ball, which is hit and lobbed back and forth over, and by, the spectators

- food and beverage sellers moving through the group

- cheerful security staff, passing up and down the line, talking to people.

To what extent can these measures be justified in the light of the evidence that you have read in this chapter?

Based on http://www.epc-pcc.gc.ca/research/scie_tech/en_crowd/ref.html

where to now?

The following are good sources of information about high-density living:

▶ **Aronson, A. (1999)** *The Social Animal*, **8th edn. New York: Worth/Freeman** – this has a good section on bystander apathy which, although it doesn't relate directly to crowding, does discuss some of the other factors that affect an individual's response to an emergency.

▶ **Marsh, P., Rosser, E. and Harré, R. (1978)** *The Rules of Disorder*. **London: Routledge and Kegan Paul** – this provides a fascinating account of the structure and rules within a group of football supporters.

Conclusions

Living in crowded conditions has a range of detrimental effects on animals, many of which are also exhibited by humans in high-density accommodation. In animals, fecundity falls, the animals' health fails, aggression increases and some individuals become highly territorial. In response to high-density living, humans also become less socially competent; they become anxious, feel helpless, avoid social situations and grow to dislike the people they have to encounter. Furthermore, they are less inclined to seek help from others when they need it, and less likely to offer help when it is required. People also become dissatisfied with their accommodation and feel crowded, especially when they are forced into social interactions. High-density living affects health, increasing blood pressure, the incidence of illness and the risk of suicide. In crowded conditions, people may become aggressive or disruptive, and suffer reduced performance on complex mental tasks.

The behaviour of people in crowds may be explained by a number of theories. Deindividuation can explain the way in which people in crowds may cease to act rationally, as they no longer feel responsible for their own actions. Emergent norm theory can also account for differences in crowd behaviour; that is, whether they are peaceful or become riotous. Finally, in emergency situations members of a crowd may fail to act as a consequence of diffusion of responsibility – or may all respond at once, causing problems with crowd mobility.

what do you know?

1 Describe and evaluate **two** theories of crowd behaviour in humans.

2 Describe, using evidence, **two** effects of high-density living on human behaviour.

3 Outline one study that demonstrates the effects of crowded conditions on animals, and discuss the extent to which the same effects could arise in humans.

4 Describe one theory that attempts to explain how behaviour in an emergency is affected by the presence of a crowd.

5 If you were asked to provide advice to improve crowd control at a forthcoming demonstration against fox-hunting, what advice would you give?

5

Encouraging Environmentally Responsible Behaviour

This chapter explores an aspect of human–environment inter-action in which people have an impact on their surroundings rather than simply being affected by them. Since the environment is a shared and limited resource, we have a duty to interact with it in responsible ways. We will consider the ways in which humans can affect the physical environment and consider the options available to encourage people into more environmentally friendly behaviour, including ways of changing attitudes and the use of promotional literature.

Environmental matters

The natural environment is occupied by ourselves and by non-human inhabitants. It is a scarce resource that humans are using up increasingly quickly. The human population, which already stands at 6.2 billion, is growing at a rate of 211,000 people per day. The consequence of this expansion is an increased demand on the natural environment to provide resources such as fuel, agricultural land and the space and materials required for building (stone, wood, metals and so on). These demands are compounded by the additional stress placed on the natural environment to absorb the destructive effects of modern existence; for example, the impact of advancing technology, deforestation, reduction in biodiversity and coastal land reclamation. Pollution alone has detrimental effects on landscapes, soils, rivers and the atmosphere, resulting in the greenhouse effect and destruction of the ozone layer. Humans, unlike any other occupants of the Earth, have a responsibility for the environment, because we are both the most destructive inhabitants and the only ones with the powers of reason to choose how we behave.

Environmentally friendly behaviour

Relevant factors

A number of factors dictate an individual's tendency to engage in environmentally friendly behaviour:

- their attitude to environmental issues
- values
- behavioural constraints
- the effort required to engage in appropriate behaviour
- commitment and moral responsibility
- information and feedback.

Attitudes

Breckler and Wiggins (1989) define *attitudes* as 'enduring mental representations of various features of the social or physical world. They are acquired through experience and exert a directive influence on subsequent behavior.' Because attitudes are internal value judgements, they cannot be seen directly; they must be inferred from their effects on thoughts (as indicated by self-reports) or on behaviour (which can be observed). Thus an opinion about recycling is an attitude, and could be measured by asking people about the feelings that they have towards the issue, or by observing the frequency and diligence of their recycling activities. People may report positive, negative or neutral evaluations of the attitude object (for example, recycling) and these may differ in intensity; that is, the strength of people's judgements will vary. Differences between people's attitudes can indicate the affective component of that attitude – that is, the emotional evaluation the individual has made regarding the concept of recycling – as well as the cognitive aspects, such as their memory for relevant information, the beliefs that they hold or mental images relating to the issue. Kaiser *et al.* (1999) view environmental attitude as the key to enabling psychology, as a discipline, to encourage people to use natural resources in a less exploitative way. In an Internet-based literature search using PsychInfo (a search facility dedicated to psychological literature) they found that almost two-thirds of all environmental–psychological publications had 'attitude' in the title.

Values

Attitudes towards the environment can be considered on a global as well as a local scale. Until recently, the dominant view of the Western world was one of human supremacy and ownership. A shift in approach to the world's resources seems now to be occurring and a new ecological paradigm is emerging. These views are summarised by Bell *et al.* (2001).

Contrasting views of the world's resources

The dominant world view holds that:

1 Humans are unique and have dominion over all other organisms.

2 We are masters of our own destiny – we have the intellectual and technological resources to solve any problem.

3 We have access to an infinite amount of resources.

4 Human history involves infinite progress for the better.

The new ecological paradigm holds that:

1 Humans are interdependent with other organisms, such that their preservation is to our advantage.

2 Many things that we do have unintended negative consequences for the environment.

3 Some things, such as fossil fuels, are finite.

4 Ecological constraints, such as the carrying capacity of an environment, are placed upon us.

Bell *et al.* (2001), page 479

Dunlap and Van Liere (1978) have developed the *New Environmental Paradigm* (NEP), a single measure of environmental attitude. This recognises that the relationship between people and the natural environment is changing from one of alienation and exploitation to one in which humans are an integral part of nature. Schultz and Zelezny (1999) measured environmental attitudes of students from 14 different countries using a revised version of the NEP. They found consistent patterns of environmental values across countries – for example, differences in the believed effect of destruction of the environment on the individual – that supported the use of the NEP as a tool. However, Kaiser *et al.* (1999) argue that NEP is partly a measure of the evaluative aspects of attitudes and is not necessarily a good predictor of environmental behaviour. Their research focuses on the role of values in determining environmental attitudes. This represents a further change in approach to the study of environmental issues. They argue that values – an individual's guiding principles – are more fundamental than attitudes.

research
now

ecological care counts

Kaiser, F.G., Wölfing, S. and Fuhrer, U. (1999) Environmental attitude and ecological behaviour. *Journal of Environmental Psychology*, 19, 1–19

Aim: To investigate whether environmental attitude is a reliable predictor of ecological behaviour.

Method: Questionnaires were sent to members of two different Swiss transportation associations which differed in their ideology (one aiming to promote minimal impact on humans and nature, and the other representing drivers' interests). The return rate for the former group was much higher than for the latter. The questionnaires measured social desirability, ecological behaviour and environmental attitude (including knowledge, values and behavioural intention). In addition, factors affecting the difficulties encountered in attempting to behave in ecologically sound ways were assessed as a measure of influences beyond people's actual behavioural control.

Results: It was found that environmental knowledge and environmental values explained 40 per cent of the variance in ecological behavioural intention (the extent to which people believe that they will make an effort to respond in ecological ways). In turn, behavioural intention predicted 75 per cent of the variance in ecological behaviour.

Conclusion: Having the intention to engage in ecological forms of behaviour is significantly related to a person's knowledge about environmental issues, and to the extent to which they have beliefs that place the environment high amongst their concerns. This intention then affects their actual performance of various kinds of ecological behaviour.

Behavioural constraints

The effort required to engage in environmentally friendly behaviour affects the extent to which people participate. Luyben and Bailey (1979) investigated the effects of rewards and the proximity of containers on newspaper recycling behaviour in four mobile home parks. In the reward condition, children earned toys for recycling: in the proximity condition, additional recycling containers were made available. Both conditions resulted in increased levels of recycling. Offering rewards increased recycling by 92 per cent over the baseline rate, while increasing the proximity of facilities increased recycling by 52 per cent. Indeed, it could be argued that both represent an increase due to reduced effort, as it was the children, rather than the adults, who generated the newpaper waste, and who were expending effort in the reward condition!

Tanner (1999) considered two specific categories of constraint that may affect pro-environmental behaviour. To investigate these, Tanner used a questionnaire with Swiss adults to determine the constraints on their environmentally friendly behaviour. She identified two factors that affected the frequency of their car use:

- *subjective factors* assumed to affect the preference for pro-environmental behavioural alternatives (such as a sense of responsibility or perceived behavioural barriers, such as getting wet and cold doing the recycling in the rain)

- *objective conditions* that inhibit the performance of pro-environmental action (socio-demographic variables, such as lack of automobile, place of residence and income).

Having a pro-environmental attitude was not sufficient to necessarily result in appropriate behaviour. The individuals also had to overcome subjective and objective barriers to pro-environmental behaviour.

Commitment and moral responsibility

The relative importance of factors other than attitude is supported by evidence that suggests that engagement in paper recycling can be induced by increasing commitment (Wang and Katzev, 1990). Using elderly residents in a retirement home and students in a dormitory, Wang and Katzev demonstrated that manipulating the commitment to recycling – for example, by asking participants to sign a pledge – is more likely to result in a sustained change in behaviour than alternative strategies (group commitment or token reinforcers). This was the case especially for individuals. Furthermore, Hormuth (1999) found that physical settings and social structures that allowed for social exchange and the establishment of social norms were better predictors of compliance with recycling rules than an individual's environmentally related attitudes. Kaiser and Shimoda (1999) found that moral responsibility predicts a considerable proportion of a person's ecological behaviour. The guilt that people feel for what they do or fail to do in respect of environmentally friendly behaviour promotes their self-ascription of responsibility and this, in turn, dictates the way in which they behave.

Information and feedback

The extent to which individuals perceive action to be necessary will depend in part on the amount of information available and whether they are aware of conflicting views about appropriate responses to a situation. For example, people may be more likely to engage in paper recycling if they are informed about the damage that virgin paper production does to the environment, but less likely to do so if they are also told that the trees grown to make paper help to combat the greenhouse effect. Conflicting information such as this may lead to cognitive dissonance – the discomfort associated with conflicting beliefs – and may disincline the public from engaging in environmentally friendly kinds of behaviour. However, an alternative response to such inconsistencies in belief may be to consolidate people's determination to behave in a particular way: having invested time and effort on recycling in the past, to abandon the habit now would suggest that their previous efforts have been wasted. Thus pro-environmental behaviour may be increased.

Brandon and Lewis (1999) investigated the effect of feedback on pro-environmental behaviour. The 120 households studied received a range of information: feedback about changes in their energy consumption, tips on energy saving either via computer or leaflets or through feedback relating to financial or environmental costs. Their energy consumption was monitored and compared to their earlier usage. Income and demographic features predicted previous usage but not changes in consumption during the study; here, environmental attitude and feedback had the most effect. The installation of computers resulted in the greatest reduction in energy consumption. People with positive environmental attitudes but who had not previously engaged in many conservation activities were most likely to change their usage following feedback. Therefore, pro-environmental attitudes are important, but without a cue such as feedback, a positive attitude alone may be insufficient to trigger environmentally friendly behaviour.

The theory of planned behaviour

Ajzen's (1985) *theory of planned behaviour* proposes that actions such as forms of environmentally friendly behaviour are determined by a combination of behavioural intention (deciding to achieve a goal) and perceived behavioural control (believing that you can or cannot perform a behaviour). Behavioural intention may be affected by attitude (which is in turn affected by knowledge) and by subjective norms that arise from our beliefs and our inclination to comply with these values. Consider recycling, for example. There may be two factors that affect the behaviour of recycling your glass bottles: first, wanting to engage in a form of behaviour that is seen to be worthwhile, perhaps to feel virtuous or to avoid feeling guilty or excluded (behavioural intention); and secondly, believing that you can participate, having the time and facilities to take your bottles to the bottle bank (perceived behavioural control). See the diagram on page 120.

The theory of planned behaviour is useful because it enables us to explain inconsistencies in people's behaviour; for example, instances in which someone behaves in an environmentally friendly way in one domain of their lives but not another (Kaiser *et al.*, 1999). Pro-environmental behaviour is affected by the factors predicted by the theory of planned behaviour. For example, a range of influences have been identified that

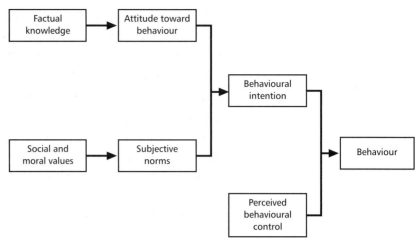

Based on: Ajzen (1985)
The theory of planned behaviour (Ajzen, 1985)

are beyond the individual's own control. Water conservation is affected by the cost of water (Moore *et al.*, 1994), recycling is affected by storage space (Williams, 1991) and energy consumption is affected by the characteristics of the home (Verhallen and Van Raaji, 1981) and by the external temperature (Olsen, 1981). Thus the theory of planned behaviour can account for both individual influences on environmentally friendly behaviour, such as attitude or intention, and local influences, such as the availability of information, some physical factors and sociocultural constraints.

The ability to predict environmentally friendly behaviour is clearly useful in planning provision; for instance, in the demand for recycling facilities and to estimate probable uptake for companies attempting to reuse recycled resources. The theory of planned behaviour can be useful here. Bamberg *et al.* (1995) had some success in predicting whether people would choose to drive or take the bus. Taylor and Todd (1995) have also used this model as a basis for modelling people's waste management behaviour. They found that both the intention to recycle household rubbish and to compost biodegradable waste were influenced by attitude and perceived behavioural control.

As environmental problems are worldwide, the resolution of these problems must be tackled at a global level. There has been surprisingly little research into cross-cultural issues, such as differences in environmental values, attitudes and behaviour. Schultz and Zelezny (1999) explored cultural differences (see p.116) and found that the NEP scores were lower for US respondents than for those in most other countries (except the Dominican Republic, Ecuador and Peru). This contradicts the view that environmental concern only emerges in developed countries. Their cross-cultural evidence suggests that the belief that pro-environmental behaviour is made possible only because wealth enables the satisfaction of basic needs such as food and shelter, thus allowing for the luxury of caring for the environment, is unfounded. In fact, Schultz and Zeleny's findings show that environmental issues are central to the culture of developing countries in Latin America, where the 'humans in nature' view prevails over the 'humans as protectors and consumers of nature' view that typifies Western attitudes.

Some patterns found by Schultz and Zelezny (1999), such as positive correlations between 'self-transcendent values' (such as social justice, responsibility and world beauty) and both NEP and ecocentrism (a belief in the inherent value of the natural environment), were consistent across all countries surveyed. We can conclude from this that one global influence on environmentally friendly behaviour is the set of values determined by sociocultural influences, but that these cannot be readily predicted.

for and against

the theory of planned behaviour

+ It takes individual variables into account, because people vary in terms of both intention and perceived control.

+ It includes the role of constraints on behaviour that are outside the individual's control.

− It does not account for how these non-volitional factors affect behaviour.

− It does not include specific effects of altruistic values.

Recycling

Pro-environmental attitudes and values are important because they affect our pro-environmental behaviour. A key example of such behaviour is the reuse of materials. Recycling has two clear environmental benefits; it reduces waste and conserves resources. We will look at this example of environmentally friendly behaviour in detail. What stops people from recycling their rubbish? Inconvenience and the demands on time are frequently cited as reasons for failing to recycle (Vining and Ebreo, 1990; Gamba and Oskamp, 1994; McCarty and Shrum, 1994). As a consequence, when recycling activities are voluntary, they tend to be low priority and the behaviour reduces with time (Grogen and Bell, 1989; Werner *et al.*, 1995). However, even mandatory requirements to recycle are not necessarily sufficient to motivate people to prepare and sort their recyclables. Unless people participate fully in recycling schemes, the output is lower in quantity and quality and so is less viable in the marketplace.

In an attempt to understand and predict people's behaviour in such situations, Sansone *et al.* (1992) proposed a model that incorporated the

What are the factors that affect your decision to recycle or not recycle waste?

factors that affect a decision to engage and persist with a task that is neither inherently rewarding nor pleasurable. They suggested that people need to redefine the task such that they transform their experience into a positive one. In the case of recycling, this may be done by:

- *changing the focus of the task*, from how time-consuming it is to how quickly recyclable material is amassed

- *adding variety to the task*, by listening to music or the radio while sorting

- *changing their definition of the task*, from an emphasis on rubbish to a means of working with a reusable resource.

research
now

recycling redefined

Werner, C.M. and Makela, E. (1998) Motivations and behaviors that support recycling. *Journal of Environmental Psychology*, 18, 373–86

Aim: To investigate factors affecting the motivation to recycle household waste as a test of Sansone *et al.*'s (1992) model of how people engage themselves in a boring but necessary task.

Method: On two occasions, 27 months apart, participants filled in questionnaires asking about their attitudes to and satisfactions associated with recycling, and how they organised their homes to accommodate domestic recycling. They were also asked to give a self-report of their recycling behaviour.

Results: The researchers found that individuals who had strong reasons to persist with recycling (such as holding pro-recycling attitudes or having a social orientation towards recycling) tended to redefine recycling activities. They shifted their focus away from the time-consuming nature of recycling and emphasised the pleasurable aspects of the various kinds of behaviour, or the sense of satisfaction they gained from contributing to the environment. These people were also more likely to have made the task manageable, so as to ensure that recycling activities did not interfere with other aspects of their lives. Finally, they were more likely to engage in both short- and long-term recycling.

Conclusion: These findings support the Sansone *et al.* (1992) model, confirming that people who make a boring but valued task more manageable and interesting are more likely to continue with the behaviour.

The combined findings of Sansone *et al.* (1992) and Werner and Makela (1998) thus help us to identify some factors that *stop* people from recycling. These might include being unable or unwilling to focus on the positive aspects of the task (such as fear of the noise of breaking glass at the bottle bank) or being unable to make the task manageable (such as in districts where insufficient recycling facilities exist).

interactive
angles

Consider the task of recycling paper. What are the problems associated with this activity that might prevent people from engaging in the task? How could a household reduce the inconveniences associated with recycling these materials? In what ways could the task be made more interesting or pleasant? What information might enable people to redefine the task to feel more positive towards the activity?

After considering the answers to these questions, design a leaflet that could be used to encourage recycling of paper in your local area.

research
now

sorted – student rubbish

Matthies, E. and Krömker, D. (2000) Participatory planning – a heuristic for adjusting interventions to the context. *Journal of Environmental Psychology*, 20, 1–10

Aims: To investigate ways to improve the sorting of rubbish for recycling by university students.

Method: Sorting of rubbish for recycling was measured at the start of the experiment in two student residences. Participants in one residence were contacted and helped to set up an action group. This group implemented measures designed to encourage better sorting of rubbish, such as information about the sorting system, providing signs and having larger containers. They also sent all students a bogus letter threatening that their residency costs would rise unless sorting improved. Participants in the second (control) area received no additional assistance with recycling. A final measure of recycling was taken in both locations.

Results: By the end of the study the amount of unsorted rubbish had fallen from 69 per cent to 53 per cent in the experimental residence, but had risen from 64 per cent to 74 per cent in the control area.

Conclusion: The involvement of students in the intervention group improved their participation in the recycling of rubbish.

Encouraging environmentally friendly behaviour

Changing attitudes towards the environment: the Yale model of persuasive communication

Hovland and his colleagues at Yale University conducted many studies that led to the development of a theory of persuasive communication, sometimes called the 'Yale model'. Whilst this laid the foundation for modern theories of attitude change, much has changed in this field since the 1950s.

Stages in persuasion

In order for a communication to be persuasive, it must first be noticed; thus *attention* is the first stage of the model. You are unlikely to be affected by a sign asking you to return your plastic cup-holder for reuse unless it is prominent. Andreoli and Worchel (1978) demonstrated the advantage of television commercials over those in print or on the radio. By using both sound and vision, the television is more likely to attract our attention. However, having attended to the message alone does not guarantee attitude change; the recipient must also be able to understand the message. *Comprehension* is required for the persuasive attempt to be successful. For example, a company may want its workers to adhere to a complex policy of sorting office waste, but if this is not clearly explained they are unlikely to follow the required procedure. Jaccoby *et al.* (1980) found that 30–40 per cent of adults who saw a 30 second television clip misunderstood the information presented. Whilst both attention and comprehension are necessary, they are not sufficient. Finally, the message must be *accepted*. Acceptance does not necessarily demand belief, but it does require that the receiver acts on his or her understanding. Thus, if you see a notice that says *Turn taps off fully after use – or we will face another water shortage*, you may not believe that the consequences of your actions will be that significant, but because you understand the sentiment of the message that you have seen, you change your behaviour accordingly and turn off the taps.

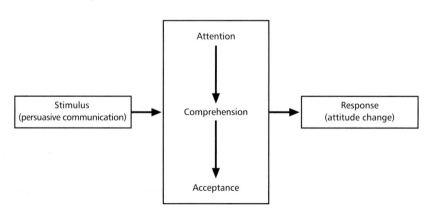

The Yale model of persuasive communication

This notion of a staged sequence in the processing of persuasive information is now referred to as *systematic processing* (McGuire, 1969), in contrast to heuristic processing (see p.00). This is believed to use a *central route to persuasion* (Petty and Cacioppo, 1986), because it requires the receiver to engage in thinking about the message, as opposed to the peripheral route to persuasion (p.00), in which the recipient is relatively passive. To account for some of the observed effects of persuasive communication, the model has been adapted to incorporate more stages. McGuire (1968) separated 'acceptance' into two stages – *yielding* and *retention* – and introduced a final stage, *action*. This version differentiates between being persuaded by the message (yielding) and retaining that changed belief (retention). You may see a poster that asks you to squash your cans for recycling so that animals can't hurt themselves on the open edges, and although you understand and accept the message you may forget why it was important after a while. Thus, initially your behaviour changes – that is, there is action – but this may revert to inaction when retention fails.

Factors affecting persuasion

In addition to describing the process of behaviour change, the Yale model also indicates the factors that can influence the acceptance of attempted persuasive communication (Janis and Hovland, 1959). These factors are as follows:

- the *communicator* of the message – the role, affiliations and intentions of the source

- the *content* of the message – the topics, appeals, arguments and stylistic features

- the *media characteristics* of the message – whether interaction is direct or indirect and the sensory modality used

- the *situational surroundings* – such as the social setting and extraneous pleasant or unpleasant stimuli

- the *characteristics* of the recipient – such as persuasibility and self-confidence (Janis and Field, 1959).

Communicator factors

Hovland and Weiss (1951) investigated the importance of the source of the message. They found that American participants were more likely to be persuaded by a message from the American physicist Robert Oppenheimer than the Soviet newspaper *Pravda*. They concluded that the credibility of the source was a key factor affecting attitude change. Expertise also affects the likelihood of attitude change. Petty and Cacioppo (1981) showed that advice about the hours of sleep that people needed was more effective when given by a Nobel Prize-winning physiologist than by a YMCA director. Other characteristics of the source that increase the believability of the message include:

- a communicator who is arguing *against* his or her own best interests – the manager of a waste incinerator who says that the emissions are dangerous is more likely to be believed than an environmental protestor who says the same thing

- *attractiveness* of the communicator – Chaiken (1979) asked students to persuade others to sign a petition, and physically attractive individuals were more effective

- the perceived *similarity* of the communicator to the recipient – this is particularly so if the similarity is deemed to be relevant to the issue

- the *likeability* of the source – we are more readily persuaded by an individual who we find pleasant than by one we do not.

One reason why such superficial characteristics, which are unrelated to the content of the message, may be effective in attitude change is that people engage in *heuristic processing* (Chaiken, 1987); that is, they reach a decision based on simple cues, without considering the available information in any depth. Petty and Cacioppo (1986) describe this as the *peripheral route to persuasion*.

Content factors

Many characteristics of the message are also important, including:

- The *emotional content* – Is it fear-arousing?

- The *medium* – Verbal or visual?

- The *argument* – Is it presented as one-sided or a two-sided debate?

Fear-arousing arguments may be effective, although a range of factors affect the likelihood that recipients will adhere to the message. Rogers (1975) suggested that these were the unpleasantness of the fear-arousing suggestion, the probability of the event occurring if the recommendation is not followed, and the perceived effectiveness of the recommended action. Persuasive communication should therefore be most powerful if the recipient finds the suggestion relatively unpleasant, really believes it will happen and expects that the evasive action will be effective. However, it is not always the case that high levels of fear-arousal are the most effective. Janis and Feshbach (1953) found the reverse, with low levels of fear-arousal producing the most behaviour change. Thus, for environmental issues such as global warming, warnings about climate change that suggest wetter weather may be more effective than threats about rising sea levels causing mass flooding.

Some additional factors have been shown to affect attitude change. Howard (1997) found that *familiarity* had a powerful influence. Students were more likely to be persuaded by an argument couched in familiar terms, such as *Don't put all your eggs in one basket* or *Don't bury your head in the sand*, than by exposure to phrases such as *Don't pretend a problem doesn't exist*.

Media factors

We both hear and see messages geared towards encouraging our environmentally responsible behaviour. Which medium is most effective, or does the efficacy of the communication depend on the message being conveyed? The answer seems to depend on the stage at which the recipient is likely to resist the message. If difficulties are likely to arise at the comprehension stage – for instance, if you are conveying a complex message – then written communications appear to be most effective. However, where problems arise with yielding to the message, more direct media, such as face-to-face communication, are more effective (Chaiken and Eagly, 1976). So, an explanation of the impact of diesel versus unleaded fuel on the greenhouse effect would be better presented on paper, since it is a complex issue. In contrast, persuading schoolchildren to walk to separate rubbish bins with different kinds of waste (paper, cans and plastic) would be more successfully tackled face to face, as the problem is not one of difficulty with comprehension but of encouraging participation.

Situational factors

Presenting a communication as either a one- or two-sided argument can be advantageous in different situations. Where your views are likely to go unopposed, a one-sided argument is likely to achieve opinion change more quickly, if only temporarily. However, in most situations where environmental issues are at stake, one view is likely to be countered by another: the environmentalists by the industrialists, the non-smokers by the smokers, and so on. In these instances, persuasive communication is more likely to be effective if both sides of the argument are acknowledged. In these instances, primacy and recency effects come into play. If the time lag between the presentation of the two sides of the issue is small, the first message should be more effective (due to the *primacy effect*). If, however, the interval is long, the later message will be better remembered, due to the *recency effect*, so is likely to result in greater attitude change (Petty and Cacioppo, 1981). Therefore, in a heated debate in a local hall about the merits of a bypass through a local site of special scientific interest, the first speaker is advantaged, because the presentations are likely to follow one another in quick succession. However, if cases are to be presented in a local magazine in successive monthly editions, running up to a referendum on an issue, there is a distinct advantage to being the last to appear.

inter**active**
angles

You are campaigning at your college for the provision of aluminium can recycling bins, but this is being opposed by the Estates Department. If you and the Estates Department can each design screensavers that will appear on every college computer monitor for a week, would your message be more persuasive if it appeared during the first week or during the second? If you and the Estates Manager are allocated an afternoon to give presentations to the students, would you rather speak first or last?

If your message were complex, would you opt for the verbal presentation or a written message on the computer?

One key issue in the context of a persuasive communication is the nature of the distractions with which it has to compete. It seems obvious that a message will be less effective if it is in competition with other stimuli for the recipient's attention, but this is not always the case. This is because distractions prevent us from rehearsing our argument. Whilst a viewpoint with which we agree may be disadvantaged by interruptions (as we are less able to focus on the additional supporting arguments), a contrary viewpoint may benefit from distractions. If we are attending to a message that conflicts with our own views but we are distracted, we will be unable to generate our own arguments against it, and thus it will seem more persuasive.

media
watch

Recycled products and packaging

In just one hour we produce enough rubbish to fill Trafalgar Square to the height of Nelson's Column, according to statistics from the Department for Environment, Food and Rural Affairs (DEFRA).

Each tonne of paper recycled equates to around 17 trees saved, not to mention the surrounding habitat and wildlife, claim the organisation Waste Watch.

Launched in January 2002, the Christmas Card Recycling Scheme is run by the Woodland Trust in partnership with WH Smith and Tesco. People have been supporting the scheme by taking advantage of special recycling bins whilst shopping in local stores.

Tesco is just one of the supermarkets working towards recycling as much of their product packaging as possible. The store has its own recycling units, recovering virtually all paper, board and plastic that might otherwise be consigned to landfill sites or incinerated. Each year the units save over 155,000 tonnes of card – the equivalent of nearly 3 million trees.

Source:http//:www.nfucountryside.org.uk

Study this extract from the NFU countryside website. What strategies for persuasive communication have been utilised? Try to obtain some promotional literature from the sources mentioned and identify the strategies used in their production.

Personal characteristics

There is little evidence that gender or self-esteem affect the tendency for an individual to be affected by persuasive communication (Bauer, 1970; Eagly and Carli, 1981), although some results are contradictory (for example, Janis and Field, 1959). These differences might be explained using McGuire's (1968) concept of substages to the process of acceptance; people with different personalities may differ in their responses to elements of the acceptance process. For example, people with better memories, or for whom the issue is more pertinent, may find retention of information easier. Another personal characteristic, self-monitoring, may affect the likelihood that a person will be persuaded. Lavine and Snyder (1996) found that high self-monitors (people who are more sensitive to the demands of a situation and adapt accordingly) were more likely to be influenced by an imaged-focused approach that concentrated on the communicator's status, popularity and attractiveness. In contrast, messages that expressed values were more effective with low self-monitors. Therefore, high self-monitors would be more likely to be persuaded to participate in an environmentally friendly scheme if it was endorsed by a celebrity. In contrast, low self-monitors would be more likely to be influenced by messages in which the communicator described his or her personal beliefs and reasons for being environmentally friendly.

for and
against

the Yale model of persuasive communication

+ There is some evidence that the process of attitude change is affected by a range of factors.

+ Attention and comprehension appear to be important factors in the effectiveness of persuasive communications.

− There may be more factors involved in the process of attitude change than envisaged by the Yale model.

− There is evidence for attitude change arising from heuristic, non-sequential processes.

interactive
angles

Global Warming
What's the problem?

The weather, like the times, is a-changing. In the next 100 years temperatures will rise 2 to 3 degrees and seas will rise by 1 metre, according to the Hadley Centre, The Met Office's climate research organisation. And if you think this won't affect you, Anthony Astbury at the Met Office predicts that traffic will grind to a halt and trains will be even more disrupted by global warming in the form of heavy rains, flash floods and land-slides. Over the past 3 years more than 20 major extreme weather events (hurricanes etc.) have cost 100,000 people their lives.

Concentrations of carbon dioxide, the main contributor to global warming, have risen from an estimated 270 parts per million in 1870 to 360 in 1990. Reasons range from deforestation (since trees absorb CO_2 and turn it into oxygen this is bad news) to the burning of fossil fuels, which release CO_2.

Carbon dioxide is a greenhouse gas: it helps to trap solar heat on earth which alters the weather and causes temperatures to rise. And it's not the only culprit: methane, water vapour, nitrous oxide from vehicle exhausts and agricultural fertilisers are also to blame.

What's the solution?

The United Nation Environment Programme's Kyoto Protocol has committed 84 coun-tries to reducing emissions of greenhouse gases by at least 5 per cent. But some sci-entists claim this isn't enough. Catherine Senior of the Hadley Centre says: 'It will not really change global warming. It won't respond instantly to things we do today. It's been building up since the industrial revolution.'

A spokesperson for the World Health Organisation sums up the mixture of fear and ignorance about this issue. 'No one really knows what climate change means. It could be a fairly benign process of global adaptation, or it could mean a kind of nuclear win-ter. We've just got to hope for the best.'

What can you do?

Future Forests, an organisation that promotes awareness about carbon management, points out that you can adopt some basic domestic practices: regularly defrost your fridge – frost build-up increases the amount of energy needed to keep the motor running – and boil water with a lid on. And instead of giving up the central heating, dishwasher and stereo, 'neutralise' them. This means paying Future Forests for a tree to be planted at one of 55 sites across the UK to offset whatever carbon dioxide you generate. For example, an average British car covering 20,000 km a year emits one tonne of carbon, so five trees would cover it. Use the calculator at **http://www.futureforests.com** to work out your personal contribution to the global greenhouse (they'll make you include everything from your lawnmower to your juicer). You can make sure you buy paper and wood products from managed woodlands.

These have the Forest Stewardship Council (FSC) label and you don't have to trek to some wierdy-beardy outpost to find them – Sainsbury's, Boots, Tesco, B&Q and WH Smith stock them. For the truly green, there's the carbon-neutral mortgage. Launched by Norwich and Peterborough Building Society in conjunction with Future Forests, the mortgage will offset your entire household carbon uptake for 5 years.

But will this do any good? Catherine Senior says: 'Reforestation is one way of ameliorating the problem, but it would be incredibly difficult to achieve *everything* through this.' So plant those trees and buy those managed products by all means but, overall, be energy efficient.

Source: *Eve*, Ocober 2000

This example of a piece of persuasive literature uses some of the strategies discussed above. Decide how this article could be changed to make it more effective in changing people's attitudes and behaviour.

Changing behaviour towards the environment

We have considered the factors that affect people's attitudes towards the environment and control the likelihood of them acting in environmentally friendly ways. So, how could we encourage more people to engage in appropriate *behaviours* or to do so more often? We could:

- *educate people so that they want to behave differently* (change attitudes to increase intrinsic rewards)

- *make appropriate kinds of behaviour easier* (alter people's surroundings)

- *offer rewards* (employ extrinsic reinforcement)

- *penalise failure* (use punishment).

Behavioural control may be *antecedent*, measures in which the intervention occurs before the behaviour arises, or *consequent*, measures in which the intervention follows the behaviour to be changed. Antecedent procedures may include education, attitude change (discussed in detail on pp.124–9) and inducing or preventing certain kinds of behaviour by controlling the triggers that cause them to occur. Consequent procedures can affect some forms of behaviour by using pleasant or unpleasant consequences to make their performance more or less likely, or through the use of feedback.

Antecedent control

- Notices reminding people to switch off lights on exit from a room

- The availability of a fast lane for car-pool users

- Provision of special bags or boxes for recyclables to be collected alongside domestic rubbish

Consequence control

Positive reinforcement (receiving a pleasant consequence)

- Sainsbury's penny back for a carrier bag

- Schools earning money through aluminium can recycling

Negative reinforcement (avoiding an unpleasant consequence)

- Reduced road tax for low-emissions cars

- No tariff for cars with two or more people in

Punishment

- Turning daytime heating off in halls of residence where electricity use exceeds a threshold

- Fines for littering

Antecedent control strategies

The antecedent control strategy of education suggests that the more informed people are on ecological matters, the more likely their behaviour is to be environmentally sound. Newhouse (1990) found that people who were better informed were more likely to have environmentally friendly views. Adopting a particular perspective does not necessarily result in a difference in behaviour, although there is some evidence that pro-environmental views do correspond to responsible behaviour. Kearney and De Young (1995) demonstrated the success of a knowledge-based intervention, as people who were better informed about car-pooling were more willing to participate in such schemes. Margai (1997) found that information increased recycling by over 30 per cent. Over a 1-year period, an educational programme used in East Harlem (a low-income urban area of New York) increased the daily volume of recycled material from 8.7 to 11.4 tons.

However, not all education-based interventions have been successful. Heberlein (1975) found no impact on energy consumption when people were given a booklet on electricity-saving tips, or a letter informing them about the personal and social costs of failing to conserve energy. This is in stark contrast to the more recent evidence from Brandon and Lewis

(1999) (see p.119). Why might these differences arise? Perhaps it is because the information provided by Brandon and Lewis was more directly relevant than that given in the earlier study. These issues are considered in more detail under 'Attitude change' on pages 124–9. Certainly, it would appear that education alone is insufficient as a strategy. Pardini and Katzev (1983–4) found that making a spoken or written statement of commitment to newspaper recycling resulted in a greater (and in the case of the written statement more sustained) increase in recycling than information alone.

classic
research

copying conservation

Cook, S.W. and Berrenberg, J.L. (1981) Approaches to encouraging conservation behaviour: a review and conceptual framework. *Journal of Social Issues*, 37, 73–107

Aim: To review the literature to search for factors affecting the tendency to engage in conservation programmes and to suggest ways to increase participation.

Method: A literature review was conducted to assess the importance of the social embeddedness of behaviour; that is, the extent to which forms of behaviour are inherently expected by a particular social group. This included social norms (moral standards of the group), conformity (following other members of the group to avoid exclusion) and modelling (learning new forms of behaviour by observing other group members).

Results: Many of the studies reviewed suggested that public scrutiny and recognition of efforts increased the effectiveness of programmes aimed at improving energy conservation.

Conclusion: As people have a tendency to respond to group pressure and recognition, these techniques can be used to increase the success of conservation programmes.

Other antecedent strategies that have proved successful include the use of triggers or prompts to remind people of appropriate behaviours and modelling. Triggers such as signs encouraging us to save energy by turning off lights and to avoid litter are antecedent controls and can be effective. Such triggers are more effective when they are polite, when they are proximate to the site of the behaviour and when they indicate the appropriate response. Thus an anti-littering slogan will be most effective when it appears on a potential item of litter (such as a sweet wrapper), and when the instruction directs behaviour such as 'place this in a bin' rather than 'keep Britain clean'.

Help the Earth

Reduce environmental pollution
(CO_2, acid rain, air pollution)

Preserve the planet's finite fossil fuels

Did you Know?
A TV on standby uses 24% of the energy when fully on.

Did you Know?
The UK wastes £11 billion of energy each year. The cost of running the UK's Universities, Colleges and Schools is £13 billion per year.

Did you Know?
Leicester University spends £1,533,000 on energy each year and a further £536,000 on water.

Seven Ways to Save the Earth

1. Switch off unwanted lights – remember to switch them off when you leave your room.

2. Use natural light where possible.

3. Switch off PCs, VDUs, TVs, Hi-Fi's and any other electrical equipment when you leave your room. (Why risk a fire?)

4. Shut doors and windows if heating is on.

5. Avoid blocking radiators with furniture.

6. Report dripping taps/flickering lights.

7. Don't overfill kettles.

Further information: http://www.le.ac.uk/earthcare/

An antecedent strategy: a polite, proximate trigger for conserving energy displayed in the University of Leicester's halls of residence

Proximity also matters in the location and attractiveness of waste receptacles. Finnie (1973) found that coloured dustbins resulted in a 14.9 per cent decrease in littering, against only a 3.15 per cent reduction with ordinary bins. As described on page 117, when recycling containers are nearby they tend to get more use; the same applies to littering. Finnie found that having a dustbin in sight could decrease littering by up to 30 per cent, which suggests that people will behave in environmentally friendly ways when the personal costs are low enough.

Consequent control strategies

Wolf and Feldman (1991) reported a very significant increase in recycling following the introduction of a 5 cent returnable deposit. Several US states introduced this deposit for soft drink and beer bottles in 1983. In New York alone, recycling rates rose from 1 per cent for plastics, 5 per cent for cans and 3 per cent for glass to 33 per cent for plastics, 59 per cent for cans and 77 per cent for glass over the first year after implementation. Thus a small potential positive outcome had a considerable effect on recycling behaviour. Other consequent strategies that have been shown to be effective are praise, such as litter bins that say 'thank you' (Bell *et al.*, 2001), and feedback (Brandon and Lewis, 1999).

One problem with behavioural control, particularly legislation and fines, is the risk that, whilst performance may be altered, attitudes may remain unchanged. Thus the effect only persists while the antecedent or consequence control measures are in place. For example, some councils, such as Eastbourne Borough Council and New Forest District Council, provide facilities for mixed recyclables to be collected alongside domestic rubbish.

If this provision were withdrawn, most people would be unlikely to continue to recycle so much of their waste. Such returns to baseline recycling levels following the withdrawal of reinforcement programmes have been recorded by De Young (1986) and Jacobs and Bailey (1982). A kerbside system does, however, have the advantage of not requiring the consumer to engage in much sorting of waste, a factor that increases participation in recycling. Oskamp *et al.* (1996) found that in a kerbside recycling scheme, 'mixed-recyclables' containers resulted in a 90 per cent participation rate amongst community residents, whereas a requirement to separate recyclables led to only 77 per cent participation.

interactive
angles

The following are examples of antecedent or consequence control (the latter using either negative or positive reinforcement or punishment). Decide which of the strategies for intervention use which mechanisms for controlling behaviour:

- giving a penny back for the return of carrier bags to a supermarket

- offering grants for loft insulation

- having bottle banks in every car park

- charging a toll for cars carrying only one person

- imposing fines for dropping litter

- reducing water rates for users who meet limited consumption targets

- placing drinks can bins all around the edge of a school playground

- having cheaper road tax for cars with lower emissions.

Ophuls (1977) has described four alternative types of strategy for putting these theoretical approaches into action, to affect the behaviour of people towards the environment:

- laws and incentives to encourage prosocial behaviour

- moral, religious or ethical appeals

- educational and informational programmes designed to produced attitude change

- encouraging prosocial behaviour through social groups and communities.

Each of these routes to encouraging pro-environmental behaviour can be put into practice, as indicated below:

Strategy for increasing prosocial behaviour (Ophuls, 1977)	Example
Laws and incentives	Variable vehicle excise duty (road tax) according to emissions
Moral, religious or ethical appeals	Friends of the Earth have employed advertising campaigns that appeal to our moral sense (see below)
Education	Many shops inform customers about recycling through leaflets and details on packaging
Encouragement through social groups sound behaviour	Organisations such as the Guides and Scouts award badges for ecologically

media watch

wasted times

Most of the things that we throw away could be a valuable resource for someone, somewhere. That's why when we call something "waste" we are making a mistake. The problem is that we are a nation addicted to chucking stuff out. The average person in the UK throws out their own body weight in rubbish every three months.

It's not just stale food and kitchen scraps that end up in the rubbish. It's also discarded coke cans, newspapers, out-of-date clothes, broken electrical goods and old toys.

This is piling up problems for our environment and future generations worldwide. Stuff that is no longer wanted ends up in landfill or being burnt in incinerators. Both methods damage the environment.

Our endless appetite for new things is adding to these problems. When we chop down forests or dig up minerals we use huge amounts of energy. Almost all manufacturing industries also rely on using energy from fossil fuels, rather than a clean energy like solar power. But burning coal, oil and gas is causing the world's climate to change. Levels of carbon dioxide are rising at a speed that threatens catastrophic change in the future.

That's why Friends of the Earth has slammed Government plans to burn up to 10 million tonnes of household waste – in 130 new incinerators to be built by 2015 – rather than concentrate on recycling, which can save energy.

We don't have to waste our waste. This booklet highlights the ways which people have found work well at reducing the amount of waste they produce. This isn't just good for the environment; it can also be very good for people because it can improve their quality of life, save money and generate jobs.

Ophuls (1977) suggested that one factor that could affect ecologically sound behaviour was to appeal to people's moral beliefs. This is one way in which campaigns such as those employed by Friends of the Earth may be effective.

interactive
angles

Every student room at the University of Michigan is provided with an individual blue plastic recycling box and it is the duty of the students to take their rubbish and recyclables to the appropriate collection point in or adjacent to the building. The students recycle all of the following materials: cardboard, paper, cans, glass and plastic bottles. Students are provided with both clear instructions about how to recycle and information about what happens to these materials after they are collected.

Guidelines for hall residence staff

Making the recycling programme a success:

1. *Actions speak louder than words*. Resident advisors are encouraged to serve as role models for their students; for instance, by recycling pizza boxes after end-of-session events, posting signs in the buildings and keeping the residents informed about the amount their hall recycles each month.

2. *Keeping them informed*. Offer educational programmes to students so that they can learn about the recycling process and raise their awareness about their own impact on the environment. This could also provide an opportunity for a sponsored 'fun' activity.

3. *Make your own paper*. Give students the chance to recycle their own paper, making hand-made cards from waste paper. The university can supply instructions and materials – you just need some waste paper!

4. *Promote events in a waste-free way*. Act as a role model and avoid wasting paper by putting a flyer under everyone's door. Instead, use bulletin boards or make invitations out of scrap card or soup tins!

5. *Conduct a tour of your hall of residence*. Show students where to put their recyclable waste and where it is taken to once it has been collected. Look inside recycling containers to ensure that materials have been appropriately segregated and check in waste bins for materials that should have been recycled. Discuss ideas with your students for new ways to increase participation in recycling.

6. *Sponsor a 'Recycle Night'*. Presenting this early in the term will avoid confusion. Encourage students to contribute to a discussion about the different recycling programmes in their home towns and whether they think recycling should be mandatory. Consider asking experts from the local community to speak.

Adapted from 'Residence Hall Recycling':
http://www.recycle.umich.edu/grounds/recycle/residence_hall_recycling.html

Can you explain the reasoning behind each of these strategies?

where to now?

The following are good sources of information about environmentally responsible behaviour:

▶ **Palmer, C. (1997) Contemporary Ethics Issues:** *Environmental Ethics.* **Santa Barbara, CA: ABC-Clio** – this provides a thorough coverage of global environmental issues and includes many excellent reference sections for resources and organisations.

▶ **Smith, E.R. and Mackie, D.M. (2000)** *Social Psychology.* **Hove: Psychology Press** – this has an excellent up-to-date chapter on attitudes and attitude change.

Conclusions

Attitude is a key issue in encouraging environmentally friendly behaviour. However, commitment, feedback, the effort required and the perceived importance of issues also play a part in determining whether people will engage in environmentally friendly behaviour. The theory of planned behaviour can help us to predict people's behaviour with regard to their environment. We can approach the need to change people's behaviour towards the environment either indirectly, by changing their attitudes, or directly, by changing their behaviour. There are several stages to attitude change, and the models of persuasive communication suggest that people must attend to and understand a message before they can accept it. In order for any change in attitude to be expressed as a change in behaviour, the recipient must both yield to and retain the information. Furthermore, in any communication a range of factors, including the characteristics of the communicator and the message, the context, media factors and situational factors, will influence its effectiveness. Behaviour change can be achieved through antecedent or consequent intervention strategies.

1   Describe and evaluate the theory of planned behaviour as applied to recycling or other environmentally responsible actions.

2   What factors should be taken into account when preparing a piece of promotional literature that aims to encourage people to recycle their waste?

3   Describe the Yale model of persuasive communication. Evaluate the extent to which this is helpful in understanding how to motivate people into engaging in environmentally friendly behaviour.

4   How effective are rewards and punishments in encouraging environmentally friendly forms of behaviour? Use research evidence to justify your answer.

5

> At Penn State University, USA, members of Eco-Action began a plan of action in conjunction with the university's officers to increase the amount of waste recycled by fellow students. The students are supposed to put plastic, newspaper and aluminium in special bins, separating these recyclables from other rubbish. They have placed more bins in some areas than others in an attempt to determine whether greater bin availability affects the incidence of recycling. If so, the university will provide more bins at all locations.
>
> Zeiber (1999)

Are the measures described above likely to be effective? Use evidence to justify your answer. What other policies could be implemented to increase the incidence of recycling?

6

Climate and Weather

what's ahead?

In this chapter we will examine the role that weather and climate – focusing on temperature and air pressure – have on our performance of tasks, our social behaviour and our health. The concept of *climatological determinism* (that climate 'forcefully' changes our behaviour and health) will be introduced, with many examples ranging from Seasonal Affective Disorder to Sudden Infant Death Syndrome.

Definitions, types and climatological determinism

What is the difference between 'climate' and 'weather'? Bell *et al.* (1996) stated that *weather* refers to the temporary conditions under which we live. These are usually rapidly changing (although in some countries, the change is not too rapid); for example, a belt of rain or a frosty morning. *Climate* refers to the 'average' weather conditions that a particular region or country has over a long period of time. So, for example, southern Spain may be currently experiencing rain today (the weather), even though it is usually warm and dry (the climate). As will become clear as this chapter progresses, it is important to understand the difference between the two, as each has a different effect on behaviour.

The extent to which the climate might affect us is still subject to debate. *Climatological determinism* refers to the belief that the climate we are used to actually changes the kinds of behaviour that we exhibit. However, not all environmental psychologists believe that this is the case. Some believe in *climatological possibilism*, whereby the climate that we are used to sets

140

up various physical limits within which our behaviour varies and changes. There is also some belief in *climatological probabilism*, which is the position in between determinism and possibilism. It is the view that the climate does not forcibly change behaviour, but that it influences the chance that some types of behaviour will occur. This chapter will focus on climatological determinism.

The effects of climate and weather on task performance and social behaviour

For some years, the weather has been linked to crime (see, for example, Rotton and Frey, 1985). Recent research has continued to unearth particular trends.

research now

does cold equal crime?

Cohn, E.G. and Rotton, J. (2000) Weather, seasonal trends and property crimes in Minneapolis, 1987–1988. A moderator-variable time-series analysis of routine activities. *Journal of Environmental Psychology*, 20, 257–72

Aim: To examine the possible link between the weather and property crime (in particular, burglary, robbery and theft) in Minneapolis, USA, between 1987 and 1988.

Method: Weather records and data from police records about crimes were analysed.

Results: The following graphs show the relationship between the time of year, the time of day and the number of crimes:

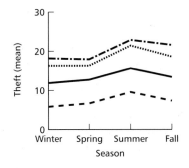
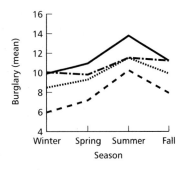

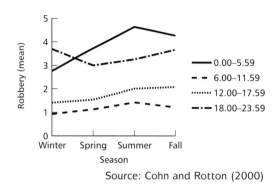

Source: Cohn and Rotton (2000)

Conclusion: As can be seen from the graphs, most crimes take place during the summer, irrespective of the time of day the crime took place. However, the results could have been due to more people being on holiday in the summer! Also, the link to temperature could be dubious, as there are many changes in weather with the seasons.

Griffit (1970) investigated the effect of temperature on a variety of measures. Participants were randomly assigned to one of two conditions. The first condition saw participants sitting in a room that had a temperature of 90.6°F (Fahrenheit) – above the threshold for tolerable temperature, which is 84.6°F (29.2°C), according to Rohles (1969). The second condition saw participants sitting in a room that had a temperature of 67.5°F (the temperature most often rated as being comfortable, according to Nevins *et al.*, 1967). All participants, however, had the same task of completing a questionnaire that measured, among other things, elation, concentration, fatigue and vigour (energy). The temperature of the room had a significant effect on these four measures. The high-temperature group (90.6°F) reported significantly less elation, concentration and vigour, but significantly more fatigue. Therefore, temperature appears to affect task performance, with higher temperatures causing the most change. However, it should always be noted that we can adapt to temperature change and that perceptions of temperature are subjective, so the effects of temperature could be relative and not absolute.

Hancock (1986) reviewed research into people's attention when under 'thermal stress'. His main conclusion was that performance on a task is affected by any long-term variation in temperature. For example, Viteles and Smith (1946) asked participants to check pairs of numbers and report when the numbers were identical. There were three temperature conditions: 73°F, 80°F and 87°F. Although there was no significant difference in the number of errors committed, the rate of 'output' (number of pairs looked at) was affected by temperature, as shown on the graph opposite:

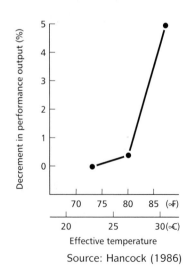

Source: Hancock (1986)

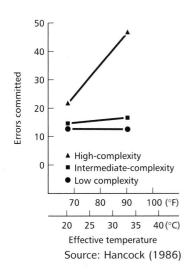

Source: Hancock (1986)

As can be seen, there was a marked detriment in performance output between 80°F and 85°F.

Carlson (1961) examined the relationship between temperature and errors committed in low-, intermediate- and high-complexity tasks. Two temperature conditions were assessed: 68°F and 91.4°F. It was hypothesised that as temperature increased so would the number of errors committed, as there would be excessive stimulation from the task *and* due to the temperature. As can be seen from the graph below, only the highly complex task was affected by temperature. The participants reported decreased vigilance in the face of such a high temperature and such a highly complex task.

As can be seen, the high-complexity task was affected by temperature, but the low- and intermediate-complexity tasks were not: in fact, in the case of the low-complexity task, a high temperature appeared to improve performance slightly!

Air pressure

Nicolas *et al.* (1999) examined the anxiety levels and personalities (among other measures) of volunteer climbers, who were placed in a 'hypobaric' chamber that changed pressure as if the climbers were ascending Mount Everest. A total of eight experienced climbers took part in the study, all of whom had actually climbed to the altitude that the chamber was simulating. They lived in a chamber that decompressed as if the climbers were reaching high altitudes (decompression refers to the process of lowering barometric pressure, which can cause certain inert gases – mainly nitrogen, which is normally dissolved in body fluids and tissue – to come out of physical solution and form bubbles if the process is too rapid). In addition, the climbers were to experience less and less oxygen in the chamber. Nicolas *et al.* wanted to see what psychological effects this would have on the climbers. The study lasted a total of 51 days. Measures of anxiety and personality were taken at certain intervals. State anxiety (a temporary emotional state that is a response to a situation that is perceived as threatening) increased with increased altitude. One measure of personality negatively correlated with state anxiety, that of the personality dimension of praxernia (conventional, sensitive) to autia (unconventional, listless) on the 16PF questionnaire (a measure of 16 elements of someone's personality). This suggested that those people who were more unconventional, even introverted, were less reactive to the environment around them and suffered less anxiety. Those who were more sensitive and extraverted were less successful at coping with the situation that they were in. There were no correlations between personality and symptoms of altitude sickness. Therefore, personality cannot predict people's likelihood of showing symptoms of altitude sickness.

Preti (1997) examined the link between seasonal change and suicidal behaviour in Italy. The research examined seasonal variances in suicides between 1974 and 1994. Some clear factors emerged as affecting suicidal behaviour. Preti discovered that there was a clear peak in suicides in spring, more so for males than females. Other factors included increased suicides with increased exposure to the sun and decreased suicides with increased rainfall. Therefore, one of the possible explanations for the effect of seasonal variation in suicidal behaviour could be the change in seasonal climate, which affects particular neurotransmitters in the brain.

Hribersek *et al.* (1987) analysed calls to a telephone counselling service in Belgium. They were interested to see if the weather had an effect on call content. For women, both health and interpersonal problems were related to the weather. That is, they made more calls about them as the weather improved. For men, calls about the intention to masturbate increased as the weather improved!

Finally, Brennen (2001) investigated whether there were seasonal cognitive rhythms in a Norwegian sample.

research
now

time goes slower in the summer

Brennen, T. (2001) Seasonal cognitive rhythms within the Arctic Circle: an individual differences approach. *Journal of Environmental Psychology*, 21, 191–9

Aim: To examine whether there were summer–winter differences on a range of cognitive tasks in a Norwegian sample.

Method: A total of 100 participants (45 female, 55 male) took part in a series of latency (speed) tasks, attention tasks and memory tasks. All participants were tested in the summer (May) and in the winter (November–December). Tasks included how quickly they could respond to a yellow circle presented on a computer screen, estimating time intervals and a simple word-learning memory task.

Results: The following are some of the differences found:

● Participants were slower in reaction time tasks by 11 ms (milliseconds) in the summer.

● Participants were only slightly worse at estimating time in the summer.

● Participants were slightly worse at recalling words in the winter.

Conclusion: There appear to be some differences in cognitive performance depending on the season. That is, winter tends to reduce memory functioning, while summer appears to reduce reaction times and estimation of time.

Effects of climate and weather on health (mental and physical)

Seasonal Affective Disorder (SAD) is a condition experienced in the short days of winter by as much as 10 per cent of the population (Ferenczi, 1997). However, there can be a summer-based SAD for those who live in countries where the seasons are the reverse of those in the UK. The symptoms of SAD include severe depression, a craving for high-carbohydrate foods and sleepiness. The prevalence of SAD among people in latitudes where winter nights are very long suggests that it may be related to day length. In the Shetlands, for instance, the shortest day lasts for just 5 hours 53 minutes between sunrise and sunset, with no guarantee of any sunshine and, on average, December promises just 15 hours of sunshine all month. In the lighter, longer days of spring and early summer, the symptoms of SAD disappear.

Seasonal Pattern Specifier

Specify if:

With Seasonal Pattern (can be applied to the pattern of Major Depressive Episodes in Bipolar 1 Disorder, Bipolar II Disorder, or Major Depressive Disorder, Recurrent)

A. There has been a regular temporal relationship between the onset of Major Depressive Episodes in Bipolar I or Bipolar II Disorder or Major Depressive Disorder, Recurrent, and a particular time of the year (e.g. regular appearance of the Major Depressive Episode in the fall or winter).

Note: Do not include cases in which there is an obvious effect of seasonal-related psychosocial stressors (e.g., regularly being unemployed every winter).

B. Full remissions (or a change from depression to mania or hypomania) also occur at a characteristic time of the year (e.g., depression disappears in the spring).

C. In the last 2 years, two Major Depressive Episodes have occurred that demonstrate the temporal seasonal relationships defined in criteria A and B, and no non-seasonal Major Depressive Episodes have occurred during that same period.

D. Seasonal Major Depressive Episodes (as described above) substantially outnumber the nonseasonal Major Depressive Episodes that may have occurred over the individual's lifetime.

Winter – the quarter of the year with least daylight hours
Summer – the quarter of the year with the most daylight hours

---

from DSM-IV-TR

There has been much interest in whether SAD is seen in parts of the world that do not experience the fluctuation of daylight that is seen in places like the Shetlands, or in Arctic regions. Srivastava and Sharma (1998) examined the rate of SAD in a tropical climate in India.

research
now

does SAD exist in the Tropics?

Srivastava, S. and Sharma, M. (1998) Seasonal Affective Disorder: report from India (latitude 26 degrees 45'N). *Journal of Affective Disorders*, 49(2), 145–50

Aim: Most research into SAD had been conducted in temperate climates, with few reports from more tropical climates such as India. Therefore, the aim was to examine the prevalence and effects of SAD in a sample of Indian people.

Method: Ninety-three patients were used in the research. They had all been diagnosed with recurrent mood disorder; that is, at least two diagnosed episodes of depression in the past. The sample was split into two groups: those with a seasonal pattern of recurrent mood disorder and those without such a pattern. Both groups were assessed for various effects of their recurrent mood disorders.

Results: A total of 18 of the 93 patients (19.4 per cent) fulfilled the criteria for having a seasonal recurrent mood disorder. Males dominated this group of patients (and also the group with non-seasonal recurrent mood disorders). For those with a seasonal recurrent mood disorder, there was a marked reduction in libido (sexual drive).

Conclusion: Seasonal Affective Disorder (the seasonal recurrent mood disorder group in this study) *is* seen at lower latitudes where there is less fluctuation in the amount of daylight experienced. This questions the role of daylight in the pattern of SAD. However, there were some limitations to the study. The sample was from a very select population and therefore does not give any information about the prevalence of SAD in India. Also, patients with a winter-based seasonal recurrent mood disorder and those with a summer-based seasonal recurrent mood disorder were used as one group.

Morrissey *et al.* (1996) were interested in whether the rates of SAD reversed in Australia compared to North America due to the reverse of seasons. They aimed to examine whether SAD is predominantly summer-based in northern Australia. A total of 176 households in the city of Townsville (latitude 19°S) were sent a survey though the post. It contained a version of the Seasonal Affective Assessment Questionnaire. Nine per cent of the respondents reported symptoms that indicated they suffered from summer-based SAD, compared to 1.7 per cent who reported symptoms related to winter-based SAD. The main influential factors associated with the summer-based SAD that were reported by the sample of participants were excessive heat and excessive humidity. Therefore, the prevalence rates of summer- and winter-based SAD were the reverse to those reported in more temperate regions such as North America and Europe.

Srisurapanont and Intaprasert (1999) examined the prevalence of SAD in a northern tropical region in Thailand to see if there was a similarity to other Northern Hemisphere studies or tropical studies, where the usual SAD prevalence is reversed as already noted above.

research now

SAD in the north Tropics?

Srisurapanont, M. and Intaprasert, S. (1999) Seasonal variations in mood and behaviour: epidemiological findings in the north Tropics. *Journal of Affective Disorders*, 54, 97–9

Aim: To examine the prevalence of Seasonal Affective Disorder in the northern Tropics. No study had been conducted in this area of the world (for example, Thailand). There had only been one previous study of SAD in tropical regions (see Morrissey *et al.* 1996 on p.146).

Method: A random sample of 520 residents of Chiang Mai Municipality (latitude 19°N) in Thailand was sent the Seasonal Pattern Assessment Questionnaire (SPAQ). This is designed to measure SAD and SAD-type symptoms. One hundred and twelve people returned the questionnaire, of which 97 had completed the whole questionnaire and were used in the analysis. Participants were classified as having winter SAD if they felt worst in November, December and/or January. Summer SAD was classified as occurring if the participant felt worst in April and/or May. Participants were also asked to note in which month they felt worst.

Results: The prevalence of summer SAD (6.19 per cent of the sample) and the prevalence of winter SAD (1.03 per cent) are the reverse of research that has examined SAD in temperate regions. Those classified as being affected by SAD showed symptoms/effects similar to those with the 'usual' winter SAD (for example, increased sleep, increased appetite and decreased mood). Those participants who noted a 'worst month' (a total of 46) showed a consistent pattern of it being April ($n = 26$), indicative of summer SAD. December and January only had one participant rate it as being the worst month. The 'felt worst' response was significantly related to temperature, but not to length of daylight or humidity.

Conclusion: There was a high prevalence of summer SAD in this sample of participants from the northern Tropics. There also appears to be a link between temperature and SAD, but not length of daylight. However, Srisurapanont and Intaprasert note some limitations. The return rate was small and the SPAQ is designed to measure winter SAD. Whether this questionnaire measures summer SAD adequately is unknown at present.

Stiles (1990) has suggested that SAD is merely the response of people to publicity. He suggests that people see psychiatrists less in summer because they are on holiday. If, however, they are asked to report problems as they arise, rather than retrospectively, a different pattern emerges. Depressed patients' ratings do not vary from month to month as would be expected with SAD, but they do exhibit a tendency for Tuesdays and Thursdays to be worse than Sundays!

After reading this, many of you may feel that you have SAD, feeling miserable and hungry through the winter and losing weight in summer. This wider experience, a mild form of winter depression called *seasonality*, is experienced by a much larger percentage of people. Ennis (1997) has identified a correlation between seasonality and premenstrual syndrome. This relationship might imply a tendency for some people to respond more strongly in terms of emotions to cyclical changes in hormone levels.

Finally, Magnusson (2000) reviewed the literature on SAD and concluded that the condition is quite common, with a peak in the winter months. The disorder appeared to be more prevalent, as a whole, in the Northern Hemisphere. A series of databases were searched and any study that had examined SAD was used in the analysis. The prevalence rates for SAD from the 20 reviewed studies ranged from 9.7 per cent down to 0 per cent. All studies except one reported that SAD peaked in the climate's winter months. The disorder was also more prevalent in northern latitudes and ethnic differences were uncovered. It was also discovered that other disorders beside mood were affected by season. These included bulimia nervosa and anxiety disorders. Magnusson concluded that there is much documentation about seasonal variations in mood with a peak in a person's climate's winter months. The most extreme form of these variations, SAD, appears to be quite a common disorder. However, it would appear that there has been little research into summer-based SAD.

interactive
angles

Re-read the studies on SAD in this chapter and make a list of common results. Is there a difference between the potential causes of winter-based SAD and summer-based SAD? You may wish to find more studies yourself!

Another area of research in which the role of the weather on health and well-being has been examined is Sudden Infant Death Syndrome (SIDS). This syndrome is characterised by the sudden and unexpected death of an apparently healthy infant. The American SIDS Institute (2001) note that even after an autopsy, an investigation of the scene of the death and an exploration of the medical history of the biological family to which the child belonged, if the death is still unexplained then it qualifies as SIDS. The Institute lists many risk factors for SIDS, including the use of tobacco, heroin or cocaine during pregnancy, not breast feeding the infant and allowing the child to sleep on his or her stomach (according to The American SIDS Institute, there is a higher level of SIDS reported in children who sleep on their stomach). They mention the temperature of the room as being a risk factor (keep it at a comfortable temperature), but they do not mention the potential role of the weather as another risk factor. Nevertheless, Schluter *et al.* (1998) discovered a strong relationship between environmental temperature and SIDS.

research now

SIDS in New Zealand

Schluter, P.J., Ford, R.P., Brown, J. and Ryan, A.P. (1998) Weather temperatures and sudden infant death syndrome: a regional study over 22 years in New Zealand. *Journal of Epidemiological Community Health*, 52(1), 27–33

Aim: To examine the potential relationship between sudden infant death syndrome (SIDS) and environmental temperature in Canterbury, New Zealand.

Method: A retrospective analysis was conducted using data about hourly temperature readings and time of death from SIDS. All cases of SIDS between 1968 and 1989 that occurred in Canterbury, New Zealand, were used in the analysis.

Results: The incidence of SIDS increased significantly after a few months of prolonged cold temperatures. After controlling for the season in which the death occurred, it was discovered that in the days on which there was little fluctuation in hourly temperature *and* on which the minimum temperature experienced was warm, the amount of SIDS increased markedly. There was no other significant relationship detected between the time of death from SIDS and temperature in the day of death or for the preceding 8 days before death. There also appeared to be an age effect. Infants aged 12 weeks or over appeared to be more susceptible to the small fluctuations in hourly temperature, compared to infants less than 12 weeks old.

Conclusion: The study confirmed that environmental temperature leading up to a death from SIDS is extremely influential. Also, the temperature on the day of death is an important factor in SIDS. As a result, incidences of SIDS were elevated after prolonged periods of cold minimum temperatures followed by either a period of warmer minimum temperatures or little fluctuation in the hourly recorded temperature on the day of the SIDS death.

Other research on SIDS has shown a potential link between pollution and the incidence of SIDS (Auliciems and Barnes, 1987). A total of 369 cases of SIDS in Melbourne, Australia, over a period of 15 years were examined. Curiously, pollution levels *decreased* over the 10-day period preceding a case of SIDS. Visibility was the only other measure that also affected SIDS. Average visibility *increased* prior to cases of SIDS in both summer and winter. The researchers hypothesised that these links could be due to either light directly affecting SIDS, increased outdoor exposure affecting SIDS or changes in parental behaviour during clear weather affecting SIDS.

Temperature can have a potentially adverse effect on people's behaviour and coordination. Gribetz *et al.* (1980) examined heat stress in aerial spray pilots in Israel, as there had been a number of crashes involving these pilots.

classic
research

flying by the seat of the hot pants!

Gribetz, B., Richter, E.D., Krasna, M. and Gordon, M. (1980) Heat stress exposure of aerial spray pilots. *Aviation, Space and Environmental Medicine,* 51(1), 56–60

Aim: To examine whether heat stress was a factor in a recent increase in fatal and non-fatal air crashes of Israeli aerial pesticide spray pilots.

Method: A total of nine pilots were examined. The temperatures of their cockpits were continuously measured, they were were weighed before and after flying, their water intake was noted and their rectal temperature was taken.

Results: For all pilots, the temperature of the cockpit always exceeded 25°C, with 70 per cent of flights exceeding 26.7°C. The daily weight loss of the pilots ranged from 0.6 per cent to 1.2 per cent of total body weight and rectal temperatures consistently rose by 0.5°C. There was a wide range of water intake during flights, from less than 100 ml to over 2,000 ml.

Conclusion: Even with all of the data, it was impossible for Gribetz *et al.* to conclude whether the stress caused by the heat in the cockpit had a direct effect on the recent crashes. This was because it was not known if the current 'safe' levels of heat stress in a cockpit (which were exceeded here) could produce a decline in psychomotor performance in the pilots. It was suggested that air cooling in the cockpit would help, but filter mechanisms would have to be put in place to help prevent pesticides getting into the cockpit.

Auliciems and Frost (1989) reported on a link between cardiovascular deaths and temperature in Canada. They examined rates of myocardial infarction over a 2-year period in Montreal in relation to temperature and, in particular, snowfall. It was discovered that mortality increased when snow fell during the previous day. During anomalous cold spells, death frequencies actually decreased. This could be due to people avoiding outside activities rather than the temperature directly affecting heart function.

The weather has been shown to play a role in other health issues. For instance, Montgomery (1994) noted that the weather had an effect on headaches, eye strain and allergies in a sample of 837 students. Kresno *et al.* (1994) noted that in Indonesia, the main factors involved in acute respiratory illness in children aged under 5 years were the weather changing and experiencing a draught in the room.

for and against

climatological determinism

+ There is evidence to suggest that climate and weather play a crucial role in the development of certain health problems; for instance, Seasonal Affective Disorder.

+ Research has shown how the weather affects our psychological behaviour, such as memory and performance on tasks.

− Climatological determinism overlooks other factors that might be causing health problems, such as nutrition, education and social class.

− Climatological determinism again overlooks other factors that affect our behaviour, such as motivation and emotion.

− It is difficult to pinpoint the aspect of weather or climate that is important, as they can have differential effects.

Conclusions

The climate and weather appear to have some effect on our behaviour. Weather has been linked to criminal behaviour, and extremes in temperature appear to affect our ability to complete tasks. Other forms of behaviour that appear to be affected by the weather include suicidal behaviour and certain cognitive functions such as memory and reaction time.

Climate and weather appear to have a large effect on our health. Seasonal Affective Disorder occurs more often in the Northern Hemisphere and in the winter when light levels are low. Sudden Infant Death Syndrome appears to be related to weather conditions. The weather has also been seen to play a role in cardiovascular deaths, the onset of headaches and respiratory illnesses. However, this role may be indirect.

where to now?

The following are good sources of information about climate and weather:

▶ **Bell, P.A., Greene, T.C., Fisher, J.D. and Baum, A. (2001)** *Environmental Psychology*. **5th edn. Orlando, FL: Harcourt College Publishers** – this is a good introduction to the role that climate and weather play in our behaviour.

▶ **http://www.sids.org and http://sids-network.org** – these two websites are dedicated to researching into and reporting findings on SIDS. It will be interesting to note the risk factors to see if the weather becomes more important in their research programmes.

what do you know?

1 What have environmental psychologists discovered about the effect that climate and weather have on our performance and social behaviour?

2 Using a health problem of your choice (for example, SAD or SIDS), discuss how climate and weather play a role in its development.

3 What evidence is there that the weather affects criminal behaviour?

7

Environmental Disaster and Technological Catastrophe

what's
ahead?

In this chapter we will examine how environmental disasters and technological catastrophes affect human health and behaviour. We will look at what constitutes a 'disaster' or catastrophe, and at how people behave during them. We will also look at several specific disasters and examine the after-effects of being in such stressful events; for example, earthquakes, tornadoes, the Chernobyl incident and hurricanes. Finally, we will investigate how psychology can intervene before and after disasters have happened.

Definitions, characteristics and causes

There is a key difference between an *environmental (natural) disaster* and a *technological catastrophe*. The former are those occasions when nature takes control and causes large amounts of damage or even death, while the latter refers to incidents that are due to human factors (usually errors or mishaps), although they too may cause large-scale destruction.

interactive
angles

Examine the national papers for a week or two and keep a list of environmental (natural) disasters and technological catastrophes. Compare your list to those of the rest of the class. Did you all see the same events as disasters?

But what makes a disaster a disaster? It is relatively easy to see an event as a 'disaster' either via natural forces or human error because of the destruction or harm caused. However, are perceptions of disasters all the same? According to Bell *et al.* (1996), in the United States the Federal Emergency Management Agency tried to define a disaster as those events where the President decides that assistance is needed due to the severity of the damage (that is, destruction). If he does, then it is a true disaster. Others (see, for example, Quarantelli, 1985) believe that there is more to it than mere destruction. If the event causes major disruption, then it should be classified a disaster. Take a tornado as an example: Which of the following is a disaster – tornado A, which hits a heavily populated area and destroys numerous homes, or tornado B, which is equally powerful but misses any populated areas and destroys a disused farm? Tornado B is not a disaster. Do you agree? A disaster appears to have two main factors:

1 Destruction that requires some form of help or aid.

2 Disruption of the usual daily events in people's lives.

Walsh-Daneshmandi and MacLachlan (2000) examined people's perceptions of a variety of hazards.

research
now

hazard ratings in Ireland

Walsh-Daneshmandi, A. and MacLachlan, M. (2000) Environmental risk to the self: factor analysis and development of subscales for the Environmental Appraisal Inventory (EAI) with an Irish sample. *Journal of Environmental Psychology*, 20, 141–9

Aim: To examine how people perceive the relative risk from disasters.

Method: A total of 26 potential hazards were presented to the 159 Irish participants. They included factors such as pollution from cars, acid rain, radioactivity in building materials and earthquakes. Each hazard had to be rated on a seven-point scale, from no threat to extreme threat.

Results: Below is a list of some of the rank positions for the 26 hazards rated and their mean score:

1.	Change to the ozone layer caused by pollution	4.38
10.	Acid rain	3.11
19.	Water shortage	2.37
26.	Earthquakes	1.82

Change to the ozone layer caused by pollution was ranked the most threatening of all 26 hazards presented. Earthquakes were ranked as the least threatening.

Conclusion: This Irish sample rated hazards that were salient to their environment as the most threatening. Those with little relevance to their own environment – for example, earthquakes, soil erosion, floods and tidal waves, and water shortage – were rated as least threatening. Therefore, perceptions of risks and hazards are influenced by local experience as well as by the popular media issues (for example, ozone depletion).

It is interesting to note that, in the study conducted by Walsh-Daneshmandi and MacLachlan (2000), there were a distinct set of responses for certain groups of hazards. These groups were techno-human hazards (such as chemical dumps), natural hazards (such as floods and tidal waves) and everyday life hazards (such as fluorescent lighting). So, for example, people who found one hazard in the techno-human hazard group threatening tended to find them all threatening.

interactive angles

Generate a list of potential hazards and get people to rate them on the seven-point scale used by Walsh-Daneshmandi and MacLachlan (2000): no threat, minimal threat, mild threat, moderate threat, strong threat, very strong threat, and extreme threat. What do you find as the most threatening hazard? Are there differences by gender or age?

Examples of behaviour during disasters

This can be a very difficult area to research, as people are usually very distressed after a disaster (see p.156 onwards) and are therefore unlikely to want to discuss the behaviour that they exhibited during the disaster. The closest psychologists have got to researching this is when they have examined people's actions in crowds and emergency situations (see Chapter 4).

Examples of the psychological and physical effects of disasters on individuals

If asked, most people would probably say that there are many negative effects of being part of an environmental or technological disaster. However, is this belief true? There has been a great deal of research into the after-effects of disasters on the physical and psychological health of people exposed to them. It should be noted that most of the research has, obviously, taken place *after* the disaster, but of course no pre-disaster measures are normally taken. For instance, there has usually been no measure of mental health *before* the disaster, so we cannot be 100 per cent confident that the levels of mental health shown by people after the disaster are *due to* the disaster. For example, people could already have been depressed.

The eruption of Mount St Helens

One of the first disasters to be systematically researched was the eruption of the volcano Mount St Helens on 18 May 1980. Children were tested on pulmonary (lung) functioning 5 days after the eruption (Johnson *et al.*, 1982). There was no significant decrease in pulmonary functions recorded after the exposure to high levels of ash from the eruption. This was compared to pulmonary functions after an episode of high air pollution that was not related to the eruption. In that period, pulmonary functioning decreased significantly. However, the negligible effects of the ash on pulmonary functions could be due to the fact that all of the residents around the eruption site were advised to stay indoors for up to 4 days after the eruption. Therefore, the absence of reduction in pulmonary functioning could be due to the protective factor of not having been exposed to the ash fallout.

Buist *et al.* (1983) researched the after-effects of the eruption of Mount St Helens; in particular, the effects of volcanic ash on health. They examined a group of children who were attending a summer camp in an area in which 1.2 cm of ash had fallen after the eruption. Buist *et al.*'s main measure was also lung function. The children's lung functioning was tested on arrival at the camp, and in the morning and late afternoon of every second or third day during their stay at the camp. There was no significant reduction in the lung functioning of any of the children at the camp (not even those who had a pre-existing lung problem) even though the ash level was well in excess of 'safe' levels.

Studying the same disaster, Fraunfelder *et al.* (1983) examined the effects of volcanic ash on eye irritation 18 months after the explosion. They

The eruption of a volcano can have adverse physical health effects on nearby residents

focused on loggers who continued to work in the area up to 18 months after the eruption. These workers were compared to a group of loggers who had not been exposed to the volcanic ash. There appeared to be no difference in the two groups as to irritation levels in the eye. Those with contact lenses reported the most frequent problems with the volcanic ash. Also, there appeared to be no long-term effects of volcanic ash exposure on eye irritation in the loggers.

The Hanshin–Awaji earthquake

Fukuda *et al.* (1999) examined post-traumatic stress and lifestyle change after the Hanshin–Awaji earthquake in Japan. They were interested in the relationship between the change of lifestyle caused by the earthquake and psychological stress. A total of 108 males were asked about their lifestyle *before* and *after* the earthquake: any post-traumatic stress disorder (PTSD – see the box below) symptoms were noted, as were their current living arrangements. Those who reported that their lifestyle had changed for the worse had higher levels of PTSD compared to the 'no change in lifestyle' and 'better lifestyle' groups. Those who reported that they were still living in temporary accommodation also had higher levels of PTSD.

309.81 Post-traumatic Stress Disorder

A. The person has been exposed to a traumatic event in which both of the following were present:
  (1) the person experienced, witnessed or was confronted with an event or events that involved actual or threatened death or serious injury, or a threat to the physical integrity of self or others
  (2) the person's response involved intense fear, helplessness or horror. **Note:** In children, this may be expressed instead by disorganized or agitated behaviour

B. The traumatic event is persistently reexperienced in one (or more) of the following ways:
  (1) recurrent and intrusive distressing recollections of the event, including images, thoughts, or perceptions. **Note:** In young children, repetitive play may occur in which themes or aspects of the trauma are expressed
  (2) recurrent distressing dreams of the event. **Note:** In children, there may be frightening dreams without recognizable content
  (3) acting or feeling as if the traumatic event were recurring (includes

---

a sense of reliving the experience, illusions, hallucinations, and dissociative flashback episodes, including those that on awakening or when intoxicated). **Note:** In young children, trauma-specific reenactment may occur

(4) intense psychological distress at exposure to internal or external cues that symbolize or resemble an aspect of the traumatic event

(5) physiological reactivity on exposure to internal or external cues that symbolize or resemble an aspect of the traumatic event

C. Persistent avoidance of stimuli associated with the trauma and numbing of general responsiveness (not present before the trauma), as indicated by three (or more) of the following:

(1) efforts to avoid thoughts, feelings or conversations associated with the trauma

(2) efforts to avoid activities, places, or people that arouse recollections of the trauma

(3) inability to recall an important aspect of the trauma

(4) markedly diminished interest or participation in significant activities

(5) feeling of detachment or estrangement of others

(6) restricted range of effect (e.g., unable to have loving feelings)

(7) sense of a foreshortened future (e.g., does not expect to have a career, marriage, children, or a normal life span)

D. Persistent symptoms of increased arousal (not present before the trauma), as indicated by two (or more) of the following:

(1) difficulty in falling or staying asleep

(2) irritability or outbursts of anger

(3) difficulty concentrating

(4) hypervigilance

(5) exaggerated startle response

E. Duration of the disturbance (symptoms in Criteria B, C, and D) is more than 1 month.

F. The disturbance causes clinically significant distress or impairment in social, occupational, or other important areas of functioning.

Specify if:
Acute: if duration of symptoms is less than 3 months

Chronic: if duration of symptoms is 3 months or more

Specify if:
With delayed onset if onset of symptoms is at least 6 months after the stressor

Source: DSM-IV-TR

Fukuda *et al.* (2000) examined PTSD after the Hanshin–Awaji earthquake in a sample of 107 participants.

how stressful are earthquakes?

Fukuda, S., Morimoto, K., Mure, K. and Maruyama, S. (2000) Effect of the Hanshin–Awaji earthquake on posttraumatic stress, lifestyle changes, and cortisol levels in victims. *Archives on Environmental Health*, 55(2), 121–5

Aim: To investigate the after-effects of the Hanshin–Awaji earthquake. The research focused on post-traumatic stress, lifestyle changes and the cortisol levels (a physiological measure of stress) of victims.

Method: A total of 107 participants were given questionnaires to complete about post-traumatic stress and lifestyle change. Blood samples were taken to measure cortisol levels.

Results: There was a strong relationship between cortisol levels and lifestyle change in this group of participants. Those with the highest cortisol levels also had the highest post-traumatic stress scores. People with a large lifestyle change, and who were also experiencing profound lifestyle changes, had the highest levels of cortisol, and as a result of this they had the poorest health.

Conclusion: The psychological stress that was caused by the earthquake was, according to Fukuda *et al.*, linked to the cortisol level in the blood. The association between cortisol and stress was also affected by the amount of lifestyle change felt by the participant. The more perceived change there was, the higher was the cortisol level.

As can be seen, the impact of earthquakes on the physical and psychological health measures can be marked, especially if the event causes a lifestyle change.

The Chernobyl disaster

The nuclear power plant accident in Chernobyl, April 26, 1986

Summary

During the night between Friday April 25 and Saturday 26, 1986, an experiment was made in block 4 of the Chernobyl Nuclear Power Plant in order to test the ability of the turbine to power the cooling pumps whilst the generator was freewheeling to a standstill after its steam supply had been cut off. At about 01.23 the staff in the control-room of block 4 tried to achieve an emergency stop of the reactor normally. However, the control rods were too few and went down too slowly. The thermal effect increased to more than 300,000 MW (megawatt) and at 01.24 two violent explosions occurred, throwing the roof of the reactor building and lumps of material and radioactivity into the atmosphere.

There were eight persons in block 4 but also 268 building employees working on blocks 5 and 6 and 175 persons in blocks 1–3 and other buildings. A fire broke out and fire fighters arrived. After some hours, the fire fighters showed acute radiation sickness.

At the medical unit of the nuclear plant, situated in the administration building, patients from the plant were given acute care, iodine, tranquilisers and antiemetics. They were then sent to the hospital of Pripjat, where they were examined the same afternoon by radiological experts.

More than 100 out of about 200 patients with high radiation doses were later on taken to Moscow where Professor Angelina Guskowa was responsible for the further treatment. In addition to whole body irradiation, several patients also had local skin injuries due to beta irradiation and burns.

During the first days the dose rate in Pripjat was 1–10 mSv/h. The inhabitants received about 30 mSv as a mean dose before they were evacuated.

Acute radiation sickness was seen in more than 100 patients. Bleeding disorders were treated with platelet transfusions. Bone marrow transplantation was performed in at least 13 cases showing signs of having received high radiation doses and chromosome aberrations. All of these patients except two died.

The total number of casualties that died, as an immediate cause of the accident, was 31. Among those, two had already died at the site of the accident. In 19 cases skin injury was an important factor and in five cases the main cause of death. Seven patients died probably because of radiation pneumonitis.

After the accident a large scale medical operation took place in the Ukraine. About 2,000 physicians and 1,000 medical students took part therein. Iodine was given in doses of 250 mg to adults, 125 mg to school children and 60 mg to younger children.

According to the Minister of Health, Dr Romanenko, about 80,000 persons were listed for medical follow-up at a new research centre for radiation injuries at the University Hospital of Kiev. About one million Soviet inhabitants were reported to have been medically examined in January 1989; among these about 32,000 had received medical treatment.

The consequences and risks of low dose radiation are discussed in this report.

Some of the more important experiences from the accident can be summarised as follows: Information to the inhabitants should be immediate and in accordance with the truth; Intervention levels and road barriers should at first be adjusted at sufficiently great distances from the site of the accident that off-limit can later be contracted; Immediate measures must be undertaken as to drinking water supply and food distribution; Supply of clothes, shoes and blankets are needed in evacuation situations; In order to reduce radiation doses, sufficiently large rescue forces are needed in fire fighting and rescue work, minimising working hours for the personnel; Except for a limited group exposed to high doses, the immediate medical effects of the irradiation were insignificant. For most inhabitants in the Ukraine and White Russia the consequences were mostly caused by evacuations, disruption of services, lack of confidence in the information given by the authorities, uncertainty and anxiety.

Adapted from http://www.sos.se

The accident at Chernobyl has been well-researched to see what effects it had on nearby residents, workers and people further afield geographically

Bertollini *et al.* (1990) examined birth rates in Italy after the Chernobyl accident. There was a reduction in births during the first 3 months of 1987 (9 months after the disaster occurred), particularly in February (7.2 per cent decrease). This was observed throughout Italy. During the next 3 months there was an observed increase in births (4.8 per cent). There were also increases in abortions straight after the disaster in areas of Italy, some as high as 12.7 per cent compared to average figures. Overall, this study suggested that there was a voluntary decrease in the number of planned pregnancies and an increase in abortions in the first few weeks following the Chernobyl disaster (that is, the disaster led to a reduced desire for children). Therefore, this shows that the disaster affected people's behaviour.

Havenaar *et al.* (1997) researched into the health effects of Chernobyl. They examined participants 6.5 years after the disaster in a seriously contaminated area near Chernobyl and in a comparable but unaffected area in the Russian Federation. A total of 3,044 participants completed a variety of self-report questionnaires. The results indicated that those in the seriously contaminated area scored significantly higher on the questionnaires indicating poorer physical and psychological health. However, any of the disorders that were more prevalent in the contaminated area could be directly attributed to radiation exposure. Therefore, they could be linked to the stress of the disaster occurring. In conclusion, Havenaar *et al.* noted that 'the Chernobyl disaster had a significant long-term impact on psychological well-being, health-related quality of life, and illness behaviour in the exposed population' (p.1533).

research
now

children of Chernobyl

Bromet, E.J., Goldgaber, D., Carlson, G., Panina, N., Golovakha, E., Gluzman, S.F., Gilbert, T., Gluzman, D., Lyubsky, S. and Schwartz, J. (2000) Children's well-being 11 years after the Chornobyl catastrophe. *Archives of General Psychiatry*, 57, 563–71

Aim: Bromet *et al.* had noticed that there had been few studies examining the after-effects of a technological catastrophe on children. This is what the study focused upon.

Method: A total of 300 children aged 10–12 who were either *in utero* or infants and who lived near Chornobyl at the time of the disaster were evaluated. 'Chornobyl' is spelt this way because most of the research team involved in this study were Ukrainian – this is the Ukrainian spelling. Another 300 children who did not live near the disaster area were also assessed. A total of 92 per cent of the Chornobyl group and 85 per cent of the non-Chornobyl group agreed to take part. Data was gathered from the children, their mothers and their teachers on the children's well-being and risk factors for psychopathology (mental disorders). A physical examination and blood test was also conducted.

Results: There were a few significant results reported by Bromet *et al.*:

- The mothers in the Chornobyl group rated their children's well-being as lower than that of the non-Chornobyl group.

- The children in the Chornobyl group rated themselves lower on educational competence than the non-Chornobyl group.

- The mothers in the Chornobyl group rated their children as having more somatic complaints and thought problems and fewer delinquency problems compared to the non-Chornobyl group.

Some of the non-significant results included no differences on social competence, self-rated depression, mothers' reports on attention problems and self-worth.

Conclusion: Bromet *et al.* noted that even though there were multiple stressors happening at the time of the Chornobyl disaster, the small differences uncovered point towards some protective factors that occurred in the children's lives at that time.

Polyukhov *et al.* (2000) noted that there was evidence of accelerated ageing in workers at Chernobyl after the incident. They assessed 306 persons working at Chernobyl after the accident happened. They discovered that in 81 per cent of men and 77 per cent of women there was an accelerated rate of ageing (measured by biological and partial cardiopulmonary age). In some participants, the increased acceleration was over 5 years and the most vulnerable group were those aged 45 years or younger. Polyukhov *et al.* concluded that the radiation exposure could be accelerating the ageing process in this sample. This shows a direct physical effect of the disaster on people, or that stress is affecting the body after the event.

As can be seen from the studies reported here about the effects of the Chernobyl disaster, people of all ages suffered some detrimental psychological and/or physical after-effects. However, in some studies (see, for example, Bromet *et al.*, 2000, p.162), some measures did not generate significant differences between the 'exposed' group and the control group. Therefore, it would appear that the effects of the disaster were focused on certain psychological and physical health issues; for example, educational competence and their well-being. It is necessary to know this so that good post-disaster interventions can be put into place (see the section on this from p.169 onwards).

media watch

'Myth' of Chernobyl suffering exposed

By A. Browne

Relocation and hand-outs have caused more illness than radiation, a new UN study concludes. Anthony Brown reports.

It is seen as the worst man-made disaster in history, killing tens of thousands, making tens of millions ill, and afflicting generations to come. Exhibitions of photographs and of the deformed victims have toured the world, raising funds and awareness.

Now a report from the United Nations on the consequences of the Chernobyl nuclear disaster 15 years after the event comes to a very different conclusion. It says the medical effects of radiation are far less than was thought. The biggest damage to health has instead come from hypochondria and well-meaning but misguided attempts to help people.

The report suggests the re-location of hundreds of thousands of people 'destroyed communities, broke up families, and led to unemployment, depression, and stress-related illnesses'. Generous welfare benefits, holidays, food and medical help given to anyone declared a victim of Chernobyl have created a dependency culture, and created a sense of fatalism in millions of people. The Human Consequences of the Chernobyl Nuclear Accident, published by the UN Development Programme and Unicef, is a challenge to those who seek to highlight the dangers of nuclear energy.

More than 100 emergency workers on the site of the accident on 16 April 1986 suffered radiation sickness, and 41 of them died. The biggest direct consequences of the radiation are increases in childhood thyroid cancer, normally a very rare disease, that increased 60-fold in Belarus, 40-fold in Ukraine, and 20-fold in Russia, totalling 1,800 cases in all.

The report says other evidence of increases in radiation-related diseases is very limited. 'Intensive effort to identify an excess of leukaemia in the evacuated and controlled zone populations and recovery workers were made without success. There remains no internationally accredited evidence of an excess of leukaemia.' There is also no evidence of an increase in other cancers, and there has been no statistical increase in deformities in babies. The only deformities related to radiation were among babies of pregnant women working on the site at the time of the explosion.

The UN believes most of the deformed babies photographed by Western charities to raise funds have nothing to do with Chernobyl, but are the normal deformities that occur at a low level in every population. 'The direct effect of radiation is not that substantial,' said Oksana Garnets, head of the UN Chernobyl programme. 'There is definitely far more psychosomatic illness than that caused by radiation.'

The evacuation of hundreds of thousands of people, particularly from less contaminated areas, is seen as an over-reaction, which in some cases did more harm than good. 'The first reaction was to move people out. Only later did we think that perhaps some of them shouldn't have been moved. It has become clear that the direct influence of radiation on health is actually much less than the indirect consequences on health of relocating hundreds of thousands of people,' Garnets said.

Among relocated populations, there has been a massive increase in stress-related illnesses, such as heart disease and obesity, unrelated to radiation.

The UN is concerned about the corrosive effects of handouts to those classified as Chernobyl victims. In Russia, Belarus and Ukraine, they get more than 50 different privileges and benefits, including monthly payments and free school meals, medical treatment and holidays. In Ukraine, 'victims' get up to $100 a month.

In Ukraine, 92,000 people have been officially designated as permanently disabled, and half of the population says their health has been affected.

'There is an incentive to get classified as a victim. People getting benefits think they should get more and more. They think everything should be done for them by someone else – it creates a huge sense of fatalism and pessimism, which means they don't get on with their life,' Garnets said.

In the largely deserted village of Chernobyl, 18 km from the reactor and deep inside the government's total exclusion zone, the UN's report was welcomed among the 600 people who have illegally returned to their old homes.

Nina Melnik, 47, who edits a local newsletter, said: 'I don't just know that relocating people killed more than the radiation did, it is scientifically proven. It was totally the wrong thing to do. They should open up the area and let everyone come back.'

Source: The Observer, 6 January 2002

Other disasters

Lutgendorf *et al.* (1995) researched into the effects of Hurricane Andrew on people who already had chronic fatigue syndrome (CFS: symptoms include having chronic fatigue for 6 months or longer alongside physical illnesses such as a sore throat, joint pain, unrefreshing sleep and psychological problems such as lack of concentration and poor short-term memory all lasting more than 24 hours). A total of 49 CFS patients were interviewed, 25 in the hurricane zone and 24 outside the zone as a control group. Lutgendorf *et al.* hypothesised that the CFS patients in the hurricane zone would have exacerbated symptoms of CFS. Their results supported the hypothesis. Those in the hurricane zone showed increases in relapse of CFS and also showed heightened frequency of symptoms related to CFS. The strongest predictor of a relapse was the patient's post-hurricane distress level. That is, the higher the distress level, the more likely it was that a relapse would occur. Conversely, if the patient was optimistic and had high levels of social support, then he or she felt less burdened by his or her illness after the hurricane. Therefore, social support played a key role in the effects of the disaster in this sample of people. This also highlights the need for social support in post-disaster intervention efforts (see the section on this from p.169 onwards).

Goenjian *et al.* (2000) examined the similarities and differences between two types of stressors: an earthquake and political violence.

research now

earthquakes versus violence: which is more trauamatic?

Goenjian, A.K., Steinberg, A.M., Najarian, L.M., Fairbanks, L.A., Tashjian, M. and Pynoos, R.S. (2000) Prospective study of posttraumatic stress, anxiety and depressive reactions after earthquake and political violence. *American Journal of Psychiatry*, 157(6), 911–16

Aim: Goenjian *et al.* (2000) examined the after-effects of a mild and a severe earthquake and people's reactions to political violence to look for similarities and differences.

Method: A total of 78 participants were given a series of questionnaires to be completed by themselves. Two groups were examined: the first consisted of people exposed to the Armenian

Spitak earthquake of 1988 (1.5 or 4.5 years after the earthquake), while the second consisted of people exposed to the violence against the Armenians in Azerbaijan in 1988. The questionnaires measured post-traumatic stress, anxiety and depression.

Results: Those who were exposed to severe trauma, either the earthquake or violence, had high post-traumatic stress scores. In both groups, depression subsided with time. There was no significant difference in post-traumatic stress scores between the two groups.

Conclusion: Being exposed to a severe trauma, irrespective of its cause, places adults at high risk of developing chronic post-traumatic stress symptoms.

Dougall *et al.* (2000) examined the effects of disasters on disaster workers. They were interested in the cumulative effects of experiencing the trauma of a disaster. A total of 108 workers were examined four times over a year after they dealt with an airplane crash. In particular, Dougall *et al.* were concerned with the role of previous disaster experience on physiological arousal following this particular disaster. It was discovered that those workers whose prior experience was dissimilar to the airplane crash experienced stress more often at all times, assessed over the year. Those who had accumulated a variety of disaster experiences appeared to be desensitised to the current airplane crash, and so could cope better with the new stressor, again at all times during the year.

Finally, Foster *et al.* (1995) were interested in discovering whether the research methods used in disaster research have an effect on the results. They researched into why certain participants of a survey about the after-effects of the grounding of a tanker off the Shetland Islands chose not to respond. Foster *et al.* interviewed 75 non-responders and asked them why they had chosen not to take part in the original study. The main reasons were that they felt that their health was not affected by the disaster and that they thought the study was not useful. Others did not want to go through biological tests, while some found the appointment times difficult to attend. So, if those who are least affected remove themselves from the sample, the effects of the disaster may be over-emphasised. A similar pattern appears to have arisen in Bromet *et al.* (2000), where more of the affected than the non-affected group responded.

Overall, it would seem that there are both psychological and physical after-effects of a disaster (depending, perhaps, on the type of disaster), and that social support may lessen these effects. However, samples of participants may be biased, with more of the affected group than the control group taking part (as in Foster *et al.*, 1995; Bromet *et al.*, 2000).

Psychological intervention before events

In Chapter 4 we discussed how strategies might be employed to reduce the risks to crowds in emergency situations. Similarly, in the context of disasters, some preparations are possible that could help to minimise the impact.

Balluz *et al.* (2000) investigated whether there were any predictors of people's responses to a tornado warning in America.

research now

are you ready for that tornado?

Balluz, L., Schieve, L., Holmes, T., Kiezak, S. and Malilay, J. (2000) Predictors of people's responses to a tornado warning: Arkansas, 1 March 1997. *Disasters*, 24(1), 71–7

Aim: Balluz *et al.* examined the predictors of people's responses to a tornado warning.

Method: A total of 146 participants were questioned about their actions during the tornado warning. Demographic details were also taken.

Results: A total of 64 participants responded positively to the warning by seeking shelter, with 58 of those doing so within 5 minutes of the siren. Balluz *et al.* discovered that four factors were associated with seeking shelter:

1   Having graduated from high school.
2   Having a basement in one's house.
3   Hearing the siren.
4   Having prepared a plan of response once a siren is heard.

Conclusion: From this study, it is clear that a predetermined plan of action is necessary for increased safety in a tornado-prone area. Also, local public health officials should educate people more about what to do when a siren is heard, as only 45 per cent of this sample responded positively to it. Finally, emergency-management officials should plan some form of protection measures for vulnerable areas, as people have limited time to respond to the siren. They could strategically erect shelters to reduce the time taken from a person starting to respond to reaching a place of safety.

Duclos and Ing (1989) examined the after-effects of a tornado in Illinois in 1982, but their findings can be used to aid intervention *before* another tornado may hit the region. The researchers telephoned participants who were in the path of the tornado, to ask them about their response to the tornado warning. They also examined the emergency room log books and the admission files of hospitals, to investigate the types of injuries that occurred. A total of 19.3 per cent of participants who were in the path of the tornado had become injured, 39 per cent of these as a direct result of the tornado. The remaining 61 per cent were injured during the clear-up, while rescuing people or just when walking through the post-tornado areas. Duclos and Ing noted certain kinds of behaviour that appeared to be the most protective of injury. These were being on the lowest floor in a house, staying underground during the tornado, protecting one's body (for example, with a blanket) and staying away from windows.

inter**active** angles

Using the findings of Duclos and Ing (1989) above, what could now be done to intervene before the next tornado in Illinois? How would you intervene?

Sattler *et al.* (2000) examined disaster preparedness at the peak of the hurricane season in America. In one of their studies, they gave questionnaires to 257 participants who were preparing for Hurricane Emily. Questions were asked about demographics, the extent of property damage from a previous hurricane, the amount of distress felt after a previous hurricane and preparedness for the impending Hurricane Emily. The questionnaires were completed 1 or 2 days before Hurricane Emily was due to hit Charleston, where the survey was taking place. One of the measures taken was that of preparation for the hurricane. About half of the participants had petrol for the car (59 per cent), flashlights (57 per cent), bottled water (52 per cent), candles and matches (51 per cent), batteries (51 per cent) and either canned or dried food (49 per cent). Sattler *et al.* also correlated demographics and previous hurricane experience with the degree of preparation for Hurricane Emily. The following factors correlated strongly with preparation:

- age – the older the participant, the more prepared he or she was

- income – the higher the person's income, the more prepared he or she was

- following the news broadcasts on the television

- knowing the evacuation route

- the distress level from a previous hurricane – the more distress experienced, the more prepared the person was.

So, as can be seen, there are a number of factors that affected disaster preparedness in this sample of Americans.

Psychological intervention after events

As we have already seen, when people are asked to take precautions after a disaster they usually do, and this has positive effects on health (Johnson et al., 1982).

Chemtob et al. (1997) examined the effectiveness of psychological intervention after Hurricane Iniki in Hawaii. Two groups of participants ($n = 43$ overall) who had been exposed to the hurricane were assessed before and after being involved in a 'multihour debriefing group'. This allowed the participants to discuss their feelings about the hurricane and to be educated about the normal psychological reactions to disasters. To provide some control for the passage of time, the two groups overlapped their debriefings, so the assessment before the debriefing of the second group took place at the same time as the assessment after the debriefing of the first group. Irrespective of the group that the participants were in, the debriefing reduced psychological distress, lending support for psychological debriefing as being useful after disasters.

Weaver et al. (2000) reported on how the Red Cross in America recognises the need for an organised plan for post-disaster intervention. The service that they provide helps victims of disasters and Red Cross workers who assist at the scene of the incident. It aims to help them to cope with the overwhelming stress experienced by both groups. The Red Cross coordinates a diverse group of professionals to aid in post-disaster psychological intervention. These include mental health professionals from psychology, marriage and family therapy, counsellors, nurses and social workers.

Carmichael (2000) reported on a rather novel approach to post-disaster psychological intervention. A counsellor used the *Wizard of Oz* as a focal point for a group of survivors after a tornado in a small US community. During the last hour of a 3 hour meeting attended by 30 residents, the counsellor began to use the story of the *Wizard of Oz* as metaphors to help alleviate the stress of the disaster. The counsellor used Dorothy's shoes as a metaphor for inner strength, the dog as significant people and the Yellow Brick Road as the trauma recovery process. After this introduction, the residents began to discuss their own experiences in the light of the *Wizard of Oz*. The common focal point of the story appeared to be effective in aiding the recovery process of the residents.

Carmichael (2000) used the story of the *Wizard of Oz* to counsel people after a tornado hit a small US community

inter**active**
angles

Examine a specific disaster, perhaps through newspaper reports or on the Internet, and see what interventions take place when people are trying to rebuild their lives. Are any of the interventions similar to the ones you have just read about?

Two separate studies to examine interventions were set in place after the Hanshin–Awaji earthquake already discussed on page 157 (Kusuda *et al.*, 1995; Nagao *et al.*, 1995).

Kusuda *et al.* (1995) examined the provision for perinatal care (care around the time of pregnancy and for a short while afterwards) after the Hanshin–Awaji earthquake. Most resources in a disaster area are focused on people without special needs (for example, those with injuries from the disaster only). Therefore, any specific medical care – for example, perinatal care – must come from outside the disaster area. The day after the earthquake happened, a hospital and a child health centre in Osaka were established as the key facilities for perinatal care. Most telephone calls to the hospital came 2 days after the earthquake, and concerned pregnant women and information for new-born infants. As a result, any high-risk pregnancies and new-born infants were taken out of the disaster zone within the following month. Even though the emergency responses to perinatal concerns were quick and efficient, Kusuda *et al.* noted that some improvements could be initiated for future post-disaster intervention to alleviate anxiety. These were:

- to establish a mechanism to handle a large volume of communications from people affected by a disaster and to give information to these people

- to make helicopter transport easily available

- to have pre-established known facilities, so that people know where to go to after a disaster.

Nagao *et al.* (1995) examined the psychological intervention for the treatment of early mental health and post-traumatic symptoms of children after the Hanshin–Awaji earthquake. The researchers believed that the most important aspect of post-disaster intervention was to aid coping in a confused situation. No transport was available and medical efforts had also been paralysed. Nagao *et al.* noted that contact with other people outside the disaster area was a great help immediately after the earthquake had finished.

Initially, parents were worried about the mental health of their children, as many appeared to be psychologically confused about the situation. However, only a few people went to their doctors to seek help. When the children were examined 5 months after the earthquake, feelings of terror and uneasiness had subsided and those who appeared to be traumatised by the situation had begun to recover. Very few children had difficulties adapting to day nurseries and elementary schools. However, Nagao *et al.* (1995) reported that the number of bone fractures had increased rapidly post-disaster, perhaps due to a decrease in bodily resistance as a result of the stress of the earthquake. Also, some children were still exhibiting symptoms of post-traumatic stress, and so rapid recognition of children's mental health problems is essential in post-disaster treatments. Finally, the level of maternal and family support appears to be important in buffering the effects of a disaster. Remember that we have already discussed the role of social support on page 165, with reference to the study by Lutgendorf *et al.* (1995).

Finally, Lesaca (1996) noted a down side to post-disaster counselling for the counsellors themselves. He compared 21 counsellors who provided their services after a major air disaster with counsellors who provided a general counselling service. Between them, the disaster counsellors had completed 38 hours with the victims' families and 58 hours with airline employees. Lesaca took measures of post-traumatic stress disorder (PTSD) and depression in both groups 4, 8 and 12 weeks after the disaster. At 4 and 8 weeks, the disaster counsellors reported significantly more PTSD symptoms and depressive symptoms compared to the general counsellors. The most common symptoms included feeling emotionally numbed, feeling as if in a daze, or dream and memory problems, such as forgetting to do important things. Other differences included difficulty in

Counsellors may exhibit PTSD symptoms after counselling the survivors of disasters

sleeping, having poor concentration, feeling agitated, and being restless and lacking energy. However, these differences had disappeared by the time of the 12 week assessment.

Conclusions

Environmental disasters and technological catastrophes are characterised by the large amounts of damage and even death that they cause. These events have profound effects on the people involved in them, both physically and psychologically. Many suffer post-traumatic stress disorder, but other disasters bring about different problems. For instance, the Chernobyl incident appeared to accelerate the ageing process of the majority of the clean-up workers and to adversely affect children's educational competence and general well-being. For disaster workers, it would appear that exposure to previous similar disasters helps them to cope with new crises.

Psychological intervention before a disaster occurs also appears to be linked to previous experience of a similar disaster (for example, a tornado). Psychological intervention after the disaster usually takes the form of counselling or psychological debriefing and can claim some success. However, research on the counsellors themselves shows that they require counselling after helping disaster victims, due to the unusual amounts of stress experienced. Finally, the level of social support after a disaster also appears to aid the recovery of those involved in the after-effects.

where to now?

▶ **The following are good sources of information about environmental disaster and technological catastrophe:**

▶ **Cave, S. (1998)** *Applying Psychology to the Environment*. **London: Hodder & Stoughton** – some good examples of behaviour linked to disasters are introduced and debated.

▶ **http://www4.ncbi.nlm.nih.gov/PubMed/** – go to MEDLINE and search for specific disasters to see how psychology has helped survivors. Abstracts can be printed.

what do you know?

1   How have environmental psychologists attempted to define disasters and catastrophes?

2   Using examples, how has physical health been affected by natural disasters and technological catastrophes?

3   Using examples, how has psychological health been affected by natural disasters and technological catastrophes?

4   Using empirical evidence, discuss the usefulness of psychological intervention before a natural disaster or technological catastrophe.

5   Using empirical evidence, discuss the usefulness of psychological intervention after a natural disaster or technological catastrophe.

8

Environmental Cognition

How do we remember information about our spatial environment and how do we utilise this information to find our way? In this chapter we will be discussing aspects of *environmental cognition*; that is, our ability to imagine and think about our spatial world. In particular, we will describe cognitive maps and look at the behavioural and physiological evidence for their existence in humans and animals. We will be evaluating the function of cognitive maps, the errors they lead us to make and the individual differences between people's maps. We will explore the process of way-finding in humans and the implications for producing better maps. Finally, we will look at the role that the scenic environment plays in our lives.

Cognitive maps

The nature of cognitive maps

You're having a party, but not all of the guests know how to get to your house. What do you do? Draw a map! We can do this, adequately if not accurately, even without the experience of having seen a map of the area: it is not simply a matter of recall – we appear to generate a pictorial representation of the local area for ourselves. It is as though we have some kind of internal model of a geographical space. This was described by Tolman (1948), who was the first to use the term *cognitive map*, which he defined as an internal representation that animals develop about the spatial relationships within their environment.

interactive
angles

Before we go any further, you might like to draw a sketch map of the layout of your college or university department and another of the local geography of the area in which you live, such as a plan of your town. These will be useful later.

What, then, is the evidence that our spatial knowledge is 'map-like' rather than, say, a sequence of instructions for various routes? Evidence comes from a range of sources, including both animal and human studies. Human and animal studies can draw on the ability (or not) of the individual to navigate; that is, to use knowledge of their current geographical location and that of their goal as a means to direct movement from one to the other. Alternatively, studies using people can ask the participants to make their internal map explicit by drawing it or describing it.

classic research

city limits

Lynch, K (1960) *The Image of the City*. Cambridge, Massachusetts: The MIT Press

Aim: Lynch's interest was in town planning; he aimed to investigate people's feelings and knowledge about their environment and how their perceptions could be used to guide environmental design.

Method: Data was gathered from three American cities: Boston, Jersey City and Los Angeles. Participants were asked to draw sketch maps of their city, to list the vivid and distinctive features of the city and to provide detailed descriptions of routes, such as that taken from home to work.

Results: There were common elements in the maps that participants produced of the three cities. Similarities between the maps suggested that five key categories of features could be used to describe and analyse maps:

- *paths* – shared conduits for travel, such as footpaths and roads
- *edges* – boundaries, such as walls of buildings or coastlines
- *districts* – large spaces with a shared characteristic, such as Soho, the West End or an industrial estate
- *nodes* – points on a map that act as a focus for behaviour, such as town squares, roundabouts or major road junctions
- *landmarks* – distinctive features, used as reference points, which are generally visible from a distance, such as the London Eye, Nelson's Column or a particular church spire.

Conclusion: Cognitive maps seem to be constructed in similar ways, tending to be built up of elements from five categories, although some features may fall into more than one category for different people; for example, a canal may be a path for some people but an edge for others.

Further evidence has supported the concept of Lynch's five categories, although they appear to be more suited to city environments (from which they were derived) than to smaller- or larger-scale maps, such as of buildings or countries. For example, Aragones and Arredondo (1985) demonstrated the presence of all five categories by testing the ability of participants to classify elements from Madrid City into groups. They were spontaneously able to cluster examples of each type of feature together; for instance, the palace, museum and post office were put together by the participants and fell into the category of 'landmarks', and similarly plazas were identified as nodes.

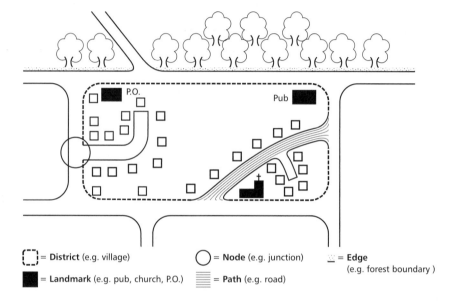

Individuals seem to differ in the type of map they construct. Some focus on paths and nodes, generating a map that relates to journeys between places: these are called *sequential maps*. Others create a map that more closely resembles a 'bird's eye view', emphasising spatial organisation; these are called *spatial maps*. Appleyard (1970) found that, for people living in cities, sequential maps were more common.

interactive angles

If you followed the interactive angles on page 175 and drew sketch maps, return to them now. Have you included features from each of the categories identified by Lynch (1960)?

Animal studies

Tolman (1948) tested cognitive maps using mazes. He argued that animals that could demonstrate a capacity to find their way around an environment that they had been allowed to explore must have an internal representation of the local geography rather than having simply learned a series of left and right turns.

classic research

a maze-ing rats!

Tolman, E.C. and Honzik, C.H. (1930a) 'Insight' in rats. *University of California Publications in Psychology*, 4, 215–32

Aim: To demonstrate that rats could make navigational decisions based on knowledge of the environment, rather than their directional choices simply being dictated by the effects of rewards.

Method: A maze was used as illustrated below. Initially, rats had access to the whole maze: later it was obstructed at point A, then at point B. The alternative route selected by each rat on each trial was recorded.

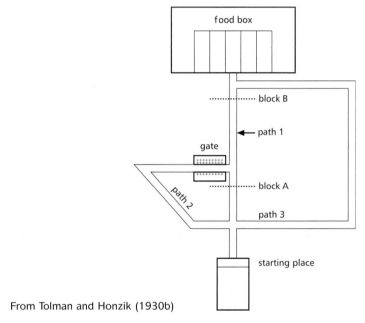

From Tolman and Honzik (1930b)

Results: Initially, rats learned their way from the start to the food box without obstructions and reliably used route 1, the shortest. When their path was blocked at A, the rats selected route 2 to avoid the obstruction and reached the food on 92 per cent of the trials. When the path was obstructed at B, 93 per cent of the rats chose route 3 on the first test trial.

Conclusion: Although the results of obstructing the maze at A could be interpreted as a simple response to reinforcement – the rat chose the route that would most quickly lead to the food, as it was the shortest available – the same cannot be said of the results of obstructing the maze at B. Here, the rats did not select the next shortest route (2), which would also have been blocked, but used their cognitive maps to deduce that the only available route was 3.

A radial arm maze has a central platform and several alleys leading out from it, like spokes from the hub of a wheel. When placed in the centre of such a maze, a rat must make a choice based on past experience. Although simple conditioning could explain correct choices when there are only a few arms, this explanation breaks down when trying to understand behaviour in a multiple-arm maze. In this situation, rats are unable to learn which arm to choose to find food and begin to show a stereotyped response pattern. Using a 24-arm radial maze, Roberts (1979) found that rats could learn to find food but did so by employing a fixed search pattern; for instance, always turning right when they had re-entered the central area. While this strategy enables the rats to find the food, it indicates that they had reached capacity for remembering particular locations; this may represent the limits of complexity for a rat's cognitive map.

As a further test of the effects of rewards on cognitive map formation, Tolman and Honzik (1930b) studied the learning demonstrated by rats in the absence of food. This too showed that rats appear to acquire information about the geography of their environment without the need for reinforcement.

classic research

a maze-ingly hungry rats!

Tolman, E.C. and Honzik, C.H. (1930b) Introduction and removal of reward, and maze performance in rats. *University of California Publications in Psychology*, 4, 257–75

Aim: To investigate the occurrence of learning in the absence of a reward.

Method: Rats were divided into three groups, each spending time in a maze each day. One group received food in the goal box every day; another was allowed to explore the maze for the same amount of time, but received no food in the goal box until the 11th day; and the third group never received food in the maze.

Start   Goal box

Based on Tolman and Honzik (1930b)

Results: The first group gradually learned to run to the goal box to find the food, while the third group continued to travel around all parts of the maze, not directing their movement towards the (empty) goal box at all. The behaviour of the second group resembled that of the third group until the day after food was made available. These rats were then able to direct their movement towards the goal box much more quickly than the first group had done.

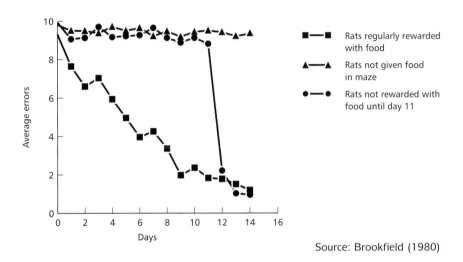

Source: Brookfield (1980)

Conclusion: The behaviour of the second group suggests that, during the days on which they had been exploring the maze, they had acquired latent information about its layout; that is, they had formed a cognitive map in the absence of reinforcement. Once motivated to find a particular location, they were able to do so more quickly because they could rely on the map that they had already developed.

In much the same way as Tolman and Honzik's rats, you have probably acquired a lot of 'latent' information about the geography of your college or university. Think about a room or department that you know exists but have never been into: Could you direct someone there? We will discuss human cognitive maps and way-finding later in the chapter.

The function of cognitive maps

How might animals benefit from having cognitive maps? If an animal explores and develops an understanding of the spatial relationships between parts of an area or maze, this could be used to minimise travelling time by taking the shortest route, thus enhancing safety and making more time available for other activities such as feeding. In addition, an animal with a cognitive map should be able to find a detour if its route is blocked. Therefore, animals with cognitive maps should be able to locate a goal and re-route on discovering an obstruction.

Evidence from Tolman and Honzik (1930b) and, more recently, Holtzman *et al.* (1999), has demonstrated that animals that have had the opportunity to explore a maze are faster than those that have not. Similarly, Regolin and Rose (1999) have shown that animals such as chicks can learn to take a detour (see below). Rats can also use cognitive maps to shorten their journey (Maier and Schneirla, 1935) as illustrated in the box below. More recently, Groberty *et al.* (2000) have demonstrated the ability of rats and humans under similar conditions to develop new routes to a goal using information from the surrounding environment.

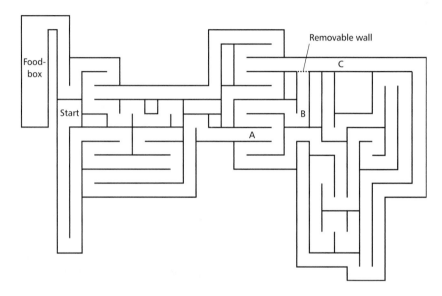

Maier and Schneirla (1935) allowed rats to explore the maze and learn to find the goal box containing food. One wall was then removed, making a short-cut available between the alleys B and C. Some rats noticed the change to alley C and explored alley B. These rats ran straight from A to B on subsequent trials, thus shortening their journey

Adapted from: Maier and Schneirla (1935)

research
now

chicken run

Regolin, L. and Rose, S.P.R. (1999) Long-term memory for a spatial task in young chicks. *Animal Behaviour*, 57, 1185–91

Aim: To test chicks' long-term memory for a spatial task.

Method: Two-day-old chicks (*Gallus gallus domesticus*) were put in a large box. Their task was to find their way around a barrier to reach a group of chicks on the other side. Each chick made one detour trial and was then re-tested after 30 minutes and 24 hours. In a second part of the experiment, the chicks' first choice of direction past the barrier was blocked on the next trial, 24 hours later. They were then given five more trials with the obstruction in place.

Results: On each re-test, the chicks were quicker to solve the task, which suggests that they had learned to find their way around the detour. When their chosen route (going left or right around the barrier) was blocked, they were quicker to find their way to the goal box when re-tested. Even those chicks that failed to find their way the first time and were removed from the apparatus after 600 seconds were able to make the detour more quickly when retested.

Conclusion: As the chicks could solve the first task progressively more quickly, this suggests that they were able to learn to find their way. When required to alter their route, they were again faster on the second test, which shows that they had incorporated this new information into their understanding of the spatial relationships within the experimental setting.

As an alternative to laboratory experiments using mazes, animals can be tested using field studies. To investigate the use of cognitive maps in a naturalistic environment, Menzel (1971) studied chimps living in a large outdoor enclosure. The chimps were held indoors and, one by one, they were taken to see food being hidden in 18 locations outside. When each chimp was released in the centre of the area to find the hidden food it took a route that minimised the distance it had to travel; it did not retrace the complex path that it had previously followed. The chimps' choices enabled them to find most of the food in the minimum time by exploiting their knowledge of the area. Therefore, they must have been using cognitive maps, as they did not employ the previously encountered route.

Furthermore, it would appear that the chimps' cognitive maps were more than just records of relationships between places. In a second part of the experiment, Menzel (1971) took the chimps to 18 new locations, half of which contained fruit (which chimps prefer) and the other half vegetables. Upon release, the chimps went to the locations where fruit had been hidden before those locations containing vegetables. Therefore, it seems that the cognitive maps provide information about the places as well as their geographical locations.

In another study, Jacobs and Linman (1991) investigated the role of the cognitive map in allowing animals to search for food that they had stored themselves. Each grey squirrel (*Sciurus carolinensis*) was released into a 45 m^2 area to bury 10 hazelnuts. The location of each food item was recorded and the nuts were then removed. The squirrels were returned to the area individually 2, 4 or 12 days later. New hazelnuts had been placed in the individual's own hiding places and at an equal number of randomly chosen sites that had been used by other squirrels (see the accompanying figures). The squirrels were more likely to find nuts in places where they had buried them, even when they had to pass the sites chosen by other squirrels.

Although the squirrels could clearly locate buried nuts by smell alone, they were preferentially seeking the ones that they had hidden on the basis of recalling each location, which suggests that they were using cognitive maps.

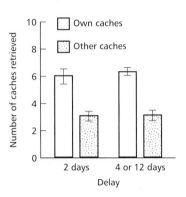

The success of squirrels at finding food at locations in which they, or other squirrels, had buried it

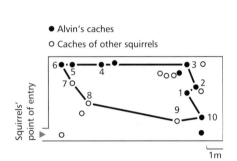

A diagrammatic representation of the route taken by one squirrel (Alvin) to retrieve buried hazelnuts

Source: Jacobs and Linman (1991)

Cognitive maps and brain structure

You may already have heard of a case study conducted by Milner *et al.* (1968) of an amnesic known as HM. Following surgery for epilepsy, HM experienced some specific memory problems. This seemed to be the result of the removal of a brain area called the hippocampus. When HM's parents moved house, he could not learn how to find the way home. Rats with lesions to the hippocampus, like HM, find tasks that require them to find their way very difficult. Morris *et al.* (1982) compared the performance of rats with hippocampal lesions with control (non-lesioned) rats. The task required the rats to find a platform concealed under the surface of water made murky by mixing it with powdered milk. Initially, any rat had to find the platform by chance. A control rat rapidly learned to swim to where the platform was situated, but rats with hippocampal lesions failed to learn the location of the platform, simply swimming until they chanced upon it on each trial. Both HM and the experimental rats appeared to have deficiencies in building cognitive maps to enable them to find their way around a new area.

However, recent evidence with another amnesic patient (Teng, 2000) suggests that even with virtually complete hippocampal damage it may still be possible for humans to *retrieve* spatial memories, although not necessarily to create new ones. Teng (2000) also investigated the role of the hippocampus in monkeys in relation to spatial and non-spatial tasks, and found that hippocampal lesions did indeed impair spatial memory, supporting the role of the hippocampus in spatial tasks such as navigation (as well as non-spatial ones).

Whishaw and Tomie (1997) showed that lesions to the fimbria-fornix (a region of the hippocampus) affected rats' navigational abilities. The rats were trained to collect food pellets from one location and take them to their home base. The locations of the release point and home base were then moved. If the new home base location was visible, the lesioned rats were able to take the food home accurately. If, however, the new location was hidden from view, these rats continued to return to the old home base location unlike the control rats that learned the reversal of locations after one trial. The rats with hippocampal lesions seemed unable to update their cognitive maps when the spatial relationships changed in the environment.

The importance of the hippocampus in navigation is also supported by evidence from natural variations in hippocampal volume. Animals that have a large territory (Gaulin and Fitzgerald, 1989) and people who navigate daily (Maguire *et al.*, 2000) have a larger hippocampus (see p.188).

Using *Positron Emission Tomography* (PET), a brain scanning technique that provides information about the activity of brain areas, Maguire *et al.* (1998) identified an area of the cortex involved in way-finding. Their participants navigated through a virtual town while being PET scanned and showed activation of the left frontal cortex while performing a detour task. This area of the brain is involved in general planning and decision-making, so the activation seen may relate to strategy choices being made during the dynamic spatial task.

Human studies

Human cognitive maps can be studied in the same ways as those of animals, by testing their usage, although this is only one of the available methods. The following review discusses a range of techniques that have been used with people. Measures of *way-finding*, our ability to move in a goal-directed way through our environment, are discussed later in the chapter.

Measures of cognitive maps

Drawing sketch maps

This technique, pioneered by Lynch (1960) (see p.175), enables the researcher to gather much detailed information about people's sketch maps and has been used extensively. It aims to reproduce the individual's internal image of the environment and is relatively easy in essence. However, there are some major drawbacks with this method. One of the biggest difficulties is that the sketch maps of different individuals will vary not only because their cognitive maps differ but also as a consequence of variation in drawing ability, the perspective from which the map has been drawn, the scale and the type of map (spatial or sequential; see p.176). By asking an unbiased question such as 'Draw a map of your home town', the researcher has introduced the risk of such idiosyncrasies arising. Despite these problems, this method is still used, such as by Pinheiro (1998), who studied Brazilians' cognitive maps of the world through sketch maps (see p.188).

If you can, compare the sketch maps of the same area drawn by yourself and other students. Are they all drawn from the same perspective? Do they all cover the same extent of the district or do some cover a much wider area? It's unlikely that, unless specified, everyone has even used the paper in the same orientation. If you wanted to combine the information, how might you overcome these problems? Could you compile a list of the paths and landmarks that have been correctly identified? How would you deal with ones which were correctly located but unlabelled or, conversely, were identifiable but in the wrong place? Such errors are called *distortions* and quantifying these offers another way to measure the accuracy of cognitive maps.

Rovine and Weisman (1995) took participants to the business area of a small town, where they were taken on a tour and asked to draw a sketch map. The sketch map was assessed in three ways:

- the frequency of landmarks, paths and nodes

- the complexity of the map (spatial maps showing appropriate inter-connections being better than sequential maps; see p.176)

- accurate placement of the 20 target buildings seen on the tour.

Other variables were also measured, such as orientation, sense of direction, self-efficacy and the ability to visualise. The participants were then asked to find eight buildings. The quality of the sketch map was the best indicator of way-finding ability; that is, the better the sketch map, the more likely the participants were to find their way to the eight buildings via a direct, short route with few turns.

Gouldian maps

One way to overcome the problems of analysis of sketch maps caused by individual differences is to begin with an accurate base map. Participants can then be asked questions with reference to this and for information about their reactions. For example, a map of their local town may be provided marked with districts; participants can then be asked to rate these for desirability as residential areas. Such a technique can then be used to investigate differences; for instance, in perceptions of people living in different locations. Gould and White (1982) used this technique to assess the evaluations that US residents made of their own and other parts of the United States. The participants rated their own area more highly than other parts of the country.

Recognition tasks

Participants can be shown illustrations depicting different landmarks, and asked whether they recognise or can identify them when they are interspersed with illustrations of unknown locations. Whilst, like Gouldian mapping, such recognition tasks overcome the problems of individual differences inherent in sketch maps, they do not provide the same richness of data. A recognition task cannot be used to measure internal representations of distances or orientation and, of course, it can only measure *recognition* – that is, an ability to identify a familiar item – rather than *recall*, being able to retrieve information without cues such as pictures. This means that the technique may overestimate participants' ability: whilst you might be able to recognise many buildings that you have seen on various holidays, you are unlikely to be able to place them with any certainty on a sketch map that you have drawn. However, this does examine a real-life aspect of our navigation in environments that we know: when we are fairly familiar with an area, we rely on recognition to guide us as we move around. Since this technique offers some advantages over sketch maps, it is also used. For example, Milgram and Jodelet (1976) used recognition tasks in their study of residents' cognitive maps of Paris.

Estimating distances

One aspect of the environment encoded in our cognitive maps is the distance between places. This information can be accessed by asking participants to estimate distances between locations. This technique avoids problems encountered with other methods, such as differences in drawing ability or reliance on recognition. Computer-based analysis allows the researcher to produce a map based on the estimated distances, as in Moar's study of British housewives. Moar (1978) demonstrated that women living in Glasgow overestimated distances in Scotland compared to distances in southern England, whereas for housewives from Cambridge the errors were reversed.

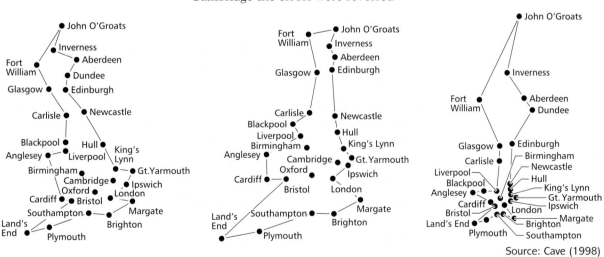

Source: Cave (1998)

The UK with towns and cities correctly located

The UK as represented by participants in Cambridge

The UK as represented by participants in Glasgow

Moar (1978) found that British housewives differ in their estimation of distances between cities depending on where they live

185

Hanyu and Itsukushima (1995) used distance estimation to gauge people's *cognitive distances*; that is, the time they perceive a journey to take. However, such studies also suffer from problems. People may differ as much in their ability to estimate distances as in their drawing skills, and it is likely that estimates of outward and return journeys will differ! Think how differently you might have experienced the distance walking to school and the distance walking home again.

interactive angles

You can try to construct a map from distance estimates without a computer. Ask a group of people to estimate the distances between 10 locations, such as major landmarks, buildings or road junctions. Work out the mean for each distance and then cut lengths of elastic band to represent these averages on a scale that you can work with. Pin out one piece of elastic band and try to fit the rest around it, in approximately the correct locations. If your estimates were accurate, you should end up with a realistic layout of the 10 landmarks. This is unlikely, as we tend to make consistent errors. For example, you may find that the group has scaled up – that is, overestimated – journeys that they dislike or make only occasionally (hence you may need to stretch some pieces to make them fit together). You could compare different groups of participants estimating the same distances, perhaps students who live in different areas or those who drive versus those who travel by bus. Try to predict the differences that you would expect from these groups.

for and against

techniques for studying cognitive maps

+ Human and animal maze studies allow us to test whether a cognitive map enables the individual to find the way to a goal around an obstruction, thus indicating that they have not simply learned a route.

+ Animal lesion studies and human case studies have demonstrated the role of key brain areas such as the hippocampus in the formation of cognitive maps.

+ Sketch maps provide a way to externalise the cognitive map in humans.

− Sketch maps may not reliably indicate the detail of a person's cognitive map, reflecting instead the individual's drawing ability.

− Analysing sketch maps may be difficult due to variations in the perspective from which they are drawn, the scale and the orientation of the paper chosen by the participant.

+ Gouldian maps and recognition tasks overcome some of the problems with analysis of sketch maps.

− Recognition tasks cannot be used to measure internal representations of distances, nor do they provide as much detail as sketch maps.

+ Recognition tasks have good validity, as we rely on recognising familiar locations to navigate in real-world environments.

+ Estimation of distances also avoids problems with drawing ability and reliance on recognition.

− Individuals may vary in the accuracy of their estimations, thus lowering the validity of this technique, and estimates of the same journey in the inward and outward directions may differ.

Errors and cognitive maps

Cognitive maps are internal *representations*; thus they are not accurate replicas of the real world – they contain mistakes. The nature of the errors in cognitive maps is itself interesting. First, our cognitive maps are *incomplete*: we tend to omit minor and sometimes even major details. For example, if you compare your sketch map from the *interactive angles* on page 175 to a street map of the area, you will find that many small paths and roads are missing. You may also find that you have left out a whole district or key location!

Secondly, our cognitive maps may be *distorted*; for example, the distances between locations may be too small or too great, and the relationships between road junctions may be simplified. Roads that meet at a junction tend to be represented as closer to right angles than they really are (Byrne, 1979).

Even though the roads at this junction do not meet at right angles, they are likely to be represented as such on a sketch map

187

Thirdly, our maps are *disproportionate*: we tend to exaggerate the size of places that we know well or prefer. Thus Milgram and Jodelet (1976) found that participants overestimated the size of their own neighbourhoods compared to other districts of the city, while Moar (1978) found that Glasgow residents overestimated distances in Scotland compared to those in England (see p.185). Pinheiro (1998) found that the appearance and size of countries on students' sketch maps of the world were related to factors such as military and economic power as well as their actual size. Seibert and Anooshian (1993) reported that participants omitted from their sketch maps areas or landmarks that they did not like. Look back at your own sketch map. What is more likely to be missing from your version – the pub, the church, the police station, the recycling centre, the shops or a dark alley?

Finally, we may *augment* our maps; that is, add non-existent features to them. For example, we may put in a set of traffic lights at a junction we know to be dangerous, even though there are none there. Appleyard (1970) cites an example of an engineer adding a railway line to his sketch map even though there was no such line in the real world. He had linked a mining port and a steel mill, a logical but incorrect assumption. This enables us to recognise another potential problem with the use of sketch maps as a measure of cognitive maps; people may lack actual geographical knowledge but make correct inferences, leading to augmentations that are accurate. This means that individuals are inappropriately credited for aspects of their maps that are the result of augmentation rather than experience with the environment. For example, I may imagine that two bridges cross the same river, so I might join the river up between these two locations. I may be correct, but I could just as easily be wrong: the accuracy of my map would be accidental.

Individual differences in cognitive maps

Animal species show a huge variation in their ability to use cognitive maps. This is not surprising, as their varied lives will place different adaptive advantages on the ability to remember specific locations. One interesting example is the difference between two closely related species, the meadow and prairie voles, and the influence of sex on this difference. Male meadow voles (*Microtus pennsylvanicus*) occupy larger territories than females, so place greater demands on their cognitive maps and have a larger hippocampus. The male and female prairie vole (*M. Ochrogaster*), however, share a territory. Gaulin and Fitzgerald (1989) compared the males and females of each species and found, as expected, that male meadow voles, but not prairie voles, were better at learning a maze (see the accompanying graph).

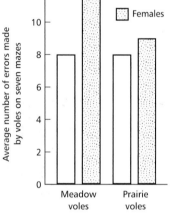

Source: Gaulin and Fitzgerald (1989)

Gaulin and Fitzgerald (1989) compared the errors made by male and female voles in a maze. As predicted, the prairie voles, which share a home range, made similar errors, but in the case of the meadow vole, where the male's territory is four times that of the female, the males made significantly fewer errors. This shows that animals that have evolved to occupy larger territories – therefore placing greater demands on their spatial memories – have a larger hippocampus and make fewer errors

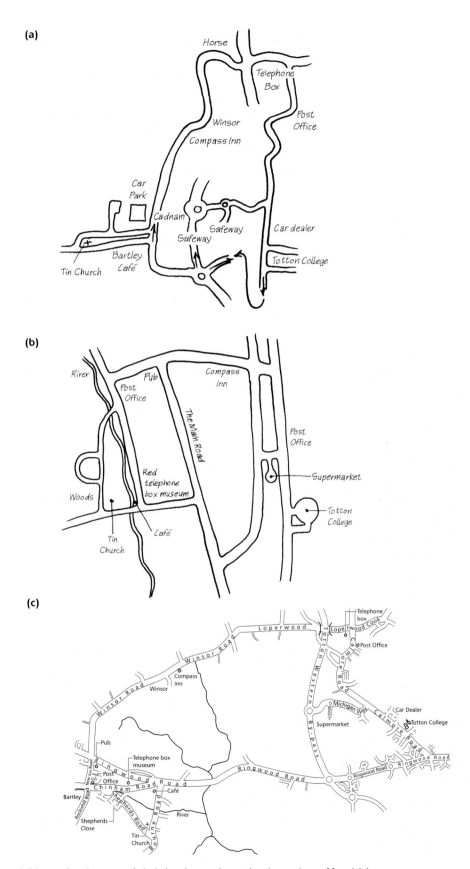

Maps (a) and (b) are sketch maps of their local area drawn by the authors. Map (c) is an accurate representation of the same district. What errors can you identify?

Like voles, humans seem to differ in their hippocampal volume, as suggested by the findings of Maguire *et al.* (2000).

research now

clever cabbies

Maguire, E.A., Gadian, D.G., Johnsrude, I.S., Good, C.D., Ashburner, J., Frackowiak, R.S. and Frith, C.D. (2000) Navigation-related structural changes in the hippocampi of taxi drivers. *Proceedings of the National Academy of Sciences, USA*, 97, 4398–403

Aim: One of the aims of this study was to examine whether London cab drivers have an increased hippocampal volume the longer they have been in the occupation.

Method: The taxi drivers had their hippocampal volumes recorded using a brain scan and they were asked how long they had been taxi drivers. These two measures were then correlated.

Results: Maguire *et al.* found a strong positive correlation: the longer the participants had worked as taxi drivers, the larger their hippocampus.

Conclusion: These results suggest that hippocampal volume is related to experience of navigation. Unlike the situation in voles, where differences between sexes and species are likely to be the product of evolution, this cannot be the case for taxi drivers. The individual differences between drivers seem to be directly related to their experience of navigating around the capital in their cabs. Of course, as these data are correlational, it is equally possible that a cab driver with a larger hippocampus is better and so stays in the job longer.

Differences between men and women

Gender differences in navigation are somewhat contentious. Appleyard's (1970) research in Venezuela found that males' cognitive maps were slightly more accurate and extensive, but concluded that this was a consequence of greater familiarity with the city. Other research has suggested that, while there are few differences in accuracy, men's and women's maps seem to differ in style. Sketch maps produced by women seem to focus on landmarks and districts, whilst those of men are based on paths (see, for example, McGuinness and Sparks, 1979; Galea and Kimura, 1993). Research has also shown that women may know more information about a district than they include on their sketch maps (McGuinness and Sparks, 1979; Ward *et al.*, 1986).

Self-reports by men and women also reveal differences in their reliance on way-finding information. Lawton (1996) conducted an indoor way-finding exercise in an unfamiliar building (the Economics Department of a university) with psychology undergraduates. She found that men preferred orientation strategies that use global references, such as compass points or the position of the sun. Women reported using route strategies, relying on local references such as sequences of left and right turns and landmarks. As a consequence, the removal of local cues to position affects way-finding women more than men, as demonstrated by Sandstrom *et al.* (1998) using a virtual maze.

Harrell *et al.* (2000) investigated differences in the way that students directed visitors around their university campus. They found that men provided more complete sketch maps but they were no more likely than women to include landmarks or labelled buildings. The men were also more confident and willing to lead visitors to their destinations. Lawton (1996) found that the women showed greater spatial anxiety when asked to rate how they would feel in situations such as 'finding your way out of a complex arrangement of offices that you have visited for the first time'. Schmitz (1997) obtained similar results with a sample of 10–17-year-olds, with girls showing higher anxiety and slower way-finding in a walk-through maze. So differences in way-finding performance may be affected by emotions or confidence, as well as by navigational ability.

Older women know how to get there, but can't tell where they are

By Alexandra Frean and Alan Hamilton

You know the scene. He's driving, she's got the map. Before you know it, they're hopelessly lost. Male road rage ensues.

New research published today suggests that men should be more understanding of their female navigators, who are prisoners of their hormones. Once a woman has passed the menopause, her map-reading skills are likely to improve.

But there is a down side. The older woman may be better at finding her way to a given destination but she is less likely to recognise where she is once she gets there. Having experimented with rhesus monkeys, the American Psychological Association suggests that the decline in oestrogen levels associated with the menopause can improve the spatial memory skills needed for tasks such as reading maps or negotiating a maze.

Six old monkeys aged 19 to 27, who had their ovaries removed, were compared with eight monkeys of the same age with intact ovaries, the main source of oestrogen, as well as a control group of five young monkeys. Rhesus monkeys were used because they share numerous cognitive and physiological characteristics with humans. Researchers at

Emory University in Atlanta, Georgia, and Boston University gave the monkeys tasks that tested their visual recognition and spatial memory.

No monkey, however, was asked to drive a car, plot a route across Los Angeles or tell a Tesco from an Arndale Centre. The older monkeys with no ovaries were marginally more impaired than their intact cousins in object recognition tests but significantly better in the spatial memory tests. In other words, they could get to the supermarket but once inside might not be able to tell Sainsbury's from Safeway.

Agnes Lacreuse, of Emory University and co-author of the study, said the results suggested that the absence of oestrogen may be protecting the older monkeys with no ovaries against the decline in spatial memory which goes with age.

She added that high oestrogen levels during the menstrual cycle had previously been associated with impaired spatial performance in young women. 'This may generalise to human females and suggest that prolonged absence of the ovaries may prevent or lessen age-related decline in certain aspects of spatial memory.'

Dr Lacreuse said that the findings, published in *Behavioural Neuroscience*, may have important implications for the design of hormonal replacement therapies for post-menopausal women.

Are hormones responsible for gender differences in navigation?

Groen *et al.* (2000) investigated gender differences in brain activation during visuospatial navigation. Using MRI, participants were studied as they searched for a way out of a complex three-dimensional virtual-reality maze. Although activation during navigation was identified in six different brain areas, these were not the same areas for men and women. In males, the left hippocampus showed distinct activation, while in females the right parietal and right prefrontal cortex were consistently activated. This has provided a neural basis for the well-established gender differences observed in spatio-cognitive performance.

In general, men seem to be better at navigating through virtual environments than women, but this may be a consequence of their greater experience with computer games, rather than reflecting a real-world difference in way-finding ability (Moffat *et al.*, 1998). Astur *et al.* (1998) demonstrated significant gender differences in ability to navigate in a virtual Morris water maze and found that the men had greater experience with games that had computer graphics similar to the task. Nevertheless, they concluded that gender, rather than computer game experience, was responsible for this difference.

Differences between men's and women's navigational ability may also depend on more general spatial skills. Malinowski (2001) replicated typical findings showing that men outperform women on tests of mental rotation. For example, they are better at judging whether an object that appears to have been turned in three-dimensional space is in fact the same or is a mirror image.

research now

finding our way in the real world

Malinowski, J.C. (2001) Mental rotation and real-world wayfinding. *Perceptual Motor Skills*, 29, 19–30

Aim: There is almost no evidence to suggest that the well known gender differences in spatial ability relate to real-world abilities, such as finding your way around a strange place. This study therefore aimed to test whether differences in spatial ability relate to navigational competence.

Method: Two hundred and eleven military college students were tested on two tasks; a measure of spatial ability (a mental rotation test measuring whether the participant can make accurate judgements about visual objects turned in three-dimensional space) and a test of navigational skill (a 6 km orienteering task).

Results: Mental rotation ability correlated positively with way-finding performance and typical gender differences were found on the spatial ability task, with men scoring higher than women on average, although some women performed as well as men.

Conclusion: The results suggest that while the spatial skills demonstrated by mental rotation may be important to way-finding in men, they may not be so essential for effective way-finding in some women; they must be using strategies related to other skills.

Familiarity

One of the most significant factors affecting the accuracy of our cognitive map is our familiarity with the environment and so individual differences arise due to differences in how well people know the locality. Sketch maps of familiar areas thus tend to be more detailed and accurate (see, for example, Appleyard, 1970), so participants who have been resident in an area for longer produce more detailed sketch maps. These also tend to be of a spatial nature compared to the more sequential maps produced by newcomers to the area. Evans *et al.* (1981) found that, as time progresses, our maps develop from a focus on nodes and paths to inclusion of landmarks as an area becomes more familiar. Therefore, it is not surprising that children's cognitive maps tend to include fewer landmarks than adults' maps (Bell *et al.*, 2001). The importance of familiar landmarks in navigation is supported by work with animals. Prados *et al.* (1999) found that rats pre-exposed to the location of landmarks were quicker to learn to swim to a hidden platform in a Morris milk maze. However, if the landmarks were moved during pre-exposure, the rats were slower to learn to find the platform. The stability of spatial relationships between landmarks is important if they are to assist in navigation.

Of course, our familiarity with our environment does not have to be visual: other cues may also assist our way-finding. Sommer (1998) describes the importance of auditory cues to navigation for a blind student shopping at a co-operative where the range of noises typical of different locations helped his orientation compared to the 'muzak' played in every aisle of commercial supermarkets.

Abu-Obeid (1998) investigated the way-finding ability of students at the Jordan University of Science and Technology (JUST), because they complained that they couldn't get to lectures on time as they kept getting lost around the campus! The JUST campus consists of a grid-like layout, with regular, continuous and symmetrical buildings. The study aimed to compare way-finding in repetitive and non-repetitive environments, and to suggest solutions to navigational problems experienced in repetitive environments such as JUST. Students from JUST were compared to those from two other universities with different, less repetitive campus designs. Students from each university were tested on tasks measuring abstract imagery (for example, drawing a route map) and scenographic imagery (for example, putting photographs of a route in order). It was found that familiarity with the *type* of environment may also affect way-finding ability; participants from JUST (with the grid-patterned, repetitive layout) made more errors on the scenographic imagery task than students from the other universities.

The findings suggest that pictorial information, from variety in the shape, texture, contours and entrances of buildings, helps to differentiate landmarks. Therefore, the way-finding problems at JUST may arise as a result of insufficient visually memorable cues to aid the building of an effective 'environmental image' or cognitive map. Thus, to improve way-finding in repetitive environments, distinguishing features need to be added to enable people to separate otherwise similar areas of their locality.

Another factor that affects familiarity with the local environment is socio-economic status (SES); in Ramadier and Moser's (1998) study, higher-SES participants drew more thorough maps than those of lower SES. This may arise because wealthier people have a greater opportunity to experience the environment, and perhaps because they are more likely to be driving than walking or using public transport, another factor that increases the accuracy of our maps (Appleyard, 1970; Bell *et al.*, 2001).

for and against

cognitive maps as an explanation for human navigation

+ The concept of cognitive maps can explain the ability to recall routes and select detours when a path is obstructed.

+ Cognitive maps seem to hold information on both routes and landmarks.

– Individual differences in cognitive maps may in part explain gender differences in navigation and the effects of familiarity on accuracy of way-finding.

– The possession of a cognitive map is not in itself sufficient to account for all of our spatial abilities.

Way-finding

Possession of a cognitive map may neither be necessary for nor guarantee successful *way-finding*, the process of navigating through an environment. We may use published maps, ask others for directions, or obtain other experience or information to help us to find our way. In the absence of these, or an ability to understand them, we may become lost. In reality, this is relatively rare. We may indeed 'lose ourselves', but this tends to be short-lived. By keeping moving until we find somewhere familiar, or by returning to a known location, we can re-establish effective way-finding.

A cognitive map needs only to provide a path with appropriate nodes in order to be effective in enabling us to engage in successful way-finding along a single predetermined journey. However, if we wish to take alternative routes or find our way to new locations, we would need a more sophisticated cognitive map with landmarks and networks of paths, or we could seek further navigational aids. How do we use the available information to find our way?

Action plans

According to Gärling *et al.* (1986), way-finding is a decision-making process that operates through a four-step action plan:

- determine the location
- localise the destination
- select a route
- decide how to travel.

This model suggests that we pre-plan our behaviour in the environment, rehearsing the journey that we will make.

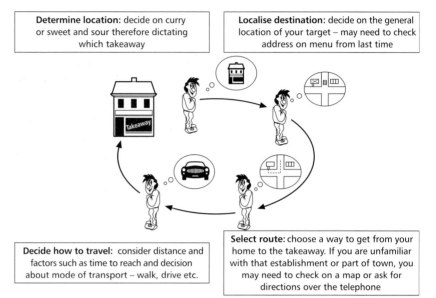

Determine location: decide on curry or sweet and sour therefore dictating which takeaway

Localise destination: decide on the general location of your target – may need to check address on menu from last time

Decide how to travel: consider distance and factors such as time to reach and decision about mode of transport – walk, drive etc.

Select route: choose a way to get from your home to the takeaway. If you are unfamiliar with that establishment or part of town, you may need to check on a map or ask for directions over the telephone

Gärling *et al.* (1986) proposed an action planning model of way-finding

Adapted from: Bell et al. (2001)

Action plans may be spatially asymmetrical; that is, we may plan journeys such that we leave by one route and return via another. The author, for example, travels to work past fields and forest, but returns home along the shortest route. Such route asymmetries may be governed by practical matters such as traffic flow at different times of day or by *'road climbing'*, a phenomenon described by Bailenson *et al.* (1998) such that people prefer routes that are initially long and straight (even if they cover a much greater total distance).

Assisting way-finding

Even with cognitive maps and action plans, we may still need assistance. What else can be done to help the navigator to find his or her way?

Characteristics of the physical environment

Gärling *et al.* (1984) have identified three features that contribute to successful navigation. *Differentiation* is the extent to which different parts of the environment are similar or distinguishable. Evans *et al.* (1982) demonstrated that buildings with high differentiation, such as ones that stood alone or were of an unusual shape, were remembered better. So, if buildings differ in appearance we can differentiate them, making way-finding more effective. If all the buildings look the same, we are more likely to get lost. Multi-storey cars parks in which the floors are colour coded have higher differentiation, so that finding your car is made easier.

Way-finding is also facilitated by a high degree of *visual access*; that is, being visible from different perspectives. In a hilly town we are likely to be able to obtain different views of buildings and streets, increasing visual access. Conversely, underground, such as in car parks or particularly on tube trains, our visual access is limited, and thus it is difficult to assimilate information about the relationships between locations.

How difficult an area is to understand in terms of the amount of detail and its intricacy is referred to as the *complexity of spatial layout*. Way-finding is hampered in environments with a very complicated spatial layout. Within a building this may result from having several floors, unpredictable interconnections both across and between floors and a different floor plan at each level. Complex spatial layouts such as this may be encountered in large shopping centres. Since it may also be difficult to gain a high degree of visual access, and because shop fronts are all essentially similar, lowering differentiation, it may be very difficult to learn our way around shopping centres.

Maps

A map offers a bird's-eye view of an area, providing us with *survey knowledge*; that is, spatial information about locations and distances. This can allow us to acquire a sufficient understanding of the environment for successful way-finding. However, the information on a map is not necessarily useful. Have you seen 'you are here' maps, such as are provided as town plans in holiday destinations? A common experience is to come away knowing just that; 'I am here'... but where is *here*? Unless the map has enabled you to locate yourself in the surrounding environment, you are no better off. Butler *et al.* (1993) found that maps were less effective than signs in assisting people to navigate around a complex building: maps take longer to study and have to be remembered, whereas signs are instant. Similarly, in a study of way-finding errors made by drivers, Burns (1998) suggested that problems could be alleviated by improving road signs.

Implications for improving maps

Levine (1982) and Levine *et al.* (1984) have suggested strategies for improving the usefulness of 'you are here' maps. To aid their navigation, users need to know where they are in relation to the map. This can be achieved if they can correctly identify a minimum of two features both on the map and in the environment. This is called *structure-matching* and it enables users to place themselves accurately on the map. For example, a 'you are here' dot may pinpoint your position along a road running down the map. However, without indicators of direction, such as buildings that are both visible in the environment and appear on the map, it would be impossible to decide whether your side of the pavement was to the left or right of the map – you would be unable to navigate.

Many passengers travelling from north to south prefer to hold their maps upside down to assist navigation. This restores the map to its correct *orientation*; that is, it achieves direct correspondence between the map and the real world – what is ahead on the road is 'up' on the map (*forward-up equivalence*) and features to the left on the map are on the left-hand side of the road. Levine *et al.* (1984) demonstrated experimentally that if way-finding maps are not displayed with forward-up equivalence, they are misleading and will disrupt way-finding even when people are made aware of the non-equivalence. Levine *et al.* also found that the presentation of maps in airports and offices often fails to achieve forward-up equivalence. The consequences of this could range from mild inconvenience or delay to a serious threat to life in emergency evacuations.

Visual and virtual experiences

Clearly, being able to see features in the environment helps way-finding. Philbeck *et al.* (2001) demonstrated experimentally that visual previews of an environment assist accurate navigation even when subsequently navigating blindfold. Photographs of routes can help people to gain experience without having to see a new environment for themselves. Hunt (1984) compared the way-finding skills of elderly people in an unfamiliar building. One group were taken on a tour around the building; another were shown photographs of locations in the same order as experienced by those who visited the site, and saw a three-dimensional model of the internal and external layout; and a third, control group, had no prior experience. On-location tasks revealed that both experimental groups had superior navigational abilities to the control group. Thus simulations, as well as actual experience, can assist in way-finding. It is interesting to note that while both groups could follow known routes successfully, the simulation group were superior at finding their way to new locations. This may be because exposure to the scale model provided more information that could be used in developing a cognitive map of the area than the tour.

what's new?

way-finding in virtual space

One new approach to testing people's way-finding ability is to use computer models of environments. Sophisticated computer graphics can be used to simulate 'virtual environments' through which participants can navigate – you may already be familiar with this if you have played games such as ' Tomb Raider'.

Janzen *et al.* (2001) tested participants' ability to find their way through a virtual maze when provided with either a field perspective (a view as if the person were in the scene) or an observer perspective (a bird's-eye view). A third group of participants saw the field perspective, but were asked mentally to transform this into an observer perspective during the tasks. The participants learned a route through the maze (see illustrations (a) below) and could find a new path around an obstruction. The participants were also asked to draw sketch maps of

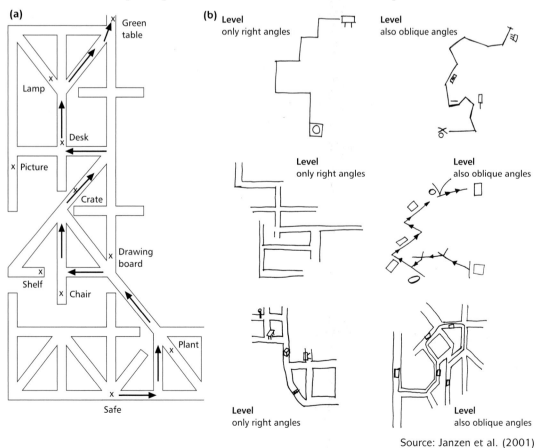

Source: Janzen et al. (2001)

the virtual environment (see illustration b). Participants who saw a bird's-eye view of the maze made fewer errors than those with a field perspective but the 'transformation' group drew the best maps. There were no gender differences in number of errors or time taken, although men drew more elaborate sketch maps than women.

Gamberini and Bussolon (2001) discuss the problems for users of virtual environments (such as used in games and metaworlds on the Internet) and hypertext (for example, the World Wide Web). A common problem is disorientation; users have difficulty reaching specific locations and remembering paths. This, Gamberini and Bussolon suggest, is caused by difficulties with forming a cognitive map of the destinations visited. One way to assist people is illustrated by the *Percepta* system, which allows people to utilise the cognitive systems of navigation that are used in the real world. The Percepta virtual museum is a virtual environment of visual illusions and effects. As one explores the galleries, the spatial dimension represented by the virtual environment accompanies the navigator, so that spatial, perceptual and cultural landmarks from the museum can be used to construct a detailed cognitive path. The importance of landmarks to spatial cognition was demonstrated by Werner and Schmidt (1999), who showed that, even when *imagining* locations, information 'ahead of you' was easier to access than information about spatial locations 'behind you'.

Developing maps without actual spatial experience, be they of geographical locations or abstract ideas, is difficult. Computers may offer new resources to help in way-finding for the visually impaired, for whom cognitive map development cannot be based on visual landmarks. Loomis *et al.* (2001) describe the development of a portable, global positioning systems (GPS)-based navigation system. This was tested with blind participants, who could use an acoustic information system for route guidance.

Despite the potential problems, cognitive map development has been demonstrated in entirely non-spatial situations. For example, you may have the equivalent of a cognitive map to guide you through a complex assignment. You may be able to identify 'routes' (your action plan), 'landmarks' (sub-goals in the completion of the task) and you may even be able to take 'detours' (short-cuts such as borrowing someone else's work or asking your tutor when you get stuck). The importance of such non-spatial 'cognitive maps' has been tested in real-life settings. Nair (2001) studied the effectiveness of problem-solving behaviour in managers of a factory in India. Those managers with the most complex cognitive maps of the issues had the greatest ability to solve complex simulated problems.

Magnetoreception

Evidence from animals suggests that one important source of information about way-finding is the use of an internal compass that detects the Earth's magnetic field, a process called *magnetoreception*. This is supported by physiological, anatomical and behavioural studies. Beason (1989) has found a compound called magnetite in the brains of a species of migrating bird (the bobolink, *Dolichonyx oryzivorus*). It is an iron-containing substance that is magnetic and is located in the ethmoidal region (behind the nose). When Beason placed microelectrodes in the brain of anaesthetised birds and altered the magnetic field around them, the neurones in this region responded. Although it is as yet unclear how these neurones might use this information, magnetoreception does appear to make a significant contribution to the navigational skills of many birds, such as pigeons (Larkin and Keeton, 1976; Wallcott and Brown, 1989), bobolinks (Beason, 1989) and robins (Wiltschko and Wiltschko, 1988). Remarkably, evidence suggests that humans may have a similar facility to use magnetoreception.

In an investigation to assess the use of an innate magnetic sense by humans, Murphy (1989) tested the ability of schoolchildren aged between 4 and 18 to judge direction. In a quiet room in their school, each child was shown four objects used in place of compass directions (such as a desk or a picture, in order to make the task sufficiently easy and memorable for young children). Using a spinning chair, the children were rotated clockwise and then anticlockwise, before stopping at each compass point in a random order. Each child made one estimate for each compass direction.

A comparison of males and females showed that the girls aged from nine upwards performed significantly better than chance. Boys were less accurate, achieving better than chance only in the 13–14 age group. To establish whether this ability was dependent on detecting the Earth's magnetic field, Murphy tested 11–18-year-old girls in two conditions, with either a brass bar or a magnet attached to the side of the head. She found that the girls could reliably pinpoint compass directions in the 'brass bar' condition, but lost this ability in the 'magnet' condition. The magnets would have disrupted their interpretation of natural magnetic fields, thus limiting their ability to use this cue to position. The findings suggest that humans can indeed use magnetic information to judge orientation. This ability seems to be more effective in females, perhaps because males are taught to use other techniques and thus do not rely so heavily on this navigational strategy.

The scenic environment

The term *scenic environment* is used to refer to pleasing landscapes. If you recall or imagine beautiful scenery, what would it be like? A river bubbling between craggy rocks, or tree-clad hills as far as the eye could see, perhaps. One immediate question that this raises is whether judgements of natural beauty are universal: Do we all prefer the same kinds of scenic environment? Descriptive approaches to answering this question based on the opinions of experts such as landscape architects suggest that there are indeed general characteristics that people prefer. *Natural* landscapes are preferred over those affected by human activity.

(a)

(b)

High-contrast natural scenes (a) generally receive more positive evaluations than low-contrast man-made ones (b)

Another factor judged to be an indicator of natural beauty is *contrast*; for example, scenes with obvious differences in colour are preferred, and thus we find dark hills with snowy peaks and purple heather against a backdrop of green trees appealing. Colour, shape, forms and textures could all contribute to creating contrast in an environment.

interactive angles

For this task you need either to create descriptions of scenes or find photographs (magazines such as *National Geographic* and Sunday supplements are a good starting place, or you could access a photo library on the Internet). Obtain a sufficient range to have an equal number of natural landscapes (such as beaches, deserts, forests, moors and cliffs) and man-made landscapes (for example, houses, shops, industrial sites, factories and mines). Ask two groups of participants to rate the scenes, one group judging contrast and the other scenic beauty. What differences would you predict between ratings of contrast and scenic beauty for the two types of environment?

Psychologists have also contributed to the study of scenic evaluation through empirical approaches. Landscape assessments conducted by psychologists have focused on measurable variables, such as the existence of water or vegetation in the scene, that may help to predict people's preferences. Evidence suggests that these environmental features do affect liking for a scene. For example, Herzog and Chernick (2000) explored the relationship between perceived tranquillity and danger in urban and natural environments. Participants were shown photographs of environments such as fields and forests, and rated these to be more tranquil and less dangerous than the urban settings. In addition, they found that in both natural and urban scenes, the participants were more likely to identify 'open' scenes (where their view was unobstructed) and 'natural' scenes (ones with some foliage or vegetation) as higher in tranquillity and lower in danger.

Real et al. (2000) studied factors affecting the perceived scenic quality of 31 different landscape types, including beaches, cliffs, islands, lakes, canyons, waterfalls, rivers, mountains, rocks, forests and grasslands. The participants preferred landscapes that contained water, did not appear to have been transformed by human intervention, were 'powerful' (for instance, rugged) and that, in general, showed little evidence of human presence.

Therefore, Herzog and Chernick (2000) and Real et al. (2000) have – in common with many researchers before them – identified physical, perceptual and cognitive variables that can affect landscape choice. How could such universal preferences have arisen? Kaplan and Kaplan (1989) suggest that evolutionary factors may be responsible. One theory that could explain the adaptive advantage of particular landscape preferences is the concept of *affordance*. Gibson (1979) suggests that some features of the environment offer – that is, 'afford' – us vital resources such as food or shelter. We may have evolved preferences for particular landscape features (Heerwagen and Orians, 1993) or tree shapes (Summit and Sommer, 1999) because their characteristics offered better potential for survival than alternative environments. So, our *biophilia*, or need for contact with nature (Wilson, 1984), may be an example of biological preparedness (for a discussion of preparedness in relation to phobias, see Jarvis et al., 2000). The converse of biophilia is *biophobia*, in which we tend to fear natural objects and situations, such as snakes, spiders, heights and the dark, more than artificial ones (see, for example, Ohman et al., 1976). This provides further evidence for the evolutionary influence on our environmental preferences.

How might judgements of environmental preference be made? To answer this question, general models of aesthetics can be applied to the environment. Berlyne (1974) proposed four factors that contribute to our judgements of aesthetics:

- *complexity* – the variety of components in an environment

- *novelty* – the extent to which the components of the scene are new to us

- *incongruity* – whether there is a mismatch between features of the environment and their context

- *surprisingness* – the extent to which our preconceptions about the environment are contradicted.

In addition, Berlyne proposed that our aesthetic judgements can be placed along two dimensions. The *uncertainty–arousal* dimension suggests that as uncertainty increases so does arousal, while *hedonic tone* (degree of pleasant feelings) changes along an inverted U: at low levels of uncertainty, hedonic tone is low; it then rises with increasing uncertainty but falls again when uncertainty is very high. Together, these dimensions suggest that we should prefer environments that provide an intermediate level of arousal. Since the above four factors could generate uncertainty about an environment, they should be present in moderation in preferred landscapes, thus achieving an optimal level of stimulation.

Viewers do seem to be sensitive to the complexity of the visual environment. Patsfall *et al.* (1995) showed participants 63 photographic slides of landscapes with vegetation in the foreground, middleground and background, to be rated for scenic beauty. The middle and background vegetation in the centre of the photograph were important contributors to perceived scenic beauty. So, in addition, was foreground vegetation on the right of the picture. To determine whether this was a right–left bias, all of the images were presented to different participants with the slides reversed. This resulted in a reversal of the preference to vegetation on the left; clearly (although coincidentally) there were more photographs that were indeed aesthetically pleasing with vegetation on one particular side! Patsfall *et al.* concluded that the viewers were sensitive to the foreground content and its position in the scene. Such a high degree of perceptual analysis of images suggests that complexity is one feature that makes natural scenes attractive.

One problem with applying Berlyne's model to natural scenes is that it is difficult to see why artificial environments with equivalent levels of complexity, novelty, incongruity and surprisingness are not as attractive. An information-processing approach (see, for example, Kaplan, 1975) suggests that, in terms of evolution, people needed to be able to process information in order to survive. It would thus be adaptive to prefer environments that facilitate our ability to see clearly (for example, openness) and that we understand (for example, of moderate complexity). Kaplan (1987) proposed four components that contribute to scenic appreciation:

- *coherence* – whether the parts of the environment seem to be organised

- *legibility* – the distinctiveness that affords understanding of the scene

- *complexity* – the number and variety of components in the environment

- *mystery* – the extent to which the scene suggests hidden information.

In each case, the greater the extent of the factor, the greater is the preference for the scene.

(a)   (b)

Complexity (a) and mystery (b) are two components that contribute to our appreciation of a scene

If environmental preferences were adaptive, some similarities would be expected across cultures, as adaptive choices should persist regardless of cultural differences such as in architecture. Hull and Revell (1995) found some similarities between Balinese people and tourists visiting Bali from other nations (mainly Australia and the USA). Both groups demonstrated preferences for natural, green, open landscapes, which supports the idea of an evolutionary determinant in scenic appreciation.

With respect to information-processing, there were, however, some cross-cultural differences in landscape perception demonstrated by Hull and Revell (1995), which seem to be a function of understanding. They found that the Western tourists' misinterpretation or ignorance of the meaning attached to some aspects of the Balinese landscape could explain the differences. Balinese culture stresses public access, so the Balinese valued the scenes with appropriate roads, tracks or orientations of buildings more highly than did the tourists. Similarly, Balinese house-building follows highly valued, traditional rules, and thus the landscapes containing such buildings, rather than non-traditional ones, would be preferred by Balinese participants but not Western tourists. Therefore, differences in the perceived scenic quality of the environments may arise from differences in capacity to understand information that are affected by culture.

Whilst there are clear similarities between the models of Berlyne and Kaplan, the Kaplan model focuses on two distinct aspects. These are the informational properties of the environment (such as coherence and legibility) that enable us to make sense of the scene, and involvement with the environment (such as through complexity and mystery) which engages us and motivates us to explore and understand the environment. While mystery can be attractive in a natural scene, it is perceived to be threatening in an urban environment (Herzog and Miller, 1998). Consider how you might feel differently towards a winding river disappearing out of sight compared to a dark passageway between high buildings.

Shocking Plans

Eyesores or eye candy? Pylons often provoke strong opinions. Now a new breed of electricity carriers could change the landscape forever, says Sarah Shaddick

Electricity pylons have had a rotten press down the years. Deriding the towers as ugly monstrous giants, campaigners have called for cables to be buried underground. But now new voices can be heard, championing the humble pylon and even lauding its beauty.

The number of pylon enthusiasts in Britain – whose hobby involves model identification and collecting numbers from identity plates as well as admiring the structures – has mushroomed in the last few years since the release of the film *Among Giants*, starring Pete Postlethwaite and Rachel Griffiths in the role of pylon painters.

Fresh developments could yet see people flocking to the towers like birds – and birds really love their pylons, as enthusiasts are quick to tell their environmental antagonists. Foster and Partners, the award-winning company behind London's Millennium Bridge and the new Wembley Stadium, have designed an environmentally sensitive pylon.

Abandoning the conventional Christmas-tree configuration, they have adopted a minimal structure with cables neatly grouped in an open V-form. The result? An aesthetically-pleasing tower that could see even the most ardent pylophobes reaching for their binoculars.

Adapted from *Hotline*, 2000

So powerful is the effect of a positive landscape that investigations have sought to test the restorative properties of positively evaluated scenes. Ulrich (1979) showed that simply seeing scenes of nature help to relieve the stress experienced by students' examinations. The view does not even have to be spectacular. Ulrich (1984) subsequently investigated the effect on post-operative recovery for patients whose windows overlooked either a brick wall or some trees. Patients with a natural view recovered faster, needed fewer painkillers and suffered fewer post-operative complications. These effects may be the consequence of directing attention towards the scene and away from the source of stress. Ulrich *et al.* (1991) tested this by comparing physiological and psychological measures of stress during a two-stage experiment. First, participants watched an unpleasant video, followed by either natural or urban scenes. Those viewing natural environments reported feeling more positive and this was reflected in physiological measures of stress; they had lower blood pressure, skin conductance and muscle tension. The urban scenes did not induce stress recovery, nor were they associated with the lowered pulse rate (indicative of attention) associated with both the stressful and natural scenes. This effect may be mediated by the parasympathetic nervous system (see p.41). The natural scenes may assist recovery by diverting attention away from the cause of distress, allowing the parasympathetic nervous system to break the cycle of physiological arousal.

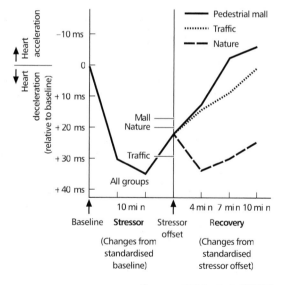

A stressful video reduces heart rate, as does one of nature, whereas an urban scene raises heart rate, which suggests that it is the least effective in drawing attention

Source: Ulrich et al. (1991)

In addition to reducing stress, natural environments may be able to enhance our experiences. Fredrickson and Anderson (1999) used a range of techniques including on-site observations, diaries and interviews to examine the qualitative aspects of a wilderness experience and its role as a source of spiritual inspiration. The participants were two groups of women on outdoor recreation trips to Boundary Waters, Minnesota, and the Grand Canyon, Arizona. Two key features of the environment that seemed to contribute to a meaningful wilderness experience which could act as spiritual inspiration were the expansiveness of the landscape and an awareness of the power of nature. Similarly, Frey Talbot and Kaplan (1995) reported that wilderness experiences provide people with benefits such as an enhanced ability to cope with daily challenges, feeling more considerate and open towards others and being able to prioritise in their own lives.

Finally, our knowledge of the factors that affect landscape preferences can be used to guide environmental preservation. It should be possible to use this knowledge to guide decisions such as restricting access to sites to prevent damage and limiting overspill from towns into countryside areas. The number of people seeking to enjoy natural resources such as national parks and forests is increasing and resources are reaching their limits (Mitchell, 1994). Even careful users may cause long-term damage to the environment, thus environmental management with recreation in mind is a necessity (Pitt and Zube, 1987). One consideration is the recreational carrying capacity (the maximum user density that a region can sustain) and the extent to which overcrowding damages both the natural resource and the outdoor experience. Stewart and Cole (2001) investigated how encountering other users affected the perceived quality of the experience for visitors to the Grand Canyon National Park. They found that most backpackers were disturbed by meeting other groups, although the effect was not great. It appears that the quality of a recreational experience may be affected by user density, but the findings described above do not justify the imposition of restrictions in the belief that this will result in a higher-quality experience. Therefore, in addition to economic, ecological and other constraints, locations need to balance the effects of environmental damage by people and the negative effects of crowding on the experience against the desirability of the area – more scenic landscapes will attract more users, potentially diminishing their effectiveness as a resource. For example, it has been necessary for caves such as those at Lascaux in France to be closed to the public to avoid damage to the cave paintings that they contain.

Some of the techniques discussed in Chapter 5 may be used to heighten people's awareness of the needs of the natural environment and to promote environmental preservation. One route to achieving this aim may be through *ecotourism*, the provision of exotic holidays to natural environments which is intended to assist in conservation efforts. Such schemes may seem counterproductive – adding strain to threatened areas – but they may be beneficial, both because they may be more environmentally responsible and because they offer a way to encourage people to think about their environment (Palmer, 1997). Direct evidence from a 10-year study by Frey Talbot and Kaplan (1995) suggests that exposure to natural environments encourages people to 'consume less' and develop a 'compelling interest in the world of nature'. They conclude that, as a result of wilderness experiences, people reject the belief that humans should dominate or 'control' natural forces, but instead become convinced that living with nature is both more appropriate and more satisfying.

The following are good sources of information about environmental cognition:

▶ **Palmer, C. (1997)** *Contemporary Ethical Issues: Environmental Ethics*. **Santa Babara, CA: ABC-Clio** – this has a short discussion of ecotourism and an extensive review of resources relating to environmental issues.

▶ **Bell, P.A., Greene, T.C., Fisher, J.D. and Baum, A. (2001)** *Environmental Psychology*, **5th edn. Fort Worth, TX: Harcourt College Publishers** – this text covers in depth the topics of cognitive maps and the scenic environment.

▶ **http://perso.infonie.fr/eh/** – this is an example of a virtual environment with navigational aids that are similar to those of the Percepta museum.

Conclusions

There is good evidence that both animals and humans use cognitive maps to provide an internal representation of their spatial environments. In humans, such maps seem to be built up from consistent elements – paths, edges, districts, nodes and landmarks. The benefits of a cognitive map are to allow navigation around the environment, particularly to make detours around obstructions, take short-cuts and to recall locations of specific objects or events. Evidence for brain structures involved in cognitive mapping points towards the hippocampus as a key area, although recent evidence suggests that cortical structures may also play a role. The various techniques for investigating cognitive maps each have advantages and disadvantages, but the simplest, using mazes and drawing sketch maps, are still often used. Our cognitive maps may contain many errors, as they are only representative of geographical space. They may be disproportionate and distorted, and they may be augmented with non-existent features. Individual differences between cognitive maps arise as a function of gender and familiarity.

The process of way-finding is assisted internally by our cognitive maps, action plans and magnetic compass orientation. External aids to way-finding include maps and virtual-reality environments. The scenic environment provides us with a source of pleasure and recreation, as well as a means of reducing stress. Our preference for natural scenes over urban ones may be related to features such as complexity, novelty, legibility, openness and mystery. Such scenes may be preferable because they resemble the environments that were safest in our evolutionary history.

1. Describe and evaluate cognitive maps as an explanation for human navigation.

2. Describe evidence that suggests that there are individual differences in people's way-finding abilities.

3. Discuss experimental evidence for the use of cognitive maps by animals.

4. Identify ways in which maps may hinder our way-finding. Suggest how these problems may be overcome.

5. Describe a model that attempts to explain our preference for the natural environment. To what extent is it successful?

6. Identify **one** role that the scenic environment may play in our lives. Discuss the evidence that this is effective and explain how this outcome may arise.

Glossary

Affordance The theory that some features of the environment offer or *afford* us vital resources such as food or shelter.

Amplitude The aspect of a wave form that is related to the absolute size of the stimulus. For sound, this is the volume or intensity and is the magnitude of the air pressure change.

Anonymity A state for an individual within a crowd where each person loses their sense of individuality.

Antecedent control A behavioural measure in which the intervention occurs before the behaviour arises. Antecedent procedures include education, attitude change and inducing or preventing behaviours by controlling the triggers which cause them to occur.

Appraisal A judgement about whether a potentially stressful situation is threatening, challenging or harmful.

Attitude An evaluation, with cognitive and affective components, that relates to a specific aspect of the world and which affects our behaviour in relation to that person, idea, object or issue.

Auditory adaptation The tendency of repeated or continuous sounds to appear less loud over time. As we habituate to the stimulus of the sound its apparent loudness decreases.

Auditory fatigue Occurs on exposure to intense sounds which cause a persistent reduction in apparent loudness.

Biodiversity The variety of living species on the Earth.

Biophilia The need for contact with nature.

Biophobia Our tendency to fear natural objects and situations, such as snakes, spiders, heights and the dark more than artificial ones.

Climate Refers to the 'average' weather conditions that a particular region or country has over a long period of time.

Climatological determinism The belief that the climate we are used to actually changes the behaviours we exhibit.

Cognitive map An internal representation that animals and humans develop about the spatial relationships within their environment.

Coherence A characteristic of the scenic environment indicating the extent to which the parts of the environment seem to be organised.

Comfortable Interpersonal Distance Scale A non-invasive method used to measure people's **personal space**.

Community environmental design Differs from **urban renewal** because these projects allow the current residents in the area to have an input in the redesign of the area.

Complexity The number and variety of components in the environment.

Consequent control A behavioural measure in which the intervention follows the behaviour to be changed. Consequent procedures can affect behaviours by using pleasant or unpleasant consequences (positive or negative reinforcement or punishment) to make their performance more or less likely or through the use of feedback.

Coping A person's efforts to minimise, control or tolerate environmental demands that are judged to exceed their resources to fight or avoid.

Crowd May be to refer to a large, cohesive gathering of individuals or to the act of coming together to form a tightly-spaced group. In addition, crowding is used to refer to the psychological perceptions associated with this increase in density.

Decibels (dB) A measure of **volume** (sound intensity).

Defensible space An area that we clearly mark out as being owned by ourselves. Other people should perceive the area as being clearly owned.

Deindividuation A process through which group members cease to pay attention to individuals as individuals so losing their self-consciousness and with it the belief that they are accountable for their own actions – moral responsibility shifts from the individual to the group.

Diffusion of responsibility Occurs in groups when an individual feels less accountable because there are other people around; the responsibility is shared (i.e. diffused) so no particular individual feels responsible.

Districts Aspects of a **cognitive map** that represent large spaces with a shared characteristic, such as Soho, the West End or an industrial estate.

Edges Aspects of a **cognitive map** that represent boundaries, e.g. walls of buildings or coastlines.

Emotion-focused coping Aims to manage the negative effects of stress on the individual.

Environmental disaster These are incidences when nature takes control and causes large amounts of damage or even death, for example a volcano erupting.

Forward-up equivalence A map orientation such that there is direct correspondence between the map and the real world – what is ahead on the road is 'up' on the map and features to the left on the map are on the left-hand side of the road.

Frequency The time between the peak of one wave and the next. For sound, frequency represents pitch; sound waves with a lower frequency are 'deeper'. Frequency is measured in Hertz or 'cycles per second'.

Global warming The gradual increase in temperature of the Earth's surface over many years that is believed to be in part the result of atmospheric pollution (see **greenhouse effect**).

Gouldian map An accurate base map used as a focus for experimental investigations of human cognitive maps.

Greenhouse effect Increased levels of carbon monoxide and other atmospheric pollutants act to trap heat close to the surface of the Earth.

Habituation The relative insensitivity to repeated stimuli such as monotonous sounds.

Hearing threshold The quietest sound that an individual can detect.

Hertz A measure of **frequency**, cycles per second.

Hippocampus An area of the midbrain, present in both hemispheres, with an involvement in the formation and storage of cognitive maps.

Impersonality A state in which individuals lose their appreciation of themselves and others as people.

Jet lag The fatigue experienced by air travellers as a consequence of crossing time zones which results in their circadian rhythm becoming desynchronised from the local zeitgebers.

Landmarks Aspects of a **cognitive map** that represent distinctive features used as reference points. These are generally visible from a distance e.g. the London Eye, Nelson's Column or a particular church spire.

Learned helplessness A failure to exert control over one's own situation even when it becomes possible, because prior learning has taught that attempts at control are not effective.

Legibility A characteristic of the **scenic environment** indicating the extent to which distinctiveness assists our understanding of the scene.

Loudness A measure of the perceived intensity of the sound. Loudness approximately doubles as **volume** increases ten-fold.

Magnetoreception A source of information about **way-finding** based on the use of an internal compass which detects the Earth's magnetic field.

Map A geographical representation of a spatial layout providing a 'birds'–eye view' of an area.

Morris milk maze A circular pool filled with murky water to prevent a swimming animal from locating a hidden platform by sight. It is used to test spatial memory.

Mystery The extent to which aspects of the **scenic environment** suggest hidden information.

Natural disaster See **Environmental disaster**

New Environmental Paradigm (NEP) A measure of environmental attitude that recognises how the relationship between people and the natural environment is changing from one of alienation and exploitation to one in which humans are an integral part of nature.

Nodes Aspects of a **cognitive map** that represent places that act as a focus for behaviour, e.g. town squares, roundabouts or major road junctions.

Noise Sounds which are unpleasant. The presence of a sound is necessary but not sufficient to produce noise; a noise must in addition be 'unwanted'.

Occupational noise The unpleasant sounds to which people are exposed in the workplace.

Ozone An oxygen molecule consisting of three, rather than two, atoms (O_3). It forms a layer high in the Earth's atmosphere that protects us from some of the harmful rays from the sun.

Paths Aspects of a **cognitive map** that represent shared conduits for travel e.g. footpaths and roads.

Personal space A 'bubble' that surrounds us that we do not like people to trespass within. The bubble changes according to the situation we find ourselves in. It helps regulate interactions we have with other people.

Personalisation The process of bringing personal belongings into work to make your work space an individual area. Items may include photographs or trinkets.

Pollution Contamination with poisonous or harmful substances.

Primary appraisal An initial impression of a potentially stressful situation which generates emotions in relation to the judgement.

Primary territory A type of **territory** where there is a high degree of occupation and perception of ownership. An example would be your house.

Problem-focused coping Aims to reduce the causes of stress.

Public territory A type of **territory** where there is a low degree of occupation and perception of ownership. An example would be an area on the beach.

Reappraisal This may follow the **secondary appraisal** of a potentially stressful situation, based on new information. This may reduce the judgement of a situation from stressful to benign or suggest that a previously innocent situation is threatening.

Road climbing Describes the route asymmetry demonstrated by people when they prefer routes that are initially long and straight even if this results in covering a much greater total distance.

Road-rage Occurs when aggressive behaviour towards other road users is displayed in the absence of any direct cause other than a perception of the traffic context.

Scenic environment Used to refer to aesthetically pleasing landscapes, generally natural rather than artificial ones.

Secondary appraisal Follows a **primary appraisal** and is the formation of an impression about one's ability to cope with the situation: a consideration of the possible options, the chances of successfully employing them and whether the action will work.

Secondary territory A type of **territory** where there is a medium degree of occupation and perception of ownership. An example would be your place in the classroom.

Sequential maps **Cognitive maps** that focus on **paths** and **nodes**, relating to journeys between places.

Sketch maps A technique for investigating **cognitive maps** in which a participant is asked to draw a plan of an environment in order to provide a representation of the individual's internal image.

Social contagion A theory suggesting that when individuals within a **crowd** become aroused they respond to one another by amplifying the intensity of their interactions.

Social density Refers to the density of the population as controlled by varying the number of individuals per unit area.

Sociofugal designs Designs that are used to keep people apart.

Sociopetal designs Designs that are used to promote interaction between people.

Sound The vibration of air. Sound intensity (**volume**) increases as the **amplitude** of the waves increases.

Spatial density Refers to the density of the population as controlled by varying the available space.

Spatial maps **Cognitive maps** that map and resemble a 'birds'–eye view' of a geographical area and emphasise spatial organisation.

Spatial zones Different zones of **personal space**. They include an intimate zone, a personal zone, a social zone and a public zone.

Subsonic jet An aircraft that cannot travel faster than the speed of sound but may still be very loud on take-off.

Suggestibility The tendency of individuals to become more responsive to the ideas of others, especially when these are proposed in an authoritative manner.

Supersonic jet An aircraft capable of flying faster than the speed of sound, such as Concorde. As a consequence of their design they are both loud on take-off and generate a sonic boom as the aircraft breaks the sound barrier. This is very loud on the ground but cannot be heard from within the aircraft.

Survey knowledge Spatial information about locations and distances such as is provided by a map.

Technological catastrophe Refers to incidents that are due to human factors (usually errors or mishaps) that may cause large-scale destruction.

Territory An area that you perceive you have ownership over.

Transportation noise The unpleasant sounds generated by motor vehicles, trains, aeroplanes and other means of transport.

Urban renewal Using the principles of Environmental Psychology (e.g. **defensible space**) to aid the development of run down areas in cities, usually in an attempt to reduce crime and vandalism.

Volume An increase in magnitude of vibration in the air (measured in decibels). Sounds increase in **volume** as the **amplitude** of the wave increases.

Way-finding The process of navigating through an environment using **cognitive maps**, navigational skills, maps, or any other available information.

Weather Refers to the temporary conditions under which we live (e.g. rain).

White noise Sound of a wide range of frequencies generated in an unpatterned way like the 'static' of an out-of-tune radio or television.

Wide band (broad band) noise Unwanted sound that is composed of a range of frequencies.

references

Abu-Obeid, N. (1998) Abstract and scenographic imagery: the effect of environmental form on wayfinding. *Journal of Environmental Psychology*, 18, 159–73

Acton, W.I. (1970) Speech intelligibility in a background noise and noise-induced hearing loss. *Ergonomics*, 13, 546–54

Aiello, J.R., Epstein, Y.M. and Karlin, R.A. (1975) Field experimental research in human crowding. Paper presented at the Eastern Psychological Association

Ajzen, I. (1985) From intentions to actions: a theory of planned behaviour. In Kuhl, J. and Beckmann, J. (eds) *Action Control: from Cognition to Behavior* (pp.11–39). Berlin: Springer-Verlag

Al-Kodmany, K. (1999) The art of community design: stimulation shared neighbourhood visions. In Mann, T. (ed.) *The Power of Imagination. Proceedings of the 30th annual conference of the Environmental Design Research Association* (pp.40–5). Edmond, OK: Environmental Design Research Association

Altman, I. (1975) *The Environment and Social Behaviour*. Monterey, CA: Brooks/Cole

Andersen, P.A. and Leibowitz, K. (1978) The development and nature of construct touch avoidance. *Environmental Psychology and Nonverbal Behaviour*, 1, 18–32

Anderson, B., Erwin, N., Flynn, D., Lewis, L. and Erwin, J. (1977) Effects of short-term crowding on aggression in captive groups of pigtail monkey. *Aggressive Behavior*, 3, 33–46

Andreoli, V. and Worchel, S. (1978) Effects of media, communicator, and message position on attitude change. *Public Opinion Quarterly*, 42, 59–70

Appleyard, D. (1970) Styles and methods of structuring a city. *Environment and Behavior*, 2, 101–17

Aragones, J.I. and Arredondo, J.M. (1985) Structure of urban cognitive maps. *Journal of Environmental Psychology*, 5, 197–212

Aronson, A. (1999) *The Social Animal*, 8th edn. New York: Worth/Freeman

Arnsten, A.F.T. (1998) The biology of being frazzled. *Science*, 280, 1711–12

Asmus, C.L. and Bell, P.A. (1999) Effects of environmental odor and coping style on negative affect, anger, arousal and escape. *Journal of Applied Social Psychology*, 29, 245–60

Astur, R.S., Ortiz, M.L. and Sutherland, R.J. (1998) A characterization of performance by men and women in a virtual Morris water task: a large and reliable sex difference. *Behavioral Brain Research*, 93, 185–90

Auliciems, A. and Barnes, A. (1987) Sudden infant deaths and clear weather in a subtropical environment. *Social Science and Medicine*, 24(1), 51–6

Auliciems, A. and Frost, D. (1989) Temperature and cardiovascular deaths in Montreal. *International Journal of Biometeorology*, 33(3), 151–6

Automobile Association (1995) Road Safety Unit: http://www.reportroadrage.co.uk/aastat.htm

Bailenson, J.N., Shum, M.S. and Uttal, D.H. (1998) Road climbing: principles governing asymmetric route choices on maps. *Journal of Environmental Psychology*, 18, 251–64

Balluz, L., Schieve, L., Holmes, T., Kiezak, S. and Malilay, J. (2000) Predictors of people's responses to a tornado warning: Arkansas, 1 March 1997. *Disasters*, 24(1), 71–7

Bamberg, S., Bein, W. and Schmidt, P. (1995) Wann steigen Autofather auf den Bus um? Oder: Lassen sich aus sozialpsychologischen Handlungstheorien praktische Massnahmen ableiten? In Diekmann, A. and Franzen, A. (eds) *Kooperatives Umwelthandeln. Modelle, Erfahrungen, Massnahmen* (pp.89–111). Chur, Switzerland: Rüegger

Banbury, S. and Berry, D.C. (1998) Disruption of office-related tasks by speech and office noise. *British Journal of Psychology*, 89, 499–517

Baron, R.M., Mandel, D.R., Adams, C.A. and Griffen, L.M. (1976) Effects of social density in university residential environments. *Journal of Personality and Social Psychology*, 34, 434–46

Bauer, R.A. (1970) Self-confidence and persuasibility: one more time. *Journal of Marketing Research*, 7, 256–8

Baum, A. and Valins, S. (1977) *Architecture and Social Behavior: Psychological Studies of Social Density*. Hilldale, NJ: Erlbaum

Beard, R.R. and Wertheim, G.A. (1967) Behavioral impairment associated with small doses of carbon monoxide. *American Journal of Public Health*, 57, 2012–22

Beason, R.C. (1989) Magnetic sensitivity and orientation in the bobolink. Paper presented at the Royal Institute of Navigation Conference

Bell, P.A., Greene, T.C., Fisher, J.D. and Baum, A. (1996) *Environmental Psychology*, 4th edn. Fort Worth, TX: Harcourt Brace College Publishers

Bell, P.A., Greene, T.C., Fisher, J.D. and Baum, A. (2001) *Environmental Psychology*, 5th edn. Orlando, FL: Harcourt College Publishers

Belojevic G., Slepcevic, V. and Jakovljevic, B. (2001) Mental performance in noise: the role of introversion. *Journal of Environmental Psychology*, 21, 209–13

Benewick, R. and Holton, R. (1987) The peaceful crowd: crowd solidarity and the Pope's visit to Britain. In Gaskill, G. and Benewick, R. (eds) *The Crowd in Contemporary Britain*. London: Sage

Berk, R. (1974) A gaming approach to crowd behaviour. *American Sociological Review*, 39, 355–73

Berlognghi, A.E. (1993) Understanding and planning for different spectator crowds. In Smith, R.A. and Dickie, J.F. (eds) *Engineering for Crowd Safety*. Amsterdam: Elsevier Science

Berlyne, D.E. (1974) *Studies in the New Experimental Aesthetics: Steps Toward an Objective Psychology of Aesthetic Appreciation*. New York: Halsted Press

Bertollini, R., Di Lallo, D., Mastroiacovo, P. and Perucci, C.A. (1990) Reduction of births in Italy after the Chernobyl accident. *Scandinavian Journal of Work and Environmental Health*, 16(2), 96–101

Bickman, L., Teger, A., Gabiele, T., McLaughin, C., Berger, M. and Sunaday, E. (1973) Dormitory density and helping behaviour. *Environment and Behavior*, 5, 465–90

Bleda, P. and Bleda, E. (1978) Effects of sex and smoking on reactions to spatial invasion at a shopping mall. *Journal of Social Psychology*, 104, 311–12

Blossom, N. (2000) Connections and collaborations to sustain the environment. *Proceedings of the 16th IAPS Conference, Paris, France (4–7 July)*, p.62

Bonnes, M. and Secchiaroli, G. (1995) *Environmental Psychology: a Psychosocial Introduction*. London: Sage

Borsky, P.N. (1969) Effects of noise on community behavior. In Ward, W.D. and Fricke, J.E. (eds) *Noise as a Public Health Hazard*. Washington, DC: American Speech and Hearing Association

Brandon, G. and Lewis, A. (1999) Reducing household energy consumption: a qualitative and quantitative field study. *Journal of Environmental Psychology*, 19, 75–85

Brannon, L. and Feist, J. (2000) *Health Psychology: an Introduction to Behavior and Health*. London: Wadsworth, Thomson Learning

Breckler, S.J. and Wiggins, E.C. (1989) On defining attitude and attitude theory: once more with feeling. In Pratkanis, A.R., Breckler, S.J. and Greenwald, A.G. (eds) *Attitude Structure and Function*. Hillsdale, NJ: Erlbaum

Breisacher, P. (1971) Neuropsychological effects of air pollution. *American Behavioral Scientist*, 14, 837–64

Brennen, T. (2001) Seasonal cognitive rhythms within the Arctic Circle: an individual differences approach. *Journal of Environmental Psychology*, 21, 191–9

Brickman, P., Rabinowitz, V.C., Karuza, J., Coates, D., Cohn, E. and Kidder, L. (1982) Models of helping and coping. *American Psychologist*, 37, 368–84

Brodsky, S.L., Hooper, N.E., Tipper, D.G. and Yates, S.B. (1999) Attorney invasion of witness space. *Law and Psychology Review*, 23, 49–68

Bromet, E.J., Goldgaber, D., Carlson, G., Panina, N., Golovakha, E., Gluzman, S.F., Gilbert, T., Gluzman, D., Lyubsky, S. and Schwartz, J.E. (2000) Children's well-being 11 years after the Chornobyl catastrophe. *Archives of General Psychiatry*, 57, 563–71

Bronzaft, A.L. and McCarthy, D.P. (1975) The effects of elevated train noise on reading ability. *Environment and Behavior*, 7, 517–27

Bronzaft, A.L., Ahern, K.D., McGinn, R., O'Connor, J. and Savino, B. (1998) Aircraft noise: a potential health hazard. *Environment and Behavior*, 30, 101–13

Brower, S., Dockett, K. and Taylor, R.B. (1983) Residents' perceptions of territorial features and perceived local threat. *Environment and Behaviour*, 15(4), 419–37

Bruins, J. and Barber, A. (2000) Crowding, performance and effect: a field experiment investigating mediating processes. *Journal of Applied Social Psychology*, 30, 1268–80

Brunson, L.N. (2000) Resident appropriation of defensible space in public housing: implications for safety and community. *Dissertation Abstracts International: Section B: The Sciences and Engineering*, 60(11-B), 5831

Buist, A.S., Johnson, L.R., Vollmer, W.M., Sexton, G.J. and Kanarek, P.H. (1983) Acute effects of volcanic ash from Mount Saint Helens on lung function in children. *American Review of Respiratory Disease*, 127(6), 714–19

Burgio, L., Scilley, K., Hardin, J.M., Hsu, C. and Yancey, J. (1996) Environmental 'white noise': an intervention for verbally agitated nursing home residents. *Journal of Gerontology: Psychological Sciences*, 51B, 364–73

Burns, P.C. (1998) Wayfinding errors while driving. *Journal of Environmental Psychology*, 18, 209–17

Butler, D.L., Acquino, A.L., Hissong, A.A. and Scott, P.A. (1993) Wayfinding by newcomers in a complex building. *Human Factors*, 35, 159–73

Byrne, R.W. (1979) Memory for urban geography. *Quarterly Journal of Experimental Psychology*, 31, 147–54

Calhoun, J.B. (1962) Population density and social pathology. *Scientific American*, 206, 139–48

Calhoun, J.B. (1971) Space and the strategy of life. In Esseer, A.H. (ed.) *Behavior and Environment: the Use of Space by Animals*. Bloomington, IN: University of Indiana Press

Carlson, L.D. (1961) Human performance under different thermal loads. Technical Report No. 61-43. Aerospace Medical Center, School of Aviation, Brooks AFB, TX, USA

Carmichael, K.D. (2000) Using a metaphor in working with disaster survivors. *Journal of Specialists in Group Work*, 25(1), 7–15.

Cassidy, T. (1992) Commuting-related stress: consequences and implications. *Employee Counselling Today*, 4(2), 15–21

Cassidy, T. (1997) *Environmental Psychology: Behaviour and Experience in Context*. Hove: Psychology Press

Cassidy, T. (1999) *Stress, Cognition and Health*. London: Routledge

Cave, S. (1998) *Applying Psychology to the Environment*. London: Hodder & Stoughton

Chaiken, S. (1979) Communicator physical attractiveness and persuasion. *Journal of Personality and Social Psychology*, 37, 1387–97

Chaiken, S. (1987) The heuristic model of persuasion. In Zanna, M.P., Olson, J.M. and Herman, C.P. (eds) *Social Influence: the Ontario Symposium* (vol. 5, pp.3–40). Hillsdale, NJ: Erlbaum

Chaiken, S. and Eagly, A.H. (1976) Communication modality as a determinant of message persuasiveness and message comprehensibility. *Journal of Personality and Social Psychology*, 34, 605–14

Chan, Y.K. (1999) Density, crowding and factors intervening in their relationship: evidence from a hyper-dense metropolis. *Social Indicators Research*, 48, 103–24

Channing, C.E., Hughes, B.O. and Walker, A.W. (2001) Spatial distribution and behaviour of laying hens housed in an alternative system. *Applied Animal Behaviour Science*, 72, 335–45

Chapko, M.K. and Solomon, M. (1976) Air pollution and recreation behaviour. *Journal of Social Psychology*, 100, 149–50

Chemtob, C.M., Tomas, S., Law, W. and Cremniter, D. (1997) Postdisaster psychosocial intervention: a field study of the impact of debriefing on psychological distress. *American Journal of Psychiatry*, 154(3), 415–17

Christian, J.J. (1955) The effects of population size on the adrenal glands of male mice in populations of fixed size. *American Journal of Physiology*, 182, 292–300

Chu, C.C., Klein, H.E. and Lange, M.H. (1982) Symptomatology differentials between urban and rural schizophrenics. *International Journal of Social Psychiatry*, 28(4), 251–5

Cialdini, R.B., Reno, R.R. and Kallgren, C.A. (1990) A focus theory of normative conduct: recycling the concept of norms to reduce littering in public places. *Journal of Personality and Social Psychology*, 58, 1015–26

Cohen, S., Glass, D.C. and Singer, J.E. (1973) Apartment noise, auditory discrimination, and reading ability in children. *Journal of Experimental Social Psychology*, 9, 407–22

Cohn, E.G. and Rotton, J. (2000) Weather, seasonal trends and property crimes in Minneapolis, 1987–1988. A moderator-variable time-series analysis of routine activities. *Journal of Environmental Psychology*, 20, 257–72

Collins, D.L., Baum, A. and Singer, J. (1983) Coping with chronic stress at Three Mile Island; psychological and biochemical evidence. *Health Psychology*, 2, 149–66

Cook, S.W. and Berrenberg, J.L. (1981) Approaches to encouraging conservation behaviour: a review and conceptual framework. *Journal of Social Issues* 37, 73–107

Cooper, C.L., Cooper, R.D. and Eaker, L.H. (1988) *Living with Stress*. London: Penguin

Corah, W.L. and Boffa, J. (1970) Perceived control, self observation and responses to aversive stimulation. *Journal of Personality and Social Psychology*, 16, 1–4

Costa, G., Pickup, L. and Di-Martino, V. (1988) A further stress factor for working people: evidence from the European Community. 1. A review. *International Archives of Occupational and Environmental Health*, 60, 371–6

Cox, V.C., Paulus, P.B. and McCain, G. (1984) Prison crowding research: the relevance for prison housing standards and a general approach regarding crowding phenomena. *American Psychologist*, 39, 1148–60

Crowcroft, P. and Rowe, F.P. (1958) The growth of confined colonies of the wild house-mouse (*Mus musculus* L.): the effect of dispersal on female fecundity. *Proceedings of the Zoological Society of London*, 131, 357–65

Cunningham, M.R. (1979) Weather, mood, and helping behavior: quasi experiments with the sunshine Samaritan. *Journal of Personality and Social Psychology*, 37, 1947–56

Cuthbertson, B.H. and Nigg, J.M. (1987) Technological disaster and the non-therapeutic community: a question of true victimization. *Environment and Behavior*, 19, 462–83

Darley, J.M. and Latané, B. (1968) Bystander intervention in emergencies: diffusion of responsibility. *Journal of Personality and Social Psychology*, 8, 377–83

De Young, R. (1986) Some psychological aspects of recycling: the structure of conservation satisfactions. *Environment and Behavior*, 18, 435–49

Deaux, K.K. and LaFrance, M. (1998) Gender. In Gilbert, D.T., Fiske, S. and Lindzey, G. (eds) *The Handbook of Social Psychology*, 4th edn (vol, 1, pp.788–827). New York: McGraw-Hill

Demirbas, O.O. and Demirkan, H. (2000) Privacy dimensions: a case study in the interior architecture design studio. *Journal of Experimental Psychology*, 20, 53–64

Diener, E. (1979) Deindividuation, self-awareness and disinhibition. *Journal of Personality and Social Psychology*, 37, 1160–71

Dohrenwend, B.P. (1973) Social status and stressful life events. *Journal of Personality and Social Psychology*, 28, 225–35

dos Santos, A.L.V and Duarte, C.R. (2000) The absent home. *Proceedings of the 16th IAPS Conference, Paris, France (4–7 July)*, p.117

Dougall, A.L., Herberman, H.B., Delahanty, D.L., Inslicht, S.S. and Baum, A. (2000) Similarity of prior trauma exposure as a determinant of chronic stress responding to an airline disaster. *Journal of Consulting and Clinical Psychology*, 68(2), 290–5

Dovidio, J.F., Piliavin, J.A. and Clark, R.D. (1991) The arousal-cost reward model and the process of intervention: a review of the evidence. In Clark, M.S. (ed.) *Review of Personality and Social Psychology*, vol. 12: *Prosocial Behaviour*. New York: Academic Press

Duclos, P.J. and Ing, R.T. (1989) Injuries and risk factors for injuries from the 29 May 1982 tornado, Marion, Illinois. *International Journal of Epidemiology*, 18(1), 213–19

Duke, M.P and Nowicki, S. (1972) Diagramming the shape of personal space: a new measure and social learning model for interpersonal distance. *Journal of Experimental Research in Personality*, 6, 119–32

Dunlap, R.E. and Van Liere, K.D. (1978) The 'new environmental paradigm': a proposed instrument and preliminary results. *Journal of Environmental Education*, 9, 10–19

Durkheim, E. (1898) Representations individuelles et representations collectives. *Revue de Metaphysique et de Morale*, 6, 273–302

Dwyer, D. (2001) *Angles on Criminal Psychology*. Cheltenham: Nelson Thornes

Dyson, M.L. and Passmore, N.I. (1992) Inter-male spacing and aggression in African painted reed frogs, *Hyperolius marmoratus*. *Ethology*, 91, 237–47

Eagly, A.H. and Carli, L. (1981) Sex of researchers and sex-typed communications as determinants of sex differences in influence-ability. A meta-analysis of social influence studies. *Psychological Bulletin*, 90, 1–20

Eagly, A.H. and Crowley, M. (1986) Gender and helping behaviour: a meta-analysis review of the social psychological literature. *Psychological Bulletin*, 100, 283–308

Eiser, J.M., Podpadec, T.J., Reicher, S.D. and Stevenage, S.V. (1998) Muddy waters and heavy metal: time and attitudes guide judgements of pollution. *Journal of Environmental Psychology*, 18, 199–208

Ellison-Potter, P.A., Bell, P.A. and Deffenbacher, J.L. (2001) The effects of anonymity, aggressive stimuli, and trait anger on aggressive driving behavior: a laboratory simulation. *Journal of Applied Social Psychology*, 31(2), 431–43

Ennis, X. (1997) Seasonal variations in mood and behaviour and pre-menstrual syndrome. *Proceedings of the British Psychological Society*, 5(1), 9

Eoyang, C.K. (1974) Effects of group size and privacy in residential crowding. *Journal of Personality and Social Psychology*, 30, 389–92

Epping-Jordan, J.E., Compas, B.E. and Howell, D.C. (1994) Predictors of cancer progression in young adult men and women: avoidance, intrusive thoughts, and psychological symptoms. *Health Psychology*, 13, 539–47

Evans, G.W. (1979) Behavioral and physiological consequences of crowding in humans. *Journal of Applied Social Psychology*, 9, 27–46

Evans, G.W. (2000) Motivational consequences of environmental stress. *Proceedings of the 16th IAPS Conference, Paris, France (4–7 July)*

Evans, G.W., Hygge, S. and Bullinger, M. (1995) Chronic noise and psychological stress. *Psychological Science*, 6, 333–8

Evans, G.W., Marrero, D.G. and Butler, P.A. (1981) Environmental learning and cognitive mapping. *Environment and Behavior*, 13, 83–104

Evans, G.W., Smith, C. and Pezdek, K. (1982) Cognitive maps and urban form. *American Planning Association Journal*, 48, 232–44

Evans, G.W., Jacobs, S.V., Dooley, D. and Catalano, R. (1987) The interaction of stressful life events and chronic strains on community mental health. *American Journal of Community Psychology*, 15, 23–34

Evans, G.W., Rhee, E., Forbes, C., Allen, K.M. and Lepore, S.J. (2000) The meaning and efficacy of social withdrawal as a strategy for coping with chronic residential crowding. *Journal of Environmental Psychology*, 20, 335–42

Eysenck, H.J. (1988) Personality, stress and cancer: prediction and prophylaxis. *British Journal of Medical Psychology*, 61, 57–75

Ferenczi, M. (1997) Seasonal depression and light therapy: http://nimnet51.nimr.mrc.ac.uk/mhe97/sad.htm

Feroleto, J.A. and Gounard, B.R. (1975) The effects of subjects' age and expectations regarding an interviewer on personal space. *Experiments and Ageing Research*, 1(1), 57–61

Festinger, L., Pepitone, A. and Newcomb, T. (1952) Some consequences of deindividuation in a group. *Journal of Abnormal and Social Psychology*, 47, 382–9

Fidell, S. and Silvati, L. (1991) An assessment of the effect of residential acoustic insulation on prevalence of annoyance in an airport community. *Journal of the Acoustical Society of America*, 89, 244–7

Finnie, W.C. (1973) Field experiments in litter control. *Environment and Behavior*, 5, 123–44

Fisher, J.D. and Byrne, D. (1975) Too close for comfort: sex differences in response to invasions of personal space. *Journal of Personality and Social Psychology*, 32(1), 15–21

Fisher, M., Pastore, D., Schneider, M., Pegler, C. and Napolitano, B. (1994) Eating attitudes in urban and suburban adolescents. *International Journal of Eating Disorders*, 16(1), 67–74

Fleming, I., Baum, A., Grisriel, M.M. and Gatchel, R.J. (1982) Mediation of stress at Three Mile Island by social support. *Journal of Human Stress*, 8, 14–22

Fleming, R., Baum, A., Davidson, L.M., Rectanus, E. and McArdle, S. (1987) Chronic stress as a factor in physiologic reactivity to challenge. *Health Psychology*, 6, 221–37

Folkman, S., Larazus, R.S., Gruen, R.J. and DeLongis, X. (1986) Appraisal, coping, health status and psychological symptoms. *Journal of Personality and Social Psychology*, 50, 571–9

Foster, K., Campbell, D., Crum, J. and Stove, M. (1995) Non-response in a population study after an environmental disaster. *Public Health*, 109(4), 267–73

Fraunfelder, F.T., Kalina, R.E., Buist, A.S., Bernstein, R.S. and Johnson, D.S. (1983) Ocular effects following the volcanic eruptions of Mount St Helens. *Archives of Ophthalmology*, 101(3), 376–8

Fredrickson, L.M. and Anderson, D.H. (1999) A qualitative exploration of the wilderness experience as a source of spiritual inspiration. *Journal of Environmental Psychology*, 19, 21–39

Freedman, J.L., Klevansky, X. and Ehrlich, P.I. (1971) The effect of crowding on human task performance. *Journal of Applied Social Psychology*, 1, 7–26

Freedman, J.L., Levy, A.S., Buchanan, R.W. and Price, J. (1972) Crowding and human aggressiveness. *Journal of Experimental Social Psychology*, 8, 528–48

Frey Talbot, J. and Kaplan, S. (1995) Perspectives on wilderness: re-examining the value of extended wilderness experiences. In Shina, A. (ed.) *Readings in Environmental Psychology: Landscape Perception*. London: Academic Press

Fruin, J.J. (1981) Causes and prevention of crowd disasters. *Student Activities Programming*, October, 48–53

Fukuda, S., Morimoto, K., Mure, K. and Maruyama, S. (1999) Posttraumatic stress and change in lifestyle among the Hanshin–Awaji earthquake victims. *Preventative Medicine*, 29(3), 147–51

Fukuda, S., Morimoto, K., Mure, K. and Maruyama, S. (2000) Effect of the Hanshin–Awaji earthquake on posttraumatic stress, lifestyle changes, and cortisol levels of victims. *Archives on Environmental Health*, 55(2), 121–5

Fuller, T.D., Edwards, J.N., Semsri, S. and Vorakitphokatorn, S. (1993) Housing, stress and physical well-being: evidence from Thailand. *Social Science and Medicine*, 36, 1417–28

Gale, A., Spratt, G., Chapman, A.J. and Smallbone, A. (1975) EEG correlates of eye contact and interpersonal distance. *Biological Psychology*, 3(4), 237–45

Galea, L.A.M. and Kimura, D. (1993) Sex differences in route-learning. *Personality and Individual Differences*, 14, 53–65

Gamba, R.J. and Oskamp, S. (1994) Factors influencing community residents' participation in commingled curbside recycling programs. *Environment and Behavior*, 26, 587–612

Gamberini, L. and Bussolon, S. (2001) Human navigation in electronic environments. *CyberPsychology and Behavior*, 4, 57–65

Gärling, T., Böök, A. and Lindberg, E. (1984) Cognitive mapping of large-scale environments: the interrelationships of action plans, acquisition and orientation. *Environment and Behavior*, 16, 3–34

Gärling, T., Böök, A. and Lindberg, E. (1986) Spatial orientation and wayfinding in the designed environment: a conceptual analysis and some suggestions for postoccupancy evaluation. *Journal of Architectural Planning Research*, 3, 55–64

Gaulin, S.J.C. and Fitzgerald, R.W. (1989) Sexual selection for spatial learning ability. *Animal Behaviour*, 322–31

Geen, R.G. and O'Neal, E.C. (1969) Activation of cue-elicited aggression by general arousal. *Journal of Personality and Social Psychology*, 11, 289–92

Gibson, J.J. (1979) *An Ecological Approach to Visual Perception*. Boston: Houghton Mifflin

Glass, D.C. and Singer, J.E. (1972) *Urban Stress*. New York: Academic Press

Glover, D., Gough, G., Johnson, M. and Cartwright, N. (2000) Bullying in 25 secondary schools: incidence, impact and intervention. *Educational Research*, 42(2), 141–56

Goenjian, A.K., Steinberg, A.M., Najarian, L.M., Fairbanks, L.A., Tashjian, M. and Pynoos, R.S. (2000) Prospective study of posttraumatic stress, anxiety and depressive reactions after earthquake and political violence. *American Journal of Psychiatry*, 157(6), 911–16

Goldberg, E.L. and Comstock, G.W. (1976) Life events and subsequent illness. *American Journal of Epidemiology*, 104, 146–58

Gould, P. and White, R. (1982) *Mental Maps*. Boston: Unwin and Allen

Green, D.M. and Fidell, S. (1991) Variability in the criterion for reporting annoyance in community noise surveys. *Journal of the Acoustical Society of America*, 89, 234–43

Greenbaum, P.E. and Rosenfeld, H.M. (1980) Varieties of touching in greetings: sequential structure and sex-related differences. *Journal of Nonverbal Behaviour*, 5, 13–25

Gribetz, B., Richter, E.D., Krasna, M. and Gordon, M. (1980) Heat stress exposure of aerial spray pilots. *Aviation, Space and Environmental Medicine*, 51(1), 56–60

Griffit, W. (1970) Environmental effects on interpersonal affective behaviour: ambient effective temperature and attraction. *Journal of Personality and Social Psychology*, 15(3), 240–4

Griffith, J., Steptoe, A. and Cropley, M. (1999) An investigation of coping strategies associated with job stress in teachers. *British Journal of Educational Psychology*, 69, 483–96

Groberty, M.C., Morand, M. and Schenk, F. (2000) Cognitive mapping in rats and humans: the tent-maze, a place learning task in visually disconnected environments. In Nullain, S.O. (ed.) *Spatial Cognition: Foundations and Applications: Selected Papers from Mind III, Annual Conference of the Cognitive Science Society of Ireland, 1998. Advances in Consciousness Research* (pp.105–26). Amsterdam: John Benjamins

Groen, G., Wunderlich, A.P., Spitzer, M., Tomczak, R. and Riepe, M.W. (2000) Brain activation during human navigation. *Nature Neuroscience*, 3, 404–8

Grogen, P. and Bell, R. (1989) Local impact of state recycling laws. *Biocycle*, 30(5), 50–5

Gulain, E., Matthews, G. and Glendon, A.I. (1989) Dimensions of driver stress. *Ergonomics*, 32, 585–602

Hall, E.T. (1963) A system for the notation of proxemic behaviour. *American Anthropologist*, 65, 1003–26

Haller, J., Fuchs, E., Halasz, J. and Makara, G.B. (1999) Defeat is a major stressor in males while social instability is stressful mainly in females. Towards the development of a social stress model in female rats. *Brain Research Bulletin*, 50, 33–9

Ham-Rowbottom, K.A., Gifford, R. and Shaw, K.T. (1999) Defensible space theory and the police: assessing the vulnerability of residences to burglary. *Journal of Environmental Psychology*, 19, 117–29

Hanazato, T. (2000) Pencil-houses or apartments: alternatives of urban dwelling in Hanoi. *Proceedings of the 16th IAPS Conference, Paris, France (4–7 July)*, p.78

Hancock, P.A. (1986) Sustained attention under thermal stress. *Psychological Bulletin*, 99(2), 263–81

Hanyu, K. and Itsukushima, Y. (1995) Cognitive distance of stairways: distance, traversal time, and mental walking time estimations. *Environment and Behavior*, 27, 579–91

Harrell, W.A., Bowlby, J.W. and Hall-Hoffarth, D. (2000) Directing wayfinders with maps: the effects of gender, age, route complexity, and familiarity with the environment. *Journal of Social Psychology*, 140, 169–78

Harris, L. (1999) Irritable Bowel Syndrome and stress. *Gut Reaction: the Journal of the IBS Network*, 34, 6

Harris, L. and Associates (1980) *The Steelcase National Study of Office Environments, II: Comfort and Productivity in the Office of the 80s*. Grand Rapids, MI: Steelcase Inc.

Havenaar, J., Rumyantzeva, G., Kasyanenko, A., Kaasjager, K., Westermann, A., van den Brink, W., van den Bout, J. and Savelkoul, J. (1997) Health effects of the Chernobyl disaster: illness or illness behaviour? A comparative general health survey in two former Soviet regions. *Environmental Health Perspective*, 105(6), 1533–7

Haynes, S.G., Feinleib, M. and Kannel, W.B. (1980) The relationship of psychosocial factors to coronary heart disease in the Framingham study. III: Eight year incidence of coronary heart disease. *American Journal of Epidemiology*, 111, 37–58

Health and Safety Executive (1995) *Noise*. Circular AS8(rev.): http://www.hse.gov.uk/pubns/as8.htm

Heberlein, T.A. (1975) Conservation information: the energy crisis and electricity consumption in an apartment complex. *Energy Systems and Policy*, 1, 105-17

Heerwagen, J.H. and Orians, G.H. (1993) Humans, habitats and aesthetics. In Kelert, S.R. and Wilson, E.O. (eds) *The Biophilia Hypothesis* (pp.138–72). Washington, DC: Island Press

Helbing, D. (2000) quoted in Taming the herd: Beyond 2000, Engineering-Safety Security. Accessed electronically at: http://www.beyond2000.com/news/Oct_2000/story_800.html

Henley, N.M. (1973) Status and sex: some touching observations. *Bulletin of the Psychonomic Society*, 2, 91–3

Herzog, T.R. and Chernick, K.K. (2000) Tranquility and danger in urban and natural settings. *Journal of Environmental Psychology*, 20, 29–39

Herzog, T.R. and Miller, E.J. (1998) The role of mystery in perceived danger and environmental preference. *Environment and Behavior*, 30, 429–49

Holmes, T.H. and Rahe, R.H. (1967) The social readjustment rating scale. *Journal of Psychosomatic Research*, 11, 213–18

Holtzman, D.A., Harris, T.H., Aranguren, G. and Bostocks, E. (1999) Spatial learning of an escape task by young corn snakes, *Elaphe guttata guttata*. *Animal Behaviour*, 57, 51–60

Hoogland, J.L. (1979) Aggression, ectoparasitism and other possible costs of prairie dog (Sciuridae: *Cynomys* spp.) coloniality. *Behavior*, 69, 1–35

Hoppe, R.A., Greene, M.S. and Kenny, J.W. (1972) Territorial markers: additional findings. *Journal of Social Psychology*, 88(2), 305–6

Hormuth, S.E. (1999) Social meaning and social context of environmentally relevant behaviour: shopping, wrapping and disposing. *Journal of Environmental Psychology*, 19, 277–86

Horton, P.B. and Hunt, C.L. (1976) *Sociology*. New York: McGraw-Hill

Hovland, C.I. and Weiss, W. (1951) The influence of source credibility of communication effectiveness. *Public Opinion Quarterly*, 15, 635–50

Howard, D.J. (1997) Familiar phrases as peripheral persuasion cue. *Journal of Experimental Social Psychology*, 33, 231–43

Hribersek, E., van de Voorde, H., Poppe, H. and Casselman, J. (1987) Influence of the day of the week and the weather on people using a telephone support system. *British Journal of Psychiatry*, 150, 189–92

http://www.allergicchild.com/images/holidays.htm

http://www.epc-pcc.gc.ca/research/scie_tech/en_crowd/ref.html

http://www.recycle.umich.edu/grounds/recycle/residence_hall_recycling.html.

Hull, R.B. and Revell, G.R.B. (1995) Cross-cultural comparison of landscape scenic beauty evaluations: a case study in Bali. In Shina, A. (ed.) *Readings in Environmental Psychology: Landscape Perception*. London: Academic Press

Hunt, M.E. (1984) Environmental learning without being there. *Environment and Behavior*, 16, 307–34

Huston, T.L., Ruggiero, M., Conner, R. and Geis, G. (1981) Bystander intervention into crime: a study based on naturally-occurring episodes. *Social Psychology Quarterly*, 44, 14–23

Ising, H. and Melchert, H.U. (1980) Endocrine and cardiovascular effects of noise. In *Noise as a Public Health Problem: Proceedings of the Third International Congress* (pp.194–203). ASHA Report no. 10. Rockville, MD: American Speech and Hearing Association

Jaccoby, J., Hoyer, W.D. and Sheluga, D.A. (1980) *Miscomprehension of Televised Communications*. NewYork: American Association of Advertising Agencies

Jacobs, H.E. and Bailey, J.S. (1982) Evaluating participation in a residential program. *Journal of Environmental Systems*, 13, 245–54

Jacobs, L.E. and Linman, E.R. (1991) Grey squirrels remember the locations of buried nuts. *Animal Behaviour*, 41, 103–10

Janis, I.L. and Feshbach, S. (1953) Effects of fear-arousing communications. *Journal of Abnormal and Social Psychology*, 48, 78–92

Janis, I.L. and Field, P.B. (1959) A behavioral assessment of persuasibility: consistency of individual differences. In Hovland, C.I. and Janis, I.L. (eds) *Personality and Persuasibility* (pp.29–54). New Haven, CN: Yale University Press

Janis, I.L. and Hovland, C.I. (1959) An overview of persuasibility research. In Hovland, C.I. and Janis, I.L. (eds) *Personality and Persuasibility* (pp.1–26). New Haven, CN: Yale University Press

Janzen, G., Schade, M., Katz, S. and Herrmann, T. (2001) Strategies for detour finding in a virtual maze: the role of visual perspective. *Journal of Environmental Psychology*, 21, 149–63

Jarvis, M. (2001) Teacher stress: a critical review of recent findings and suggestions for future research directions. **In press**

Jarvis, M., Russell, J., Flanagan, C. and Dolan, L. (2000) *Angles on Psychology*. Cheltenham: Nelson Thornes

Johnson, K.G., Loftsgaarden, D.O. and Gideon, R.A. (1982) The effects of Mount St. Helens volcanic ash on the pulmonary function of 120 elementary school children. *American Review of Respiratory Disease*, 126(6), 1066–9

Johnson, N.R. and Feinberg, W.E. (1997) The impact of exit instructions and number of exits in fire emergencies: a computer simulation investigation. *Journal of Environmental Psychology*, 17, 123–33

Johnson, N., Feinberg, W.E. and Johnson, D. (1994) Microstructure and panic: the impact of social bonds on individual action in collective flight from the Beverly Hills Supper Club fire. In Tierney, K. and Dynes, R. (eds) *Collective Behavior and Social Organization*. Newark, DE: Delaware University Press

Johnson, R.D. and Downing, L.L. (1979) Deindividuation and valence of cues: effects on prosocial and antisocial behaviour. *Journal of Personality and Social Psychology*, 37, 1532–8

Joint, M. (2000) http://www.reportroadrage.co.uk/experts.htm

Jones, J.W. and Bogat, A. (1978) Air pollution and human aggression. *Psychological Reports*, 43, 721–2

Kaiser, F.G. and Shimoda, T.A. (1999) Responsibility as a predictor of ecological behaviour. *Journal of Environmental Psychology*, 19, 243–53

Kaiser, F.G., Wölfing, S. and Fuhrer, U. (1999) Environmental attitude and ecological behaviour. *Journal of Environmental Psychology*, 19, 1–19

Kalat, J.W. (1998) *Biological Psychology*. London: Brooks/Cole

Kaplan, R. and Kaplan, S. (1989) *The Experience of Nature: a Psychological Perspective*. New York: Cambridge University Press

Kaplan, R. (1987) Validity in environment/behavior research. *Environment and Behavior*, 19, 495–500

Kaplan, S. (1975) An informal model for the prediction of preference. In Zube, E.H., Brush, R.O. and Fabos, J.G. (eds) *Landscape Assessment*. Stroudsburg, PA: Dowden, Hutchinson & Ross

Karasek, R.A., Baker, D., Marxer, F., Ahlbom, A. and Theorell, T. (1981) Job decision latitude, job demands and cardiovascular disease: a prospective study of Swedish men. *American Journal of Public Health*, 71, 694–705

Karasek, R.A., Theorell, T. and Schwartz, J. (1988) Job characteristics in relation to the prevalence of myocardial infaction in the U.S. HES and HANES. *American Journal of Public Health*, 78, 910–18

Karlin, R.A., Rosen, L. and Epstein, Y. (1979) Three into two doesn't go: a follow-up of the effects of overcrowded dormitory rooms. *Personality and Social Psychology Bulletin*, 5, 391–5

Katz, P. (1937) *Animals and Men*. New York: Longmans Green

Kaya, N. and Erkíp, F. (1999) Invasion of personal space under the condition of short-term crowding: a case study on an automatic teller machine. *Journal of Environmental Psychology*, 19, 183–9

Kaya, N. and Erkíp, E. (2001) Satisfaction in a dormitory building: the effects of floor height on the perception of room size and crowding. *Environment and Behavior*, 33, 35–53

Kearney, A.R. and De Young, R. (1995) A knowledge-based intervention for promoting carpooling. *Environment and Behavior*, 27, 650–78

Knowles, E.S. (1980) Convergent validity of personal space measures: consistent results with low intercorrelations. *Journal of Nonverbal Behaviour*, 4, 240–8

Kocher, S. and Levi, D. (2000) Social impact assessment of Alvia Beach clean-up. *Proceedings of the 16th IAPS Conference, Paris, France (4–7 July)*

Kose, V. (2000) Housing for an ageing society: adapting housing design towards universality. *Proceedings of the 16th IAPS Conference, Paris, France (4–7 July)*, pp.45–6

Kovess, V., Murphy, H.B. and Touisgnant, M. (1987) Urban–rural comparisons of depressive disorders in French Canada. *Journal of Nervous Mental Disorders*, 175(8), 457–66

Kresno, S., Harrison, G.G., Sutrisna, B. and Reingold, A. (1994) Acute respiratory illnesses in children under five years in Indramayu, West Java, Indonesia: a rapid ethnographic assessment. *Medical Anthropology*, 15(4), 425–34

Kusuda, S., Fujimara, M. and Takeuchi, T. (1995) Perinatal medical support in the area surrounding the Hanshin–Awaji earthquake. *Acta Paediatrica Japan*, 37(6), 731–4

Larkin, T.S. and Keeton, W.T. (1976) Bar magnets mask the effect of normal magnetic disturbance on pigeon orientation. *Journal of Comparative Physiology*, 110, 227–31

Larsen, K.S. and LeRoux, J. (1984) A study of same sex touch attitudes: scale development and personality predictors. *Journal of Sex Research*, 20, 264–78

Latané, B. and Darley, J.M. (1970) *The Unresponsive Bystander: Why Doesn't He Help?* New York: Appleton Century Croft

Lavine, H. and Snyder, M. (1996) Cognitive processing and the functional matching effect in persuasion: the mediating role of subjective perceptions of message quality. *Journal of Experimental Social Psychology*, 32, 580–604

Lawton, C.A. (1996) Strategies for indoor way-finding: the role of orientation. *Journal of Environmental Psychology*, 16, 137–45

Lawton, M.P., Nahemow, L. and Teaff, J. (1975) Housing characteristics and the well-being of elderly tenants in federally assisted housing. *Journal of Gerontology*, 30(5), 601–7

Lazarus, R.S. and Folkman, S. (1984) *Stress, Appraisal, and Coping*. New York: Springer-Verlag

Le Bon, G. (1879) *The Crowd: a Study of the Popular Mind*. London: Unwin

Lee, T.R., MacDonald, S.M. and Coote, J.A. (1993) Perceptions of risk and attitudes to safety at a nuclear reprocessing plant. Paper presented at Society for Risk Assessment (Europe) Fourth Conference, Rome

Lepore, S.J., Evans, G.W. and Schneider, M.L. (1991) Dynamic role of social support in the link between chronic stress and psychological distress. *Journal of Personality and Social Psychology*, 61, 899–909

Lercher, P., Hortnagel, J. and Kofler, W.W. (1993) Work noise, annoyance and blood pressure: combined effects with stressful working conditions. *International Archives of Occupational and Environmental Health*, 65, 23–8

Lesaca, T. (1996) Symptoms of stress disorder and depression among trauma counselors after an airline disaster. *Psychiatric Services*, 47(4), 424–6

Levine, M. (1982) You-are-here maps: psychological considerations. *Environment and Behaviour*, 14, 221–37

Levine, M. (1999) Rethinking bystander non-intervention: social categorization and the evidence of witnesses at the James Bulger murder trial. *Human Relations*, 52, 1133–55

Levine, M., Marchon, I. and Hanley, G. (1984) The placement of you-are-here maps. *Environment and Behaviour*, 16, 139–57

Lewis, J., Baddeley, A.D., Bonham, K.G. and Lovett, D. (1970) Traffic pollution and mental efficiency. *Nature*, 225, 95–7

Little, K.B. (1968) Cultural variations in social schemata. *Journal of Personality and Social Psychology*, 10(1), 1–7

Loftus, E.F. and Palmer, J.C. (1974) Reconstruction of automobile destruction: an example of the interaction between language and memory. *Journal of Verbal Learning and Verbal Behaviour*, 13, 585–9

Loftus, E.F., Miller, D.G. and Burns, H.J. (1978) Semantic integration of verbal information into a visual memory. *Journal of Experimental Psychology: Human Learning and Memory*, 4, 19–31

Loomis, J.M., Golledge, R.D. and Klatzky, R.L. (2001) GPS-based navigation systems for the visually impaired. In Barfield, W. and Caudell, T. (eds) *Fundamentals of Wearable Computers and Augmented Reality* (pp.429–46). Mahwah, NJ: Lawrence Erlbaum Associates

Low, D.J. (2000) Statistical physics: following the crowd. *Nature*, 407, 465–6

Lutgendorf, S.K., Antoni, M.H., Ironson, G., Fletcher, M.A., Penedo, F., Baum, A., Schneiderman, N. and Klimas, N. (1995) Physical symptoms of chronic fatigue syndrome are exacerbated by the stress of Hurricane Andrew. *Psychosomatic Medicine*, 57(4), 310–23

Luyben, P.D. and Bailey, J.S. (1979) Newspaper recycling: the effects of rewards and proximity of containers. *Environment and Behavior*, 11, 539–57

Lynch, K. (1960) *The Image of the City*. Cambridge, MA: The MIT Press

Macarthur, C., Saunders, N. and Feldman, W. (1995) *Heliobacter pylori*, gastro-duodenal disease, and recurrent abdominal pain in children. *Journal of the American Medical Asssociation*, 273, 729–34

MacDonald, J.E. and Gifford, R. (1989) Territorial cues and defensible space theory: the burglar's point of view. *Journal of Environmental Psychology*, 9(3), 193–205

Mace, B.L., Bell, P.A. and Loomis, R.J. (1999) Aesthetic, affective and cognitive effects of noise on natural landscape assessment. *Society and Natural Resources*, 12, 225–42

Machleit, K., Eroglu, S. and Mantel, S.P. (2000) Perceived retail crowding and shopping satisfaction: What modifies the relationship? *Journal of Consumer Psychology*, 9, 29–42

Magnusson, A. (2000) An overview of epidemiological studies on Seasonal Affective Disorder. *Acta Psychiatrica Scandinavia*, 101(3), 176–84

Maguire, E.A., Burgess, N., Donnett, J.G., Frackowaik, R.S., Frith, C.D. and O'Keefe, J. (1998) Knowing where and getting there: a human navigation network. *Science*, 280, 921–4

Maguire, E.A., Gadian, D.G., Johnsrude, I.S., Good, C.D., Ashburner, J., Frackowiak, R.S. and Frith, C.D. (2000) Navigation-related structural changes in the hippocampi of taxi drivers. *Proceedings of the National Academy of Sciences, USA*, 97, 4398–4403

Maier, N.R.F. and Schneirla, T.C. (1935) *Principles of Animal Psychology*. New York: McGraw-Hill

Maier, R.A. and Ernest, R.C. (1978) Sex differences in the perception of touching. *Perceptual and Motor Skills*, 46, 577–8

Major, B. (1981) Gender patterns in touching behaviour. In Mayo, C. and Henley, N.M. (eds) *Gender and Nonverbal Behaviour* (pp.15–37). New York: Springer-Verlag

Malinowski, J.C. (2001) Mental rotation and real-world wayfinding. *Perceptual Motor Skills*, 29, 19–30

Mann, L., Newton, J.W. and Innes, J.M. (1982) A test between deindividuation and emergent norm theories of crowd aggression. *Journal of Personality and Social Psychology*, 42, 260–72

Manuck, S.B., Kaplan, J.R. and Matthews, K.A. (1986) Behavioral antecedents of coronary heart disease and atherosclerosis. *Atherosclerosis*, 6, 1–14

Margai, F.L. (1997) Analyzing changes in waste reduction behavior in a low-income urban community following a public outreach program. *Environment and Behavior*, 29, 769–92

Marsh, P., Rosser, E. and Harré, R. (1978) *The Rules of Disorder*. London: Routledge and Kegan Paul

Maschke, C., Ising, H. and Arndt, D. (1995) Nachtlicher verkehrslarm und gesundheit. *Bundesgesund Heitsldatt*, 38, 130–6

Matthews, K.E. and Canon, L.K. (1975) Environmental noise as a determinant of helping behavior. *Journal of Personality and Social Psychology*, 32, 571–7

Matthies, E. and Krömker, D. (2000) Participatory planning – a heuristic for adjusting interventions to the context. *Journal of Environmental Psychology*, 20, 1–10

McCarty, J.A. and Shrum, L.J. (1994) The recycling of solid wastes: personal values, value orientations, and attitudes about recycling as antecedents of recycling behavior. *Journal of Business Research*, 30, 53–62

McFarland, D. (1999) *Animal Behaviour*. Harlow: Longman

McGuinness, D. and Sparks, J. (1979) Cognitive style and cognitive maps: sex differences in representations. *Journal of Mental Imagery*, 7, 101–18

McGuire, W.J. (1968) Personality and attitude change: a theoretical housing. In Greenwald, A.G., Brock, T.C. and Ostrom, T.M. (eds) *Psychological Foundations of Attitudes*. New York: Academic Press

McGuire, W.J. (1969) The nature of attitudes and attitude change. In Lindzey, G. and Aronson, E. (eds) *Handbook of Social Psychology*, 2nd edn (vol. 3, pp.136–314). Reading, MA: Addison-Wesley

Medalia, N.Z. (1964) Air pollution as a socio-environmental health problem: a survey report. *Journal of Health and Human Behavior*, 5, 154–65

Medway, J. (1999) Fighting the holiday blues: http://www.dcitymag.com/blue99.htm

Meijanders, A.L., Slangen-de Kort, Y.A.W. and Dinnissen, L.A.J. (2000) Privacy and identity in non-territorial office enviornments. *Proceedings of the 16th IAPS Conference, Paris, France (4–7 July)*, p.90

Menezes, P.R., Scazufca, M., Rodrigues, L.C. and Mann, A.H. (2000) Household crowding and compliance with outpatient treatment in patients with non-affective functional psychoses in Sao Paulo, Brazil. *Social Psychiatry and Psychiatric Epidemiology*, 3, 116–20

Menzel, E.W. (1971) Communication about the environment in a group of young chimpanzees. *Folia Primatologia*, 15, 220–32

Middlemist, R.D., Knowles, E.S. and Matter, C.F. (1976) Personal space invasion in the lavatory: suggestive evidence for arousal. *Journal of Personality and Social Psychology*, 33(5), 541–6

Milgram, S. and Jodelet, D. (1976) Psychological maps of Paris. In Proshansky, H., Ittelson, W. and Rivilin, L. (eds) *Environmental Psychology*. New York: Holt, Rinehart and Winston

Milgram, S. and Toch, H. (1969) Collective behaviour: crowds and social movements. In Lindzey, G. and Aronson, E. (eds) *Handbook of Social Psychology*, vol. 4. Reading, MA: Addison-Wesley

Milner, B., Corkin, S. and Teuber, H.L. (1968) Further analysis of the hippocampal syndrome. 14-year follow-up study of H.M. *Neuropsychologica*, 6, 215–34

Mitchell, J.G. (1994) Our national parks. *National Geographic*, 186 (October), 2–55

Moar, I. (1978) Mental triangulation and the nature of internal representations of space. Unpublished PhD thesis, University of Cambridge

Moffat, S.D., Hampson, E. and Hatzipantelis, M. (1998) Navigation in a 'virtual' maze: sex differences and correlation with psychometric measures of spatial ability in humans. *Evolution and Human Behavior*, 9, 73–87

Montgomery, G.T. (1994) Headache characteristics among high school and university students. *Headache*, 34(50), 247–56

Moore, S., Murphy, M. and Weston, R. (1994) A longitudinal study of domestic water conservation behavior. *Population and Environment: a Journal of Interdisciplinary Studies*, 16, 175–89

Morgan, D.G. and Stewart, N.J. (1998) High versus low density special care units: impact on the behaviour of elderly residents with dementia. *Canadian Journal on Ageing*, 17, 143–65

Morris, R.G.M., Garrud, P., Rawlins, N.J.P. and O'Keefe, J. (1982) Place navigation impaired rats with hippocampal lesions. *Nature*, 297, 681–3

Morrissey, S.A., Raggatt, P.T., James, B. and Rogers, J. (1996) Seasonal Affective Disorder: some epidemiological findings from a tropical climate. *Australian and New Zealand Journal of Psychiatry*, 30(5), 579–86

Mullen, B. (1986) Atrocity as a function of lynch mob composition: a self-attention perspective. *Personality and Social Psychology Bulletin*, 12, 187–97

Murphy, R.G. (1989) The development of magnetic compass orientation in children. Paper presented at Royal Institute of Navigation Conference, Cardiff, April

Nagao, K., Okuyama, M., Miyamoto, S. and Hada, T. (1995) Treating early mental health and post-traumatic symptoms of children in the Hanshin–Awaji earthquake. *Acta Paediatrica Japan*, 37(6), 745–54

Nair, K.U. (2001) Cognitive maps of managers and complexity of problem solving. In Lant, T.K. and Shapira, Z. (eds) *Organizational Cognition: Computation and Interpretation*. Mahwah, NJ: Lawrence Erlbaum Associates

Navarro, P.L., Simpson-Housley, P. and DeMan, A.F. (1987) Anxiety, locus of control and appraisal of air pollution. *Perceptual and Motor Skills*, 64, 811–14

Nevins, R.G., Rohles, F.H., Speinger, W.E. and Feyerherm, A.M. (1967) Temperature–humidity chart for thermal comfort of seated persons. Paper presented at the American Society of Heating, Refrigerating and Air-Conditioning Engineers semi-annual meetings, Houston, January

Newhouse, N. (1990) Implications of attitude and behavior research for environmental conservation. *The Journal of Environmental Education*, 22, 1

Newman, O. (1972) *Defensible Space*. New York: Macmillan

Newman, O. and Franck, K.A. (1982) The effects of building size on personal crime and fear of crime. *Population and Environment: Behavioural and Social Issues*, 5(4), 203–20

Ng, B., Kumar, S., Ranclaud, M. and Robinson, E. (2001) Ward crowding and incidents of violence on an acute psychiatric inpatient unit. *Psychiatric Services*, 52, 521–5

Ng, C.F. (2000) Effects of building construction noise on residents: a quasi experiment. *Journal of Environmental Psychology*, 20, 375–85

Nicolas, M., Thullier-Lestienne, F., Bouquet, C., Gardette, B., Gortan, C., Joulia, F., Bonnon, M., Richalet, J.-P., Therme, P. and Abraini, J.H. (1999) An anxiety, personality and altitude symptamatology study during a 31-day period of hypoxia in a hypobaric chamber (experiment 'Everest-Comex 1997'). *Journal of Environmental Psychology*, 19, 407–14

Nijman, H.L. and Rector, G. (1999) Crowding and aggression on inpatient psychiatric wards. *Psychiatric Services*, 50, 830–1

Nivision, M.E. and Endresen, I.M. (1993) An analysis of relationships among environmental noise, annoyance and sensitivity to noise and the consequences for health and sleep. *Journal of Behavior Medicine*, 16, 257–76

Nolen-Hoeksema, S. and Larson, J. (1999) *Coping with Loss*. Mahwah, NJ: Lawrence Erlbaum

North, A.C., Hargreaves, D.J. (2000) Musical preference during and after relaxation and exercise. *American Journal of Psychology*, 113, 43–67

North, A.C., Hargreaves, D.J. and O'Neill, S.A. (2000) The importance of music to adolescents. *British Journal of Educational Psychology*, 70, 255–72

Novelli, P. (1997) Knowledge about causes of peptic ulcer disease – United States, March–April 1997. *Morbidity and Mortality Weekly Reports*, 46, 985–7

Ohman, A., Fredrickson, M., Hugdahl, K. and Rimmo, P. (1976) The premise of equipotentiality in human classical conditioning: conditioned electrodermal responses to potentially phobic stimuli. *Journal of Experimental Psychology: General*, 105, 313–37

Olsen, M.E. (1981) Consumers' attitudes toward energy conservation. *Journal of Social Issues*, 37, 108–31

Ophuls, W. (1977) *Ecology and the Politics of Scarcity*. San Francisco: Freeman

Oskamp, S., Zelezney, L., Schultz, P.W., Hurin, S. and Burkhardt, R. (1996) Commingled versus separated curbside recycling: Does sorting matter? *Environment and Behavior*, 28, 73–91

Page, R. (1977) Noise and helping behavior. *Environment and Behavior*, 9, 311–14

Palmer, C. (1997) *Contemporary Ethical Issues: Environmental Ethics*. Santa Barbara, CA: ABC-Clio

Pandey, S. (1999) Role of perceived control in coping with crowding. *Psychological Studies*, 44, 86–91

Pardini, A.U. and Katzev, R.D. (1983–1984) The effects of strength of commitment on newspaper recycling. *Journal of Environmental Systems*, 13, 245–54

Parsons, R., Tassinary, L.G., Ulrich, R.S., Hebl, M.R. and Grossmann-Alexander, M. (1998) The view from the road: implications for stress recovery and immunization. *Journal of Environmental Psychology*, 18, 113–40

Patsfall, M.R., Feimer, N.R., Buhyoff, G.J. and Wellman, J.D. (1995) The prediction of scenic beauty from landscape content and composition. In Shina, A. (ed.) *Readings in Environmental Psychology: Landscape Perception*. London: Academic Press

Paulus, P.B. (1988) *Prison Crowding: a Psychological Perspective*. New York: Springer-Verlag

Paulus, P.B., McCain, G. and Cox, V. (1978) Death rates, psychiatric commitments, blood pressure and perceived crowding as a function of institutional crowding. *Environmental Psychology and Nonverbal Behavior*, 3, 107–16

Pearce, G.P. and Patterson, A.M. (1993) The effect of space restriction and provision of toys during rearing on behaviour, productivity and physiology of male pigs. *Applied Behaviour Science*, 36, 11–28

Peluso, M.-L. (2000) Comfort, intimacy and privacy among the poor in Brasilia/Brazil. *Proceedings of the 16th IAPS Conference, Paris, France (4–7 July)*, p.98

Petty, R.E. and Cacioppo, J.T. (1981) *Attitudes and Persuasion: Classic and Contemporary Approaches*. Dubuque, IO: William C. Brown

Petty, R.E. and Cacioppo, J.T. (1986) *Communication and Persuasion: Central and Peripheral Routes to Attitude Change*. New York: Springer-Verlag

Philbeck, J.W., Klatzky, R.L., Behrmann, M., Loomis, J.M. and Goodridge, J. (2001) Active control of locomotion facilitates nonvisual navigation. *Journal of Experimental Psychology: Human Perception and Performance*, 27, 141–53

Piliavin, I.M., Rodin, J. and Piliavin, J.A. (1969) Good samaritanism: An underground phenomenon? *Journal of Personality and Social Psychology*, 13, 289–99

Pinel, J.P.J. (1997) *Biopsychology*. London: Allyn and Bacon

Pinheiro, J.Q. (1998) Determinants of cognitive maps of the world as expressed in sketch maps. *Journal of Environmental Psychology*, 18, 321–39

Pitt, D. and Zube, E. (1987) Management of natural environments. In Stokols, D. and Altman, I. (eds) *Handbook of Environmental Psychology* (pp.1009–42). New York: Wiley Interscience

Polyukhov, A.M., Kobsar, I.V., Grebelnik, V.I. and Voitenko, V.P. (2000) The accelerated occurrence of age-related changes of organism in Chernobyl workers: a radiation-induced progeroid syndrome? *Experimental Gerontology*, 35(1), 105–15

Postman, L. and Egan, J.P. (1949) *Experimental Psychology*. New York: Harper

Postmes, T. and Spears, R. (1998) Deindividuation and antinormative behaviour: a meta-analysis. *Psychological Bulletin*, 123, 1–22

Prados, J., Redhead, E.S. and Pearce, J.M. (1999) Active preexposure enhances attention to the landmarks surrounding a Morris swimming pool. *Journal of Experimental Psychology: Animal Behaviour Processes*, 24, 451–60

Prentice-Dunn, S. and Rogers, R.W. (1982) Effects of public and private self-awareness on deindividuation and aggression. *Journal of Personality and Social Psychology*, 43, 503–13

Preti, A. (1997) The influence of seasonal change on suicidal behaviour in Italy. *Journal of Affective Disorders*, 44(2–3), 123–30

Proulx, G. (1997) Misconceptions about human behaviour in fire. *Canadian Consulting Engineer*, March, 36–8. Accessed electronically at: http://www.nrc.ca/irc/fulltext/prac/nrcc40691.html

Quarantelli, E.L. (1985) Realities and mythologies in disaster films. *Communications*, 11, 31–44

Rahe, R.H. (1968) Life change measurement as a predictor of illness. *Proceedings of the Royal Society of Medicine*, 61, 124–6

Raloff, J. (1982) Occupational noise – the subtle pollutant. *Science News*, 121, 347–50

Ramadier, T. and Moser, G. (1998) Social legibility, the cognitive map and urban behavior. *Journal of Environmental Psychology*, 18, 307–19

Rankin, R. (1969) Air pollution control and public apathy. *Journal of the Air Pollution Control Association*, 19, 565–9

Rathbone, D.B. and Huckabee, J.C. (1999) Controlling road rage: a literature review and pilot study. Prepared for the AAA Foundation for Traffic Safety. Accessed electronically at:
http://www.aaafts.org/Text/research/RoadRageFinal.htm

Real, E., Arce, C., Sabucedo, J.M. (2000) Classification of landscapes using quantitative and categorical data, and prediction of their scenic beauty in northwestern Spain. *Journal of Environmental Psychology*, 20, 355–73

Regolin, L. and Rose, S.P.R. (1999) Long-term memory for a spatial task in young chicks. *Animal Behaviour*, 57, 1185–91

Reicher, S.D. (1984) The St Paul's riot: an explanation of the limits of crowd action in terms of a social identity model. *European Journal of Social Psychology*, 14, 1–21

Reicher, S.D. and Potter, J. (1985) Psychological theory as inter-group perspective: a comparative analysis of 'scientific' and 'lay' accounts of crowd events. *Human Relations*, 38, 167–89

Rishi, P., Sinha, S.P. and Dubey, R. (2000) A correlational study of workplace characteristics and work satisfaction among Indian bank employees. *Psychologia: an International Journal of Psychology in the Orient*, 43, 155–64

Roberts, W.A. (1979) spatial memory in the rat on a hierarchical maze. *Learning and Motivation*, 10, 117–40

Rogers, R.W. (1975) A protection motivation theory of fear appeals and attitude change. *Journal of Psychology*, 91, 93–114

Rohe, W.M. (1985–6) Urban planning and mental health. *Prevention in Human Services*, 4(1–2), 79–110

Rohles, X. (1969) Psychological aspects of thermal comfort. Paper presented at the American Society of Heating, Refrigerating and Air-Conditioning Engineers semi-annual meetings, Denver, July

Ross, C.E. and Mirowsky, J. (1979) A comparison of life-event weighting schemes: change, undesirability, and effect-proportional indices. *Journal of Health and Social Behavior*, 20, 166–77

Rotton, J. and Frey, J. (1985) Air pollution, weather, and violent crimes: concomitant time-series analysis of archival data. *Journal of Personality and Social Psychology*, 49, 1207–20

Rotton, J., Yoshikawa, J. and Kaplan, F. (1979) Perceived control, malodorous air pollution and behavioural after effects. Paper presented at the annual meeting of the Southeastern Psychological Association, New Orleans

Rovine, M.J. and Weisman, G.D. (1995) Sketch-map variables as predictors of way-finding performance. In Gärling, T. (ed.) (1995) *Readings in Environmental Psychology: Urban Cognition*. London: Academic Press

Saegert, S. (1975) Effects of spatial and social density on arousal, mood, and social orientation. *Dissertation Abstracts International*, January, 35(7-B), 3649

Sanders, J.L. (1978) Relation of personal space to the human menstrual cycle. *Journal of Psychology*, 100(2d), 275–8

Sandstrom, N.J., Kaufman, J. and Huettel, S.A. (1998) Males and females use different distal cues in a virtual environment navigation task. *Cognitive Brain Research*, 6, 351–60

Sansone, C., Weir, C., Harpster, L. and Morgan, C. (1992) Once a boring task always a boring task? Interest as a self-regulatory mechanism. *Journal of Personality and Social Psychology*, 63, 379–90

Sattler, D.N., Kaiser, C.F. and Hittner, J.B. (2000) Disaster preparedness: relationships among prior experience, personal characteristics and distress. *Journal of Applied Social Psychology*, 30(7), 1396–420

Sauser, W.L., Arauz, C.G. and Chambers, R.M. (1978) Exploring the relationship between level of office noise and salary recommendations: a preliminary research note. *Journal of Management*, 4, 57–63

Schluter, P.J., Ford, R.P., Brown, J. and Ryan, A.P. (1998) Weather temperatures and sudden infant death syndrome: a regional study over 22 years in New Zealand. *Journal of Epidemiological Community Health*, 52(1), 27–33

Schmitz, S. (1997) Gender-related strategies in environmental development: effects of anxiety on way-finding in and representation of a three-dimensional maze. *Journal of Environmental Psychology*, 17, 215–28

Schneider, H.A. (1946) On breeding 'wild' house mice in the laboratory. *Proceedings of the Society for Experimental Biology, New York*, 63, 161–5

Schneiderman, N. (1982) Animal behavior models of coronary heart disease. In Krantz, D.S., Baum, A. and Singer, J.E. (eds) *Handbook of Psychology and Health* (vol. 3, pp.19–56). Hilldale, NJ: Erlbaum

Schultz, P.W. and Zelezny, L. (1999) Values as predictors of environmental attitudes: evidence for consistency across 14 countries. *Journal of Environmental Psychology*, 19, 255–65

Schwartz, B. and Barsky, S.P. (1977) The home advantage. *Social Forces*, 55, 641–61

Seibert, P.S. and Anooshian, L.J. (1993) Indirect expression of preference in sketch maps. *Environment and Behaviour*, 25, 607–24

Seligman, M.E.P. and Visintainer, M.A. (1985) Turnout rejection and early experience of uncontrollable shock in the rat. In Brush, F.R. and Overmier, J.B. (eds) *Affect Conditioning and Cognition: Essays on the Determinants of Behavior.* Hillsdale, NJ: Erlbaum

Selye, H. (1956) *The Stress of Life*. New York: McGraw-Hill

Sherman, P.W., Jarvis, J.U.M. and Braude, S.H. (1992) Naked mole rats. *Scientific American*, 245, 102–10

Shon, S.K. and Kim, S.H. (2000) The perspective on housing policy of Korea: a transition from housing supply to stock housing management. *Proceedings of the 16th IAPS Conference, Paris, France (4–7 July)*, p.107

Sinha, S.P. and Sinha, S.P. (1991) Personal space and density as factors in task performance and feeling of crowding. *Journal of Social Psychology*, 131(6), 831–7

Skorjanc, A.D. (1991) Differences in interpersonal distance among non-offenders as a function of perceived violence of offenders. *Perceptual and Motor Skills*, 73(2), 659–62

Smith, E.R. and Mackie, D.M. (2000) *Social Psychology*. Hove: Psychology Press

Smith, H.W. (1983) Territorial spacing on a beach revisited: a cross-national exploration. *Social Psychology Quarterly*, 44, 132–7

Söderberg, S., Temihango, W., Kadete, C., Ekstedt, B., Masawe, A., Vahlne, A. and Horal, P. (1994) Prevalence of HIV-1 infection in rural, semi-urban and urban villages in southwest Tanzania: estimates from a blood-donor study. *AIDS*, 8(7), 971–6

Sommer, R. (1987) Crime and vandalism in university residence halls: a confirmation of defensible space theory. *Journal of Environmental Psychology*, 7(1), 1–12

Sommer, R. (1998) Shopping at the co-op. *Journal of Environmental Psychology*, 18, 45–53

Srisurapanont, M. and Intaprasert, S. (1999) Seasonal variations in mood and behaviour: epidemiological findings in the north tropics. *Journal of Affective Disorders*, 54, 97–9

Srivastava, S. and Sharma, M. (1998) Seasonal Affective Disorder: report from India (latitude 26 degrees 45'N). *Journal of Affective Disorders*, 49(2), 145–50

Staples, S.L., Cornelius, R.R. and Gibbs, M.S. (1999) Disturbance from a developing airport: Perceived risk or general annoyance? *Environment and Behavior*, 31, 692–710

Stevens, S.S. (1956) The direct estimation of sensory magnitudes – loudness. *American Journal of Psychology*, 69, 1–25

Stewart, W.P. and Cole, D.N. (2001) Number of encounters and experience quality in Grand Canyon backcountry: consistently negative and weak relationships. *Journal of Leisure Research*, 33, 106–20

Stiles, X. (1990) Is winter the saddest time of year? *New Scientist*, 1740, 23

Stone, N. (2001) Designing effective study environments. *Journal of Environmental Psychology*, 21, 179–90

Stroebe, N. and Stroebe, M. (1987) *Bereavement and Health*. New York: Cambridge University Press

Suedfeld, P., Bocher, S. and Wnek, D. (1972) Helper–sufferer similarity and a specific request for help: bystander intervention during a peace demonstration. *Journal of Applied Social Psychology*, 2, 17–23

Summit, J. and Sommer, R. (1999) Further studies of preferred tree shapes. *Environment and Behavior*, 31, 550–76

Swerdlow, N.R., Geyer, M.A., Vale, W.W. and Koob, G.F. (1986) Corticotropin releasing factor potentiates acoustic startle in rats: blockade by chlordiazepoxide. *Psychopharmacology*, 88, 147–52

Talbott, E.O., Findlay, R.C., Kuller, L.H., Lenkner, L.A., Matthews, K.A., Day, R.D. and Ishii, E.K. (1990) Noise-induced hearing loss and blood pressure. *Journal of Occupational Medicine*, 32, 690–7

Tanner, C. (1999) Constraints on environmental behaviour. *Journal of Environmental Psychology*, 19, 145–57

Taylor, R.B. (1978) Human territoriality: a review and a model for future research. *Cornell Journal of Social Relations*, 13, 125–51

Taylor, R.B., Gottfredson, S.D. and Brower, S. (1984) Understanding block crime and fear. *Journal of Research in Crime and Delinquency*, 21, 303–31

Taylor, S.M. (1984) A path model of aircraft noise annoyance. *Journal of Sound and Vibration*, 96, 243–60

Taylor, S. and Todd, P. (1995) An integrated model of waste management behavior: a test of household recycling and composting intentions. *Environment and Behavior*, 27, 603–30

Teare, J.F., Smith, G.L., Osgood, D.W., Peterson, R.W., Authier, K. and Daly, D.L. (1995) Ecological influences in youth crisis shelters: effects of social density and length of stay on youth problem behaviors. *Journal of Child and Family Studies*, 4, 89–101

Teng, E.H. (2000) The role of the hippocampal region in spatial and non-spatial memory: findings from behavioral studies in monkeys and humans. *Dissertation Abstracts International*, 60(9B), 4451

The American SIDS Institute (2001) What is SIDS? Accessed electronically at http://www.sids.org/btnpg.htm

Theorell, T., Lind, E. and Floderus, B. (1975) The relationship of disturbing life changes and emotion to the early development of myocardial infarction and other serious illnesses. *International Journal of Epidemiology*, 4, 281–93

Tolman, E.C. (1948) Cognitive maps in rats and men. *Psychological Review*, 55, 189–208

Tolman, E.C. and Honzik, C.H. (1930a) 'Insight' in rats. *University of California Publications in Psychology*, 4, 215–32

Tolman, E.C. and Honzik, C.H. (1930b) Introduction and removal of reward, and maze performance in rats. *University of California Publications in Psychology*, 4, 257–75

Turner, R.H. and Killian, L.M. (1972) *Collective Behavior*. Englewood Cliffs, NJ: Prentice-Hall

Turner, J. and Wheaton, B. (1995) Checklist measurement of stressful life events. In Cohen, S., Kessler, R.C. and Underwood Gordon, L. (eds) *Measuring Stress* (pp.29–58). New York: Oxford University Press

Ulrich, R.S. (1979) Visual landscapes and psychological well-being. *Landscape Research*, 4, 17–23

Ulrich, R.S. (1984) View through a window may influence recovery from surgery. *Science*, 224, 420–1

Ulrich, R.S., Simons, R.F., Losito, B.D., Fiorito, E., Miles, M.A. and Zelson, M. (1991) Stress recovery during exposure to natural and urban environments. *Journal of Environmental Psychology*, 11, 201–30

Verhallen, T.M.M. and Van Raaji, W.F. (1981) Household behavior and the use of natural gas for home heating. *Journal of Consumer Research*, 8, 253–7

Vining, J. and Ebreo, A. (1990) What makes a recycler? A comparison of recyclers and nonrecyclers. *Environment and Behavior*, 22, 55–73

Viteles, M.S. and Smith K.R. (1946) An experimental investigation of the effect of change in atmospheric conditions and noise upon performance. *Heating, Piping and Air Conditioning*, 18, 107–12

Waddington, D., Jones, K. and Critcher, C. (1987) Flashpoints of public disorder. In Gaskill, G. and Benewick, R. (eds) *The Crowd in Contemporary Britain*. London: Sage

Wallcott, C. and Brown, A.I. (1989) The disorientation of pigeons at Jersey Hill. Paper presented at the Royal Institute of Navigation Conference

Walsh-Daneshmandi, A. and MacLachlan, M. (2000) Environmental risk to the self: factor analysis and development of subscales for the Environmental Appraisal Inventory (EAI) with an Irish sample. *Journal of Environmental Psychology*, 20, 141–9

Wang, T.H. and Katzev, R.D. (1990) Group commitment and resource conservation: two field experiments on promoting recycling. *Journal of Applied Social Psychology*, 20, 265–75

Wann, D.L. and Weaver, K.A. (1993) The relationship between interaction levels and impression formation. *Bulletin of the Psychonomic Society*, 31, 548–50

Ward, N.J. and Waterman, M. (2000) Accessed electronically at: http://www.reportroadrage.co.uk.experts.htm

Ward, S.L., Newcombe, N. and Overton, W.F. (1986) Turn left at the church or three miles north: a study of direction giving and sex differences. *Environment and Behaviour*, 18, 192–213

Weaver, J.D., Dingman, R.L., Morgan, J., Hong, B.A. and North, C.S. (2000) The American Red Cross Disaster Mental Health Services: development of a cooperative, single function, multidisciplinary service model. *Journal of Behavioural Health Services and Research*, 27(3), 314–20

Wells, M.M. (2000) Office clutter or meaningful personal displays: the role of office personalisation in employee and organizational well-being. *Journal of Environmental Psychology*, 20, 239–55

Werner, C.M. and Makela, E. (1998) Motivations and behaviors that support recycling. *Journal of Environmental Psychology*, 18, 373–86

Werner, C.M., Turner, J., Shipman, K., Twitchell, F.S., Dickson, B.R., Bruschke, G.V. and von Bismarck, W.B. (1995) Commitment, behavior, and attitude change: an analysis of voluntary recycling. *Journal of Environmental Psychology*, 15, 197–208

Werner, S. and Schmidt, K. (1999) Environmental reference systems for large-scale spaces. *Spatial Cognition and Computation*, 1, 447–73

Whishaw, I.Q. and Tomie, J. (1997) Piloting and dead reckoning by fimbria-fornix lesions in a rat food carrying task. *Behavioural Brain Research*, 89, 87–97

Williams, E. (1991) College students and recycling: their attitudes and behaviours. *Journal of College Student Development*, 32, 86–8

Willis, F.N. and Rawdon, V.A. (1994) Gender and national differences in attitudes to same-gender touch. *Perceptual and Motor Skills*, 78(3, Pt1), 1027–34

Willis, F.N., Rinck, C.M. and Dean, L.M. (1978) Interpersonal touch among adults in cafeteria lines. *Perceptual and Motor Skills*, 47, 1147–52

Wilson, O. (1984) *Biophilia: the Human Bond with Other Species*. Cambridge, MA: Harvard University Press

Wiltschko, W. and Wiltschko, R. (1988) Magnetic orientation in birds. *Current Ornithology*, 5, 67–121

Winneke, G. and Kastka, J. (1987) Comparison of odour-annoyance data from different industrial sources: problems and implications. In Koelega, H.S. (ed.) *Environmental Annoyance: Characterization, Measurement and Control* (pp.129–38). Amsterdam: Elsevier Science

Wolf, N. and Feldman, E. (1991) *Plastics: America's Packaging Dilemma*. Washington, DC: Island Press

Yildirim, A. and Kulodlu, N. (2000) The planning criterias of decreasing of vandalism in urban open space. *Proceedings of the 16th IAPS Conference, Paris, France (4–7 July)*, p.120

Yinon, Y. and Bizman, A. (1980) Noise, success and failure as determinants of helping behaviour. *Personality and Social Psychology Bulletin*, 6, 125–30

Yip, P.S., Callanan, C. and Yuen, H.P. (2000) Urban/rural and gender differentials in suicide rates: east and west. *Journal of Affective Disorders*, 57(1–3), 99–106

Zautra, A.J. (1998) Arthritis: behavioral and psychosocial aspects. In Blechman, E.A. and Brownell, K.D. (eds) *Behavioral Medicine and Women: a Comprehensive Handbook* (pp.554–8). New York: Guilford

Zeiber, R. (1999) *The Digital Collegian*, 22 March. Accessed electronically at: http://www.collegian.psu.edu/archive/1999/03/-22-99tdc/03-22-99dnews-5.asp

Zimbardo, P.G. (1970) The human choice: individuation, reason, and order versus deindividuation, impulse and chaos. In Arnold, W.J. and Levine, D. (eds) *Nebraska Symposium on Motivation 1969*, 17, 237–307. Lincoln: University of Nebraska Press

Zimmer, K. and Ellermeier, W. (1999) Psychometric properties of four measures of noise sensitivity: a comparison. *Journal of Environmental Psychology*, 19, 295–302

Index

Page numbers in **bold** indicate where the term has been defined in the text